Essays on Grammatic

Universal Gra

Essays on Grammatical Theory and Universal Grammar

EDITED BY

Doug Arnold
Martin Atkinson
Jacques Durand
Claire Grover
Louisa Sadler

CLARENDON PRESS · OXFORD

Oxford University Press, Walton Street, Oxford OX2 6DP
Oxford New York Toronto
Delhi Bombay Calcutta Madras Karachi
Petaling Jaya Singapore Hong Kong Tokyo
Nairobi Dar es Salaam Cape Town
Melbourne Auckland
and associated companies in
Berlin Ibadan

Oxford is a trade mark of Oxford University Press

Published in the United States
by Oxford University Press, New York

First published 1989
Reprinted 1990
First issued in paperback 1991

British Library Cataloguing in Publication Data
Essays on grammatical theory and universal grammar
1. Grammar
I. Arnold, Doug
415
ISBN 0–19–824897–0

Library of Congress Cataloging in Publication Data
Essays on grammatical theory and universal grammar
edited by Doug Arnold . . . [et al.].
Bibliography: p. Includes index.
1. Grammar, Comparative and general. I. Arnold, Doug.
P151.E78 1978 415—dc 19 88–36441
ISBN 0–19–824897–0

Printed and bound in Great Britain by
Biddles Ltd, Guildford and King's Lynn

In memory of
Dave Kilby (1947–1985)

Royalties from sales of this volume have been donated by the contributors to the Leukaemia Research Fund

Preface

This volume and the essays in it are a tribute to Dave Kilby, who died of leukaemia in 1985, at the age of 38. The editors were all friends and colleagues of Dave at Essex University. Many of the contributors also knew Dave as a friend, student, teacher, or colleague, as well as through his published work. The articles all address, in different ways, the three themes Dave was most concerned with. First, the issue of how, and how far, syntactic categories and relations can be grounded in broadly semantic concepts (Kilby 1973, 1976a, 1977a, 1977b, 1981). Second, the search for linguistic universals, and the study of language typology (Kilby 1977b, 1982c, 1982a). Third, descriptive linguistics, and the description of particular languages, especially Russian, English, and the languages of the Caucasus (Kilby 1974, 1982b, 1984).

Before coming to Essex as a lecturer in 1973, Dave had been a student of Russian at the University of Birmingham, and a postgraduate student at the University of Edinburgh. His doctoral thesis, subsequently published as *Deep and Superficial Cases in Russian* (Kilby 1977a), was devoted to the study of case in Russian.

In later years, his primary interests were in descriptive linguistics, especially language universals and language typology, and he was a well-known figure in this field, having written a number of important articles and a textbook on English *Descriptive Syntax and the English Verb* (Kilby 1984), and co-authoring an introductory book on Linguistics, *Foundations of General Linguistics* (Atkinson, Kilby, and Roca 1982). Despite the lasting quality and importance of the work he did, he was still far from realizing his full potential. At the time of his death he was working on a book on Universal Grammar based on lectures given at Essex, which would have further established his reputation as one of the best descriptive linguists of his generation.

It was obvious to everyone who worked with him that Dave had a rare combination of qualities: a penetrating intellect of extraordinary speed and clarity, a wide range of knowledge, an apparently inexhaustible supply of patience and understanding, and an equable and optimistic temperament. This last quality was particularly evident during the last three years of his life, when, knowing that he was seriously ill, he both extended his interests in a number of directions and produced some of his most outstanding research.

D.A.
M.A.
J.D.
C.G.
L.S.

Contents

List of Contributors

John Anderson
University of Edinburgh.

Bernard Comrie
University of Southern California.

Greville G. Corbett
University of Surrey.

R. M. W. Dixon
Australian National University.

John A. Hawkins
University of Southern California.

John Lyons
Trinity Hall, Cambridge.

Jim Miller
University of Edinburgh.

S. G. Pulman
SRI Research Institute, Cambridge

Andrew Radford
University of Essex

Introduction

The papers in this volume address a variety of issues in grammatical theory. Three themes are particularly salient in the collection: first, the semantic basis for syntactic categories and relations; second, the search for linguistic universals and the study of language typology; third, the detailed description of particular phenomena, both monolingually and contrastively.

Anderson's 'Reflections on Notional Grammar' addresses the first and third of these themes. The term 'Notional Grammar' comes originally from Jespersen (1924), but its use in this context arises from Lyons (1966a). Loosely speaking, the idea is that the grammatical properties of the major 'parts of speech' are basically or prototypically determined by their semantic properties (see Lyons, this volume, for a precise formulation). For example, the fact that nouns are prototypically words (used as heads of phrases) which denote or refer to objects or individuals ('people, places, or things') provides a basis for an explanation of their most salient grammatical properties. More generally, this can be related to the well-established tradition in modern linguistics (cf. e.g. the literature on *case grammar*, Fillmore 1969, Anderson 1971a, 1977) which stresses the logical priority of classes and relations which are defined in semantic terms over syntactic or distributional classes. As noted in Anderson (1986), the relationship between syntactic categories and semantic concepts that such work suggests is analogous to the relationship between phonological classes (e.g. vowels, consonants, etc.) and the phonetic characteristics (e.g. sonority and consonantality) that define them. This paper takes the analogy further, using the theoretical apparatus developed in *dependency phonology* (Anderson and Durand 1986, Anderson and Ewen 1987).

The basic ideas of dependency phonology are that phonological segments are characterized by (unary) features which are grouped into (sub-)gestures, and which may stand in a relation of dependency, so that one may predominate over another. For example, voiceless stops might be characterized as 'pure' consonants in some sense; voiced stops are also consonantal, but there is an additional subordinate element of 'vocalicness'. Sonorant consonants also have vocalic and consonantal characteristics, but here vocalicness predominates over consonantality. Within these major classes, further distinctions are made by components such as 'linguality' or 'gravity' which are grouped in a non-categorial gesture and may also be related by dependency. Applying these ideas in the domain of grammar, the obvious candidates for 'basic' features relate to potential referentiality, which is prototypically characteristic of nouns (more precisely, proper names), and potential predicativity, prototypically characteristic of verbs. Anderson goes on to demonstrate analyses of various syntactic categories in terms of combinations of these, and other features relating to 'partitive' characteristics.

The discussion concentrates on the properties of word classes generally associated with 'noun phrases' (quantifiers, demonstratives, attributive adjectives, common and proper nouns). These are argued to belong to the same notional class {N}—the class that introduces potentially referential subsets. They differ with respect to the subcategorial feature {abl}, which indicates whether, or how, such items relate to expressions indicating the set from which the relevant subset is drawn. For example, in an expression such as 'large pigs', the noun 'pigs' can be thought of as picking out a set from which the adjective 'large' draws a subset. Attributive adjectives are inherently partitive, and thus combine with nouns directly—compare cardinal quantifiers such as 'two' which appear in constructions such as 'two pigs', and 'two of the pigs', and the quantifier 'a lot', which requires an overt partitive marker: 'a lot of pigs', but not *'a lot pigs'. Pursuing the phonological analogy further, Anderson suggests a treatment of 'agreement' features such as number and gender as 'prosodic' or 'autosegmental' features, reminiscent of those involved in the description of vowel-harmony systems. Among the theoretical consequences of this analysis which Anderson discusses is the exclusion of the possibility of catastrophic and semantically unmotivated changes in the development of languages, such as the innovation of the completely new syntactic categories 'quantifier' and 'modal', which has been suggested for English by Lightfoot (1979).

Comrie's paper 'Some General Properties of Reference-tracing Systems' relates to the second of the above themes, addressing the general issue of universals of coreference by proposing a typology of reference-tracking systems, i.e. '. . . the devices used in different languages to keep track of the various entities referred to in a discourse' (p. 37).

Comrie draws attention to two distinct approaches to the study of such devices. First, syntactic theorists have focused their attention on the distribution of anaphoric and pronominal elements in sentences, their concern being to articulate abstract, configurationally defined properties which provide the terms for an explanatory account of this distribution. The best-known account of this type appears in the Binding theory of Chomsky (1981). Second, discourse theorists have been interested in ambiguity resolution, when purely formal syntactic criteria do not provide a sufficient basis for determining the referent of, say, a pronoun. Comrie proposes to embrace both of these traditions within his discussion, bringing additional, cross-linguistic observations to bear in developing a view of the dimensions of variation of such systems.

In addition to the familiar systems of gender/class marking and anaphoric reference the less well-known systems of switch reference and obviation are discussed. The former occurs when verbal morphology is used to indicate that the subject of a clause is identical to or different from the subject of another clause, thus allowing its omission. The latter, characteristic of Algonquian languages, involves assigning discourse participants proximate or obviative status at first mention, this status being maintained throughout the remainder of the discourse by consistent morphological marking.

Comrie maintains that two parameters can readily be identified as involved in these varied systems. The first of these is whether the referential characteristics of a device are inherent or assigned. Gender/class systems epitomize inherent devices, the referential characteristics of gender/class-marked expressions being determined by the gender/class to which the expression belongs and not varying as a consequence of syntactic or discourse function. By contrast, reflexive anaphors in English refer in a manner which is clearly determined by the sentential context in which they occur, for example. The same goes for switch reference phenomena and obviation, the difference between these being that whereas switch reference appears to be syntactically determined, obviation is at the whim of the initiator of a discourse. The second parameter concerns locality and admits of gradation. Inherent devices, by their nature, are global, but amongst the assigned devices a number of possibilities appear. Thus, reflexive anaphors pick up their reference in an essentially clause-bound manner in English, but the Japanese anaphor *zibun* is sentence-bound. Switch reference also appears to be local, at least in so far as it requires a syntactic dependency between the clauses within which it operates. Obviation, however, is global and extends across a discourse.

Among the fundamental questions raised by Comrie's paper is whether it is appropriate to recognize a class of phenomena defined in semantic/discoursal terms and attempt to systematize them. Conceivably, the 'natural kinds' for scientific investigation will be defined with reference to configurational criteria, in which case we might anticipate that while the study of anaphora and switch reference will ultimately fall together under a unified set of principles, the same will not hold for the global devices Comrie discusses.

The paper by Corbett, 'An Approach to the Description of Gender Systems', is also a contribution to language typology, proposing a framework for the analysis of gender systems, and analysing data from a number of languages. As he observes, universalist and typological work on gender systems is hampered by the lack of general agreement on the definitions of terms such as 'gender', 'noun class', and 'noun classifier'.

Developing the approach of Zaliznjak (1964), Corbett takes agreement as the defining factor for the identification of gender (the notion agreement is understood in terms of a matching of features between controller and target). First the notion of agreement class is defined, relying solely on syntactic evidence. An agreement class is a set of nouns which, when they occur with the same agreement target, in the same morphosyntactic form and agreement domain, require the target to have the same morphological realization. Drawing a distinction between controller and target gender, Corbett argues that the set of agreement classes for a particular language should not be straightforwardly equated with the set of controller genders (what he calls the 'maximalist position'). Rather it is possible to derive a (smaller) number of controller genders from the agreement classes by means of principled exclusions and conflations.

The term 'target genders' refers to the distinct sets of gender agreement markers found on the agreeing elements. Again the number of target genders is restricted in a principled manner. The failure to draw a distinction between target and controller genders, Corbett observes, has been responsible for much confusion in this area. The proposed definition of gender is helpful in determining the number of genders in a particular language, an area in which there is currently little consensus. The article illustrates the approach with respect to the problematic case of Romanian, demonstrating that there are two target genders but three controller genders in that language.

Section 3 explores a number of issues in the typology of gender systems, ranging from the relationship between number and gender to the semantic basis for target genders. Section 4 of the paper addresses the issues involved in restricting the number of genders recognized by means of the agreement-class approach, introducing notions such as subgender, consistent agreement pattern, and inquorate gender.

Dixon's paper addresses issues in both *language typology* and *universals*, and the notional/semantic basis for grammatical categories, simultaneously, examining the ways in which semantic distinctions are syntactically and lexically realized in a variety of languages. His starting-point is the assumption that the fundamental function of language is to convey meaning from speaker to hearer and that by asserting the priority of semantics we can explain many otherwise puzzling or arbitrary syntactic phenomena. More specifically, he claims that verbs can be grouped in about twenty semantic types such as GIVING, TELLING, LIKING, SHOWING, AFFECT, MOTION, etc. Following the ideas put forward in Dixon (1979), he suggests that, at the level of syntax, three core functions appear to be universally required: subject of intransitive (S), subject of transitive (A), and object of transitive (O). Based on data from a variety of languages, Dixon sets out to examine some of the mappings between semantic categories and the syntactic functions. While there appears to be fairly wide agreement between languages as to which functions map onto A (usually the initiator or controller of the activity), there is far less agreement as to which of the non-A roles become O and which become a peripheral function. The bulk of Dixon's paper is devoted to an exploration of the strategies used by languages to allow for alternations with respect to the O role. Alternate lexicalizations, morphosyntactic processes, and alternate frames are examined and exemplified from a wide range of languages. One of the interesting results is that verbs of GIVING, TELLING, and SHOWING tend to permit one construction only in the majority of languages, whereas AFFECT type verbs (hit, cut, dig, rub) and verbs of MOTION (fill, shake, cover) typically allow two frames (e.g. 'dig the ground for yams', 'dig yams from the ground') with a clear difference of meaning. The paper calls for a detailed investigation of these phenomena in individual languages, noting that until now the grammars and dictionaries of most languages have scarcely mentioned the topic.

The article by Hawkins, 'Competence and Performance in the Explanation of Language Universals', makes a contribution to the explanation of *linguistic universals*, examining the interaction between principles of different sorts in the explanation of left–right asymmetries (see below). He first distinguishes between the tradition of system-internal explanation ('competence explanations') and that which appeals to aspects of performance in the explanation of linguistic universals ('performance explanations'). Performance explanations may ultimately appeal to innate predispositions or limitations (for example, processing explanations which refer to memory limitations). In the first part of the paper, Hawkins provides some background to his main theme by presenting and discussing a number of competence and performance principles which have been proposed in universalist work. Amongst competence principles, Hawkins cites Keenan's work (1978, 1979) on principles of a semantic nature and in particular his Meaning–Form Dependency Principle, which suggests that function categories (e.g. adjectives) vary their interpretations according to the choice of argument (nouns). Amongst the performance principles which Hawkins discusses, we can cite Givón's (1983) pragmatically based explanation of the ordering constraints observed in free-word-order languages, as well as the psycholinguistic principles of language processing which are put forward as explanations of linguistic universals.

The main body of the article is devoted to a discussion of the interaction between competence and performance explanations for left–right asymmetries in syntax and morphology. That is, in a number of cases, independent syntactically based principles predicting a particular word order for a construction in languages of a given type are frequently violated, while they appear to hold for languages of a different type. The result is either a leftward or a rightward skewing in the observed ordering, *vis-à-vis* the predictions of the principle in question. The article discusses and proposes explanations for three such left–right asymmetries: the position of relative clauses, the position of sentential complements, and the order of morphemes.

Section 2 discusses rightward skewing in the positioning of relative clauses with respect to the nouns they modify (the head: 'H')—the H-Rel prediction is borne out for VSO (100 per cent) and SVO (94 per cent), while the Rel-H prediction is often violated in SOV languages (only 56 per cent have Rel-H). In explanation, Hawkins suggests that the syntactically determined principles interact with processing considerations, citing the work of Antinucci *et al.* (1979), which suggests that prenominal relatives provide more opportunities for misanalysis of the subordinate constituents as part of the main clause, and the work of Frazier (1978), which proposes Minimal Attachment and Late Closure as universal parsing strategies (see Hawkins, pp. 136–7, for details). Where the grammar deviates from the syntactically motivated principle, it does so in such a way as to maximize Minimal Attachment and Late Closure, and to minimize or avoid misanalysis. Hence the processing principles and the syntactic principle interact to produce the observed rightward skewing.

Sections 3 and 4 provide further illustration of the interaction between competence and performance principles in the explanation of rightward and leftward skewing in the positioning of sentential complements with respect to simple NP objects, and rightward skewing (favouring suffixation over prefixation) in morpheme ordering. The explanation of the sentential complementation data is argued to involve Kuno's (1974) centre-embedding avoidance principle; while the morpheme ordering asymmetries are explained in terms of the Head Ordering Principle, which essentially states that, for a given language, word-internal structure observes the H-Mod order found in the syntax, and a processing constraint prefers stem-affix ordering (see Cutler, Hawkins, and Gilligan (1985) for both).

The notion of 'semantic ascent' that appears in the title of Lyons's paper 'Semantic Ascent: A Neglected Aspect of Syntactic Typology' refers to the ways in which languages facilitate an ascent to levels of abstractness higher than that which allows reference to individual entities. The purpose of the paper is to discuss a number of aspects of this, and the relationship between ontology and language generally, and to promote the typological investigation of the way languages differ in this and other aspects of semantic structure. A prerequisite of this is restating and refining the ideas first presented in Lyons (1966a), and developed in Lyons (1977) and elsewhere—what we have called 'notional grammar' above, but which Lyons here suggests should be called 'ontologically based grammar'.

More concretely, the paper aims to defend two theses by discussion of the distinction between classes of nominal which differ in their degree or kind of abstractness. The these are: (i) 'that the meaning and distribution of the major grammatical categories [are] basically, or prototypically, dependent upon and determined by the structure of the external world' (p. 153), and are hence universal; (ii) that, however, 'much of the semantically relevant syntactic structure of natural languages—and more particularly their categorial structure—is non-universal' (p. 151), because it is under-determined by the external world, and languages resolve the indeterminacy in different ways. Specifically, Lyons suggests that languages may differ in the degree to which they permit higher levels of abstraction.

The paper begins by updating and clarifying the ideas and terminology of the 1966 paper, remedying its most obvious defects (such as the failure to distinguish part-of-speech from form class, entity-referring from place-referring expressions, and the question about the universality of the category of lexical nouns from the under class of nominals, such as noun phrases). The paper then turns to the specific issue of the classification of nominals along dimensions of abstractness. The traditional formulation of this classification is in terms of the concrete–abstract distinction. Definitions from a wide variety of sources are examined, demonstrating the confused and uncritical way the distinction is applied in the traditional descriptive and theoretical literatures alike. Lyons's proposal is that the distinction should be abandoned and replaced by an ontological classification more soundly based on two dimensions: first order versus second order, and intensional versus extensional.

First order entities are the entities countenanced by 'naïve realism': individuals such as persons, animals, and physical things, which can be quantified over and have properties ascribed to them in languages such as First Order Predicate Calculus. It is in keeping with traditional and current practice to define the class of nouns in a language as the distributionally distinct class of expressions (if one exists) which prototypically denote such entities. However, it is clear that Natural Language semantics (at least for languages like English) requires us to countenance additional kinds of entity to these. In particular, there is need for such second order entities as a denotation/reference for 'singing' or 'John's singing in the bath', and more generally hypostatized properties of first-order entities, or hypostatized relations, events, situations, etc., involving first-order entities.

Moreover, apart from such extensional objects, we require (second-order) intensional entities such as propositions which are the referents of e.g. 'that' clauses. Now, it is clear that these distinctions are grammaticalized in languages like English (albeit to a limited and rather irregular extent), and Lyons makes a number of observations about relevant aspects of English grammar. But the question arises of whether they are distinguished in all languages, and whether in fact all languages provide grammatically distinct ways of referring to second-order and intensional entities. Though some related questions have been investigated, Lyons notes that this question cannot yet be answered. However, there is a real possibility that they do not, that 'semantic ascent' is a non-universal property of languages, supporting thesis (ii) above and raising the possibility that there are genuine differences between languages in terms of expressivity. This, together with a number of other aspects of the idea of semantic ascent, is taken up in the final section of the paper.

The link between grammar and meaning is further examined in Miller's paper 'Participant Roles, Synonymy, and Truth Conditions', which explores some aspects of participant roles (i.e. cases in the Fillmore (1969)/Anderson (1971a, 1977) tradition), theta roles in the terminology of Government and Binding (Chomsky 1981, 1982, 1986), with special reference to synonymy and truth conditions. Miller stresses the need to take grammatical factors into account in establishing participant roles and warns of the dangers of relying on weak notions of synonymy or referential identity in studying related sentences such as

(1) They issued rifles to the policemen.

(2) They issued the policemen with rifles.

which involve alternations between Dixon's (this volume) O position and peripheral functions. Sensitivity to patterns of grammar (morphology, choice of preposition, word order, transformational tests) recommends analyses which are closer to the surface orientation of the sentences. In particular, the direct object position correlates significantly with prototypical patienthood. Miller argues tht analyses of (1) and (2) which reduce them to trivalent structures of the form predicate (agent, theme, goal) miss an important difference of meaning: a difference which varies in salience according to the type of predicate, but which is none the less significant.

Pulman's paper 'Prepositional Relatives and Syntactic Marginality' deals with the problems of analysing such generally neglected English sentences as (3), and the theoretical and meta-theoretical issues that they raise.

(3) He gave her a cake *with icing on* (*it*).

Pulman calls the italicized portion of (3) a 'Prepositional Relative'. Prepositional relatives combine properties of a PP (e.g. the preposition) and a relative clause (e.g. the optional 'gap') in a way that is problematic for any description of English. In the second part of the paper Pulman discusses the meta-theoretical issue that this construction raises. This relates to the way in which evidence from such 'marginal' constructions can be brought to bear on theoretical issues. Pulman observes that it is possible to argue for one of two positions with respect to a marginal construction. On the one hand, one may point to evidence that shows it to be marked or peripheral in the grammar (e.g. that learners acquire it late, or with difficulty, or only on the basis of explicit instruction), and on these grounds regard as suspect evidence or arguments based on them (this position has, for instance, been taken with respect to 'tough movement'). On the other hand, one may observe that the marginality of the construction makes it unlikely that learners of the language will have had (sufficient) direct exposure to the construction to learn it in the normal sense, and that it must therefore reflect the features of Universal Grammar which enable language acquisition, in a relatively direct and hence revealing way (Chomsky has taken this position with 'parasitic gap' constructions). The theoretical importance of the construction lies in the problems it raises for the theory of Binding as presented in Chomsky (1981, 1982).

As Pulman demonstrates, neither view of marginality is entirely free of internal problems and the views themselves are contradictory.

In the final two sections of the paper Pulman describes the grammar of prepositional relatives in terms of the theory of

Government and Binding (Chomsky 1981), and Generalized Phrase Structure Grammar (Gazdar 1981, 1982). With respect to the former, he argues in detail that it is impossible to reconcile the theory of Binding with the presence of the gap in the prepositional relative without making untenable assumptions about their structure, or making otherwise problematic modifications to the theory. By contrast, he shows that given the theory of gap distribution associated with GPSG it is possible to provide an analysis which captures the main features of the construction without serious theoretical inconsistency.

Radford's paper 'The Status of Exclamative Particles in Modern Spoken French' provides a thorough investigation into the categorial status of a class of French exclamative particles. Apart from those which are clearly complementizers (*si*) and those which are clearly wh-words (*combien*), a group of these particles (*comme*, *comment que*, *que*, *qu'est-ce que*, *ce que*) has given rise to diametrically opposed positions in the work of Milner (1978) and Gérard (1980). Milner argues that they are wh-words while Gérard argues that they are complementizers, claiming that a historical change from wh-exclamatives to complementizer-exclamatives has occurred in French.

Radford observes that the issue presupposes independent criteria by which it is possible reliably to distinguish wh-items and complementizers. On the basis of an examination of non-exclamative constructions, he draws up a set of such criteria and provides a detailed discussion of the behaviour of each of the problematic particles.

In the case of exclamative *comme* and *que* it seems clear that these cannot be wh-words of the kind which normally appear in unbounded dependency constructions. If they were, then they would need to be analysed as preposed quantifiers, but there is no conclusive evidence that a quantifier gap exists. Moreover, they behave abnormally in that they appear to require that the quantified constituent should be stranded and in that they permit violations of some island constraints (the Prepositional Island Constraint and the Subjacency Condition). Radford points out that there are alternatives to the complementizer analysis, suggesting that they might best be analysed as sentential wh-adverbs.

With exclamative *comment que* and *qu'est-ce que* the evidence again provides no support for the wh-word analysis. Questioning

Gérard's assumption that these particles are indivisible units, Radford rejects the complementizer account, proposing an alternative in which *comment que* can be analysed as a wh-sentence adverb (*comment*) followed by an optional finite-clause complementizer (*que*) and where *qu'est-ce que* can be analysed as a wh-pronoun or adverb (*qu'est-ce*) followed by an obligatory finite-clause complementizer (*que*).

As for *ce que*, Radford argues that its behaviour under coordination demonstrates that it too is divisible. Furthermore, unlike complementizers, *ce que* is not invariable since *que* can be replaced by *qui* and *dont* in appropriate contexts. The most plausible analysis seems simply to be one where *que* introduces a relative clause with *ce* as its pronominal head. Further justification comes from the observation that *ce* without *que* can quite often be used with exclamative force.

In each case, then, he concludes that, though the particles are by no means typical wh-items, Gérard's thesis that they are complementizers, and hence her claim about the historical development of French, is unjustified.

I

Reflections on Notional Grammar, with Some Remarks on its Relevance to Issues in the Analysis of English and its History*

John Anderson

One strand in linguistic research has been concerned to emphasize the syntactic relevance of semantic functions ('case relations', 'θ-roles') such as 'agent', 'location', etc. This concern has been manifested within proposals whose views on other aspects of linguistic structure vary widely, ranging from e.g. those associated with 'functional grammar' (Dik 1978) to one interpretation of some recent developments of 'EST' (Culicover and Wilkins 1986; Růžička 1983). The strongest manifestation of this 'tradition', wherein many other aspects of structure (syntactic and lexical) are claimed to be subordinate to, or predictable from, information concerning semantic function, has come to be called 'case grammar' (e.g. as defined by the body of work, from the mid sixties on, described in Anderson 1977: ch. 1, or, more recently, Anderson 1986); and in deference to this I shall refer henceforth to the semantic function labels associated with arguments as *case relations* (CRs). However, what characterizes all these proposals is an acknowledgement of the role in the syntax of elements whose cross-linguistic identification depends on semantic, or notional, criteria: for instance, whatever recurrent syntactic (or lexical) properties 'agents' may be associated with, their identification as such depends on prototypical instances of the set of putative 'agents' in various languages fulfilling the semantic function of 'source of the action'.

* The usual but still not unappreciative thanks to Fran Colman for criticism and encouragement, again, as usual, blame free, as are Jacques Durand and Louisa Sadler, who provided detailed comments on the pre-final version of the paper. Belated thanks too to my former supervisors John Lyons and John Sinclair, who, in the sixties, respectively stimulated my interest in 'notional grammar' and helped instil the idea of 'prosodic syntax'.

Anderson (1986) draws an analogy here between CRs and phonological elements: the members of the universal set of elements out of which phonological representations are constructed are distinguished phonetically, by their possession or lack of certain *phonetic* properties or features; likewise, the universal alphabet of CRs is defined and distinguished in terms of combinations of *notional features*, as in Table 1.1 (cf. Anderson 1971a: § 12.3; 1972: § x; 1973a; 1977: ch. 2), where the CRs comprise the set argued for in the preceding and other places, and they are characterized by possession or lack of the unary notional features, **loc** and **abl**, or 'place' and 'source', which may be relevant to other categories than case. Indeed, it is my concern here to re-emphasize that these case-grammar proposals belong within a tradition whose concern is with the set of syntactic categories as a whole, namely the tradition of 'notional grammar'. Let us spell this out a little more carefully, before carrying even further the analogy with phonology.

TABLE 1.1

CRs	Absolutive	Ergative	Locative	Ablative
Features			**loc**	**loc**
		abl		**abl**

The cross-linguistic identification of word classes in general, not just of members of the set of CRs, depends on notional criteria. As is familiar to every beginning linguistics student, syntactic classes established on distributional grounds cannot be equated with notional classes such as are comprised, for instance, of those words which denote and can be used to make reference to 'people, places, or things'. But the equation of classes across languages invokes the words characterized in such notional terms as the prototypical members of particular syntactic classes (cf. here e.g. Lyons 1966a; 1968: § 7.6.1; 1977: § 11.3; Schachter 1985). We use the label 'noun' for that class of words in a language which is typically referential (either in itself or as part of an endocentric construction ('noun phrase')), and this class will contain as prototypical members those words characterized notionally as above. We label 'verb' that class which is typically predicative and whose prototypical members denote 'processes' (including 'actions'). There is no simple distributional characteristic of 'noun-hood' or 'verb-hood'. Within a richly articulated syntactic theory there will be universal abstract 'properties' attributable to noun and verb; yet these do not define or give substance to the notion 'noun' or 'verb', but rather constitute theorems with respect to which status as noun or verb is axiomatic. They follow from the notional characteristics of noun or verb.

Say, for instance, we have some universal definition of (syntactic) subjecthood; and let us lay aside the difficulties in arriving at such (cf. e.g. Keenan 1976, Johnson 1977) and recognize the possibility that some languages may simply fail to meet the universal definition (universal definitions may not be universally applicable—Anderson 1980a). It will universally be the case that nouns belong to the set of syntactic entities that function as subjects. But this is predictable from the essentially referential nature of nouns: referential entities are prototypical arguments and subjects are (however defined) a special argument type. This is particularly clear given the definition of subject suggested in Anderson 1977, 1979a, 1980b, whereby those arguments constituting subjects are selected in accordance with a hierarchy of CRs, each argument being primitively associated with a CR but not with presence or absence of subjecthood (however the latter is characterized). I therefore consider unwarranted claims concerning in this respect the 'autonomous' character of syntax, as, for example, Williams's (1983) denial of a semantic basis for syntactic categories: indeed, the most that his argument can be taken to show is that certain semantic distinctions perhaps do not have syntactic consequences.

Consider again our analogy with phonological representation. As with noun and verb there are distributional (in this case, phonotactic) universals associated with status as consonant or vowel (cf. e.g. Greenberg 1978a). However, segment types are defined not distributionally, but rather by their internal phonetic characteristics, their phonetic features; and the feature composition determines phonotactic potential. This is well illustrated by the role of the 'sonority hierarchy', defined in terms of the feature composition of segment types (specifically, in terms of dependency phonology, the content of the categorial gesture—cf. e.g. Anderson and Ewen 1980a, 1987: ch. 4; Anderson and Durand 1986; and see further below), in determining universal aspects of syllable structure and a range of other phenomena. This is not to deny that features are relativistic and their interpretation system-dependent (if the difficulties noted by e.g. Pike (1943: particularly ch. 5) are to be avoided); but they have a substantive basis. Representations on both planes (of phonology and syntax) are constructed out of universal substantive, interpreted alphabets.

This is just one aspect of the analogy of structural principles which Hjelmslev (e.g. 1953: 101) held to characterize the planes (though he himself would have rejected the idea of substantive alphabets) and which we shall pursue further in what immediately follows. The *structural analogy* assumption simply embodies an expectation that the structural properties of one plane will be replicated on the other, except for substantive-based differences and for distinctions that are based on the relationship between the planes (given, say, that phonology interprets syntax). (For some discussion and exemplification see Anderson 1985a, 1986, forthcoming b.) Thus, even the analogies I have been drawing so far are not simply expository conveniences but are demanded by the structural analogy assumption.

Our presentation of the internal structure of the CRs in Table 1.1 has already assumed the existence of notional features analogous to the phonetic features which characterize phonological segments. Let us now carry the analogy a little further forward. Within the notational system of dependency phonology segments are characterized by the presence and absence of unary features, grouped into subsegments or *gestures* and possibly, within gestures, related by *dependency* (rather than simple co-occurrence). Thus, we might represent a contrastive unit such as English /g/ as in (1):

(1) {**C; V**}
{**l, u**}

where the braces enclose gestures, the first being the *categorial*, in which the segment is specified as a voiced stop, and the second the *articulatory* specification for a velar. **C, V, l,** and **u** are unary features: **C** is the feature of 'consonantality' (energy reduction), **V** that of 'vocalicness' (harmonic energy), **l** is 'linguality', and **u** is 'gravity'. The semicolon indicates that in this segment type **C** predominates over (governs) **V**; in the representation for a voiceless fricative ({**V: C**}) the two features mutually govern, and in that for a sonorant consonant ({**V; C**}) the preponderance is reversed; a voiceless stop lacks the **V** altogether, and a vowel lacks **C**. These representations of categorial gestures, as presented in Table 1.2, impose a hierarchy on the various segment types in terms of the relative proportions of **V** and **C** present, from presence of **V** and absence of **C** to the converse. It is this categorial hierarchy which determines syllable phonotactics. Notice too that the representations are of varying complexity: the vowels and voiceless stops are inherently simpler than the other types. This correlates with their 'less marked' status, in terms of distribution throughout languages, for example. **l** and **u** in (1) are simply combined; **l** alone would be a denti-alveolar, **u** alone a labial, both appropriately, it would appear, less complex. (On such representations see again particularly Anderson and Ewen 1987: pt. II.)

TABLE 1.2

Features	**V**	**V; C**	**V: C**	**C; V**	**C**
Major classes	vowel	son	vl fric	vd stop	vl stop

The case features deployed in Table 1.1 are not the syntactic analogues of categorial features in the phonology; in characterizing CRs they (and other features, to do with dimensionality, orientation, and the like—distinguishing the locationals *in/on*, *before/after*—cf. Anderson 1977: ch. 2) are associated with a single word class, a class for which one might use the term *functor*, frequently realized as an adposition (as in the preceding examples) but also frequently cumulated with the noun word class and manifested morphologically (see further below): they are *subcategorial* features. The *categorial* features of the syntax distinguish word classes: analogous to **C** and **V** we might introduce a referential feature **N** and a predicative one **P**, such that we can characterize names and pronouns as categorially {**N**}, verbs as {**P**}. This correlates with their semantic functions, argument versus predicate, and with their universality (cf. Schachter 1985: §§ 1.1–2): they are the most simple to specify (like vowel and voiceless stop in the phonology).

I assume the strong position that **N** and **P** exhaust the notional categorial features: other 'classes' are distinguished by combination of these two (as with **C** and **V**) or, like the different CRs, are subcategories of classes so distinguished (as by the articulatory gesture in phonology). Thus, functors are associated with neither **N** nor **P**;

they are in themselves categorially unspecified, as neither referential nor predicative. Adjectives are more complexly specified, in being both referential (as in *large dogs*, wherein *large* invokes some subset of the set of dogs—or, less generally, as constituting arguments in e.g. *the poor* or *the beautiful*) and predicative, as in (2):

(2) John is large

i.e. categorially they are perhaps {**P, N**} (but see further below). For the reason just invoked I thus do not, *pace* Lyons (1968: §7.6.4), regard the association between adjectives and **N**, or nouns, as purely 'superficial'—indeed, the sharing of 'superficial' (morphological) properties could be taken as a reflection of a 'deeper' affinity, rather than as simply arbitrary. They are classified as sharing a property with both nouns and verbs (cf. e.g. Anderson 1973a) and as being inherently more complex than either. They are thus as a class perhaps not universally distinguished (cf. Schachter 1985: § 1.3; and, on the ontological basis for the ambivalence of adjectives, Lyons 1977: §11.3), and may figure only as a subclass of one of the major categories.

The situation of nouns clearly requires a little further consideration, once we move outside the prototypical case of names. For common nouns can also be predicative, as in (3):

(3*a*) This is meat
(*b*) This is a cow

unlike names, which even in copula sentences are arguments rather than predicates, as is evidenced by the equivalence of predicational structure of (4*a*) and (*b*), whatever the distinction(s) in information structure involved:

(4*a*) The go-between is Jonathan
(*b*) Jonathan is the go-between

(cf. Anderson 1977: ch. 2). (4) are equative; each NP is an argument, whereas in (3) only the initial one is such.

But predicative structures involving nouns display a subset of the same internal possibilities as noun arguments (thus *This is a very large cow of dubious origin*, etc.), though they do not include referential definites as in (4*b*); crucially, predicative nouns remain potential noun phrases. In view of this, common nouns might be analysed as {**N; P**}—that is, entities whose referential potential preponderates over their predicative potential. Adjectives can be appropriately distinguished from nouns by possessing the oppositely orientated dependency structure: {**P; N**}. The semicolon again indicates the presence of a dependency relation between the features in the (in this instance, syntactic) categorial gesture, such that with adjectives **P** predominates over **N,** whereas with common nouns the reverse is the case. The mere presence of **P** in a categorial gesture allows predicative position; but those predicates which also are associated with **N** typically are more restricted—for example, in their *argument structure* (the range of arguments available to them), or, in many languages, the requirement, when they are predicative, of a superordinate (simple) predicate, or copula, as in (2). We can further associate with the specification {**N; P**} for common nouns a redundancy of the form of (5):

(5) {**N; P**} ⇒ {**N**}

which allows referential positions to common nouns (but not predicative position to names, etc.), though their occurrence there entails certain restrictions (see below).

An obvious extension to the hierarchy is the inclusion of a position thereon for infinitives: if they are accorded a characterization as {**P; N**} (in recognition of the reduced 'verbalness' that goes along with their typically argument status—see Anderson forthcoming a), then adjectives can return to their central position in the hierarchy, as {**P: N**}—**P** and **N** are mutually governing. (Nouns remain as {**N; P**}.) Again the preponderances of features specify, as well as relative relatedness among classes, a hierarchy with names at one end and verbs at the other.[1]

Return now to the referential function of adjectives. Like nouns they establish potentially referential sets, as in (6):

(6) Frances adores large pigs.

But as part of the structure of an argument, i.e. as 'attributives', they specifically introduce a subset, or subpart (with 'mass' nouns—see below), in the case of (6) of the set of *pigs*. I follow the proposals put

[1] With the addition of complex categories (such as are proposed below as characterizing, say, nominalizations), the hierarchy can be considerably extended further, in such a way as to give promise of providing, for instance, for the 'squishy' phenomena described by Ross (1973). However, I shall not pursue these aspects in the present paper: for some brief discussion see Anderson forthcoming a: § 1.

forward in Anderson (1976: ch. 4—and see too 1979b) in expressing this inherently partitive character of attributive adjectives as (7):

(7) {**N**}
{**abl**}

i.e. adjectives are names which are characterised by a subcategorization feature as taking an argument specifying the source from which the subset denoted by the adjective is extracted. (Cf. e.g. Anderson 1977: ch. 2, on similar argument-specifying subcategorization for verbs.) Such a characterization rests in this instance on the assumption that a noun phrase such as the second in (6) has attributed to it a syntactic structure such as that shown in (8), wherein *large* is the

(8)

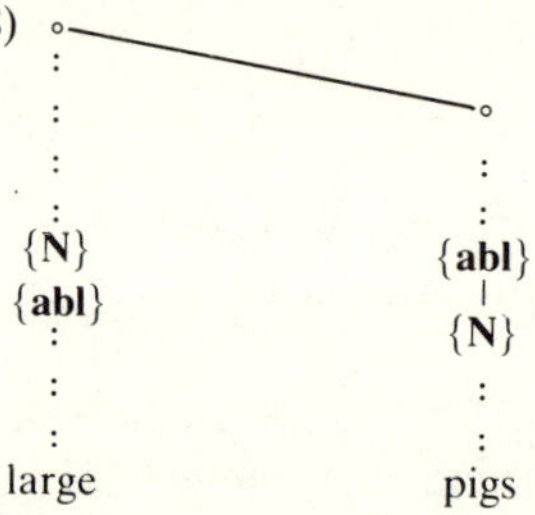

head of the construction and *pigs* realizes a dependent characterized as a functor-argument complex: the functor governs the {**N**} but is not distinct in sequence from it; the {**N**} is *subjoined* rather than *adjoined* (Anderson 1971b). In other languages such a functor is given distinct expression (Anderson 1976: ch. 4), either in the morphology of the word which realizes the complex or as an independent word (adposition); and in other circumstances in English the partitive functor is expressed by *of* (see further below). Such complexes characterize a variety of 'derived' categories, such as 'adverbs' of different types (cf. Anderson 1971b) and nominalizations (cf. Anderson 1984), as well as subclasses involving functors and other closed class items such as some we shall discuss below (and cf. here the extensive discussion in Thrane 1980).

If an overall representation such as (8) is acceptable,[2] then we can

[2] Zwicky (1985) finds analyses of the noun phrase of the kind presented in (8) 'odd' but provides no principled basis for so describing them; I suggest they are not so much 'odd' as 'unfamiliar'. Many more familiar analyses are more 'odd' in the sense of lacking motivation.

associate with adjectives the lexical redundancy in (9):

(9) $\{\mathbf{P{:}\ N}\} \Rightarrow \begin{matrix}\{\mathbf{N}\}\\ \{\mathbf{abl}\}\end{matrix}$

which suppresses **P** and introduces a subcategorial **abl**, specifying that such items take an **abl** argument. Again, the converse does not hold: there are items characterizable as in (7) which are not also predicative—such as those in *the late president*, *our beloved leader*, etc. (cf. e.g. Levi 1973).

The remainder of our discussion is concerned with various classes of $\{\{\mathbf{N}\}(\{\mathbf{abl}\})\}$ items in English, in an attempt to show the appropriateness of notional classification in a rather rich domain whose interpretation remains controversial. Given the dimensions of the present paper, many potential riches will remain unmined; but I hope at least to make something of a case for the viability and interest of notional grammar.

Some labels for a referential (sub)set signal that the identification of the (possibly one-member) set is context-dependent in some way (e.g. textually, deictically), as opposed to being part of 'background' knowledge; this is the case with personal pronouns. Let us associate these $\{\mathbf{N}\}$ forms with a notional diacritic $\boldsymbol{\delta}$. Some such $\{\{\mathbf{N}\}\{\boldsymbol{\delta}\}\}$ are, like adjectives, partitive, and thus also $\{\mathbf{abl}\}$—i.e. are $\{\{\mathbf{N}\}\{\boldsymbol{\delta}, \mathbf{abl}\}\}$; this is the case with definite articles and (optionally) demonstratives. With both these last and with adjectives in English the partitive marker is not given overt expression; as represented in (8) above it is cumulated with the set label. Let us characterize this by the syntactic redundancy, appropriate for English, in (10):

(10) $\{\mathbf{abl}\{\mathbf{N}\}\} \Rightarrow \{\mathbf{abl}\}^{\sim}\{\mathbf{N}\}\}/\{\{\mathbf{N}\}\_\}$

i.e. partitive heads ($\{\mathbf{N}\}$, whether $\{\boldsymbol{\delta}\}$ or not) take an **abl** argument in which the **abl** is not distinguished in sequence from ($^{\sim}$) its dependent $\{\mathbf{N}\}$; the $\{\mathbf{N}\}$ is subjoined to the functor, which as governor determines external distribution. (10) refers in abbreviated form to configurations of the character of: $\{\{\mathbf{N}\}\{\mathbf{abl}\}\}$; $\{\}\{\mathbf{abl}\}$; $\{\{\mathbf{N}\}\}$; and it cancels the normal expectation that syntactic elements (each unit bounded by an outer bracket) are sequenced distinctively. (I am assuming that such sequencing is non-contrastive, derivative, assigned in the course of the syntax: see Anderson 1976, 1977, 1986.)

Another group of $\{\{\mathbf{N}\}\{\mathbf{abl}\}\}$ forms, however, preserve overt expression of the partitive before a form which is itself {{**N**}{**abl**, $\boldsymbol{\delta}$}}, as illustrated in (11):

(11*a*) two peaches, some peaches
(*b*) two of the peaches, some of them

while still others uniformly retain an overt partitive:

(12*a*) a lot of peaches, groups of stragglers
(*b*) a lot of the peaches, groups of the stragglers

In the latter case we can relate the failure of (10) to the fact that the {{**N**}{**abl**}}'s involved are all inherently (rather than derivatively—see below) number-bearing, i.e.:

(13) {**sg/pl**} $\Rightarrow$ −(10)

(We return below to the distribution of number.) The pattern illustrated in (11) is characteristic of 'quantifiers', cardinal (*two*) and non-cardinal (*some*), i.e. non-$\boldsymbol{\delta}$ {{**N**}{**abl**}} forms which, like those in (12), do not bring along a denotative characteristic for the subset they introduce (as with descriptive adjectives like *large* in (6)), but which, unlike *group*, etc., do not bear an inherent number distinction. Let us abbreviate the semantic characteristic shared by forms of the (11) and (12) types as $\boldsymbol{\varepsilon}$.[3] Thus, all $\boldsymbol{\varepsilon}$-forms reject (10) if their dependent **abl** includes {{**N**}{$\boldsymbol{\delta}$}}:

(14) {$\boldsymbol{\varepsilon}$, **abl**{$\boldsymbol{\delta}$}} $\Rightarrow$ −(10)

(where the innermost bracket specifies a constraint on the **abl** argument), and (12*b*) are excluded by virtue of both (13) and (14). Number-variable numerals like *hundred* show application of (10) only in the singular, and if they do not govern a $\boldsymbol{\delta}$-form: *a hundred peaches*, *a hundred of the peaches*, *hundreds of the peaches*, but *hundreds of peaches*.

More exceptional are various 'universal quantifiers', here indicated by the presence of the additional notional diacritic $\boldsymbol{\alpha}$ (but see n. 3). *All* and *both* allow optional operation of (10) in the circumstances outlawed by (14):

[3] For attempts at a more explicit characterization of the semantics and syntax of $\boldsymbol{\varepsilon}$ see e.g. Anderson 1973b, 1974; Jessen 1975. In terms of these accounts, the 'universal quantifiers' are characterized in terms of $\boldsymbol{\varepsilon}$ but specifically its double negation rather than as involving a further ($\boldsymbol{\alpha}$) subcategorizational feature; and an interpretation is offered therein of 'scope determination', 'referential opacity', and related phenomena.

(15) all/both (of) the peaches

and, moreover, in this case show postpositioning with respect to pronouns (*they all/both*). They differ from the α-quantifier *each*, however else, by virtue of rejecting an **abl** that is {**sg**}, whereas *each* demands such:

(16*a*) all peaches, all sunshine, *all peach
(*b*) *each peaches, *each sunshine, each peach

to the exclusion of plural and mass {−**sg**, −**pl**} (where '−' denotes absence of a feature. We can therefore restrict (14) as in (17):

(17) $\{\boldsymbol{\alpha}, \mathbf{abl}\{-\mathbf{sg}\}\} \Rightarrow (-(10))$

whereby, in the case described on the left of (17), the ban on (10) is shown by the outer bracket on the right as being optional only.

More seriously still, *every*, despite, like *each*, requiring a singular partitive noun:

(18) *every peaches, *every sunshine, every peach

behaves like an unrestricted {{**N**}{**abl**}} in, as well as obeying (10), also rejecting a {$\boldsymbol{\delta}$} partitive:

(19) *every of the peach(es)

And it behaves specifically like an 'article', with which it is mutually exclusive (cf. the sequencing constraints formulated below): for instance, with respect to the positional criteria for 'quantifiers' proposed by Lightfoot (1979: §4.1) *every* shares with *a*(*n*) and *the* the distinction of failing to occur in all but one such position (the least distinctive one for quantifiers), and like them it is necessarily also partitive.

This suggests that we recognize a subclass of articles which cross-classifies with {$\boldsymbol{\delta}$}, {$\boldsymbol{\varepsilon}$}, and {$\boldsymbol{\alpha}$}, with *the*, *a*(*n*), and *every* as its respective members. (A fourth member of the article subclass might be the 'reduced *some*' of *Some politician suggested that*, as a non-cardinal equivalent to *a*(*n*).) There is certainly a notional basis for this in the case of *the* and *a*(*n*): they both involve a weakening of the characteristic properties of the subclass they belong to, *the* being only weakly deictic (cf. Thorne 1972; Lyons 1977: §15.2) and *a*(*n*) being only weakly quantifying, or, specifically, numerical (Thorne 1982). And we return to their article status below. However, this is perhaps less clear in the case of *every*, which would then have simply to be marked as a lexical exception, a non-prototypical article. At any rate, we can formulate a constraint on articles as in (20), where τ is the article diacritic shared by *the*, *a*(*n*), and *every*:

(20) $\{\tau\} \Rightarrow \{\mathbf{abl}\}$

such that an article necessarily takes an **abl** argument.

Such a brief discussion can be no more than suggestive; I have concentrated my attention on word classes associated with 'noun phrases', and the examination has been far from exhaustive (cf. again Thrane 1980). But the conclusion is clear, and worthy of further consideration. All of the classes we have been discussing, traditionally associated with the 'noun phrase', belong to the notional class {**N**}, which introduces potentially referential (sub)sets; and they are distinguished in terms of further (subcategorizational) features which are themselves notionally based (provided in some instances we allow for lexical exceptions) but which correlate in various ways with the distribution of the partitive marker *of*—and with the relative distributions of the subclasses, as anticipated in (20). That is, crucial aspects of the word order of noun phrases are determined by the notional subcategorization. These can be characterized in terms of constraints on the nature of the partitive (**abl**) argument associated with the subcategories. Let us spell this out somewhat.

TABLE 1.3

Classes	Quantifiers	Demonstratives	Adjectives	Nouns	Names
Examples	some, all	this, the	large	pig	Frances
Features	{**N**} {**abl**, $\varepsilon(\alpha)$}	{**N**} {**abl**, $\delta(\tau)$}	{**N**} {**abl**}	{**N**(;**P**)}	{**N**}

We can summarize some of our results so far in the form of Table 1.3, wherein names are distinguished from common nouns by lacking the predicative possibility ({**N**; **P**}). Neither quantifiers nor demonstratives allow a partitive quantifier:

(21) *all some pigs, *the some pigs

though quantifiers (but not normally another demonstrative or article) permit a demonstrative **abl** (11b, 15, 19); and descriptive adjectives allow neither a quantifier which lacks inherent number nor a demonstrative **abl**:

(22) *large some pigs, *large the pigs

Adjectives allow 'stacking' (a succession of **abl** relations):

(23) large brown female pigs

where again the sequence is determined by semantic factors (Bache 1978); but, as observed, quantifiers may not be stacked under quantifiers nor demonstratives under demonstratives, on account of semantic incompatibility (**that this pig*). Partitive arguments appear to the right of their heads (where appropriate, preceded by *of*). The recorded gaps are thus accounted for by the restrictions formulated in (24):

(24*a*) $*\{\mathbf{N}\}$
$\{\mathbf{abl}, \varepsilon/\delta\{\mathbf{N}\}$
$\{\varepsilon\}\}$

(*b*) $*\{\mathbf{N}\}$
$\{\mathbf{abl}, \delta/\tau\{\mathbf{N}\}$
$\{\delta/\tau\}\}$

(which accounts for (21) etc.), and by a restriction on the arguments of adjectives (simple {{**N**}{**abl**}}) that limits them to other adjectives or number inherent {**N**}'s (*pig*, *group*). Nouns, which are not subcategorized for {**abl**}, appear only on the right of such sequences. Names are excluded from all such sequences by (25):

(25) $*\{\mathbf{N}\}$
$\{\mathbf{abl}\{\mathbf{N}-(;\mathbf{P})\}\}$

given that names are {**N**}s that cannot be predicative.

Apparently exceptional here are cardinal quantifiers and non-cardinals such as *many* and *few*:

(26*a*) the two peaches
(*b*) the many peaches

whereby (24) is violated. But these differ from other quantifiers in additionally being adjectival, to the extent of also being, marginally perhaps, predicative:

(27*a*) The survivors were five (in number)
(*b*) The survivors were many

and, in the case of *many* and *few*, modifiable by *very*. Such quantifiers thus have dual category membership, and it is by virtue of their specification as {**P: N**} as well as { {**N**} {**abl, ε**} } that (26) and (27) are viable.

Also excluded from (24*a*) are quantifiers which bear inherent number:

(28) the group(s) of pigs

The number variation is also shown in (29):

(29*a*) a group of pigs
(*b*) groups of pigs

which reveals further that *group* etc. violate (24*a*) in another respect, in that they can constitute the partitive argument of another quantifier (cf. also *two groups of pigs* and the like). We must therefore impose the restriction on (24*a*) in (30):

(30) {**N**}
{**abl, ε, sg/pl**} ⇒ – (24*a*)

Exceptionally accessible to (30) to some extent are apparently *few* and *little* in *a few* and *a little*. But a consideration of their status must take us into a by now overdue discussion of number and the articles.

An examination of number introduces another analogy with the phonology. For number in English, indicating a distinction between a set of referents presented as one-membered and one that is not, is not marked by a syntactic segment, a word, but rather by a feature expressed in the morphological structure of particular words. Moreover, it may be realized at various points within a particular domain:

(31*a*) *this* large *pig*
(*b*) *these* large *pigs*

In other languages, including Old English, number may also be realized on e.g. adjectives (cf. Anderson forthcoming c):

(32*a*) se goda mann
(*b*) ða godan menn

And we can define the domain structurally: namely configurations subordinate to {**N**} (as in (31)), in the first place, and terminated by the {**N**} which allows a distinction in number to be drawn, which is inherently number-bearing (*pig* in (31)). Number spreads up a dependency tree from its initial locus to the highest {**N**} in a sequence of { {**N**} {**abl**} }'s, unless blocked by another number-bearing element which is opaque to the spread of the original number, as in (33):

(33) one of the pigs

Adjectives in modern English, though they do not realize number, are nevertheless transparent to its spread, as shown by (31). Unlike *pig*, *one* is of invariant number, and blocks number spread. Quantifiers of variable number, such as that in (29), allow spread of the original number, so that both (34*a*) and (*b*) are possible:

(34*a*) A group of pigs has escaped.
(*b*) A group of pigs have escaped.

The noun phrases in (34) are both singular and plural. (34) also illustrates the spread of the number of a subject {**N**} to a predicative element (*has*/*have*). (We return in a moment to the status of *a*(*n*).) 'Fractional' quantifiers do not spread their own inherent number (*A quarter of the cheese was edible*, *Three-quarters of the cheese was edible*) but, like other variable-number quantifiers, do not block, indeed favour, spread of number from a subordinate (*A quarter of the men like it*). So too variable-number integers: *A hundred* (*of the*) *men like it*.

The phenomenon I have been describing is familiar to any phonologist as a 'prosody' or 'autosegment', not just in outline but in detail, given that we have here the spread of a feature from a 'trigger' through a structurally defined domain, the spread being 'filtered' by opaque and transparent segments (in the senses used above) and manifested in segments which are accessible to it. Compare typical 'harmony' systems such as are described by Clements (1980), Goldsmith (1985), Anderson *et al.* (1985), Anderson and Durand (1986, 1987a), or Anderson 1987). Crudely, number constitutes a syntactic prosody (cf. the similar suggestion concerning tense made in Anderson 1965). Thus, the plurality feature associated initially with *pigs* in (31*b*) is spread to the rest of the noun phrase by virtue of being derivatively associated with the structure subordinate to the highest {**N**} as indicated in (35), plurality then being realized within any accessible word in the domain associated with the prosody. {**pl**} in (*b*) is what Anderson *et al.* (1985) refer to in the phonological plane as an 'extra-segmental' feature; the derived representation in (35) is equi-

(35a) Number spreading in noun phrases

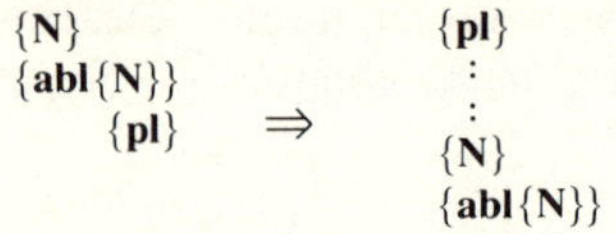

(b) . . . illustrated

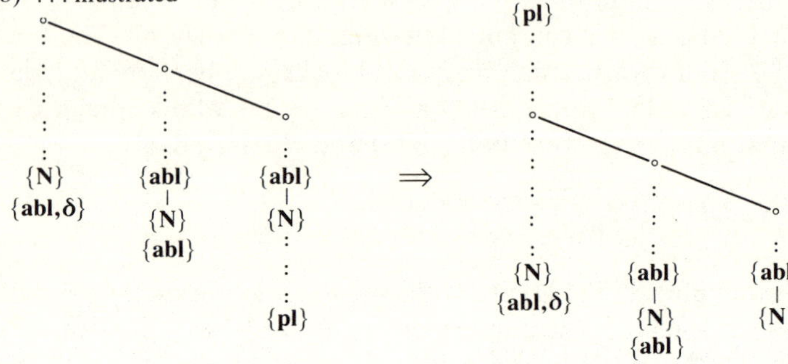

valent to a one-to-many association, those on the left being one-to-one. Thus, every representation resulting from application of (35*a*) is in turn eligible for further application with respect to its governor; {**pl**} is thus spread up the tree, iteratively.

In Old English gender shows a similar prosodic spread (though descripion is complicated by the interaction of 'grammatical' and 'natural' gender), being realized on all {**N**}s in a partitive stack and on predicative {**N**}s; and person spreads from subject to governing verb. Case marking is realized over a similar domain to gender, but in this instance the 'trigger' is not a (gender- or number-inherent) {**N**} but rather the subcategorization of the functor governing the relevant 'noun phrase' (cf. Anderson forthcoming c).

We must now consider the question of whether or not both singularity and plurality spread. Just as there are forms which are non-derivatively both singular and plural, as (36*a*):

(36*a*) A committee are considering the proposal
(*b*) A committee is considering the proposal

some {**N**}s are neither singular nor plural, the 'mass' nouns, as illustrated by the predicative in (3*a*) above. The conjunction of **sg** and **pl** allows for four possibilities as far as inherent number marking is concerned (cf. here the slightly different analysis of Anderson 1969).

Concord on the verb, however, depends on plurality versus non-plurality alone:

(37*a*) A cow is expensive.
(*b*) Meat is expensive.
(*c*) Cows are expensive.

The simple {**N**} in (37*a*) is {**sg**, −**pl**}, (*c*) {−**sg**, **pl**} but (*b*) is simply {−**sg**, −**pl**}. It is thus unnecessary to suppose that {**sg**} spreads to predicates: all that we need is a distinction between presence of {**pl**} and its absence. Similarly, we can allow for (36*b*) and the like by supposing that with { {**N**} {**sg**, **pl**} } spreading of {**sg**} does not occur but spreading of {**pl**} is optional, or by analysing (*b*) as being simply {**sg**, **pl**}, just as *the committees* would be {−**sg**, **pl**}. (However, on some additional complexities see Juul 1975: pt. II, ch. 1.) Realization of number (plurality) in the noun depends on both the presence of {**pl**} and the absence of {**sg**}: the {**N**}s in (36) and (37*a*) are both associated with {**sg**}, and (36*a*) and (*b*) both lack {**pl**}; so no number is indicated. Only (37*c*) is characterized by the conjunction {−**sg**, **pl**}.

As we have already observed in relation to universal (*α*) forms, quantifiers impose constraints on the number of their arguments. *Many* and *group* require that their **abl** argument be {−**sg**, **pl**}:

(38*a*) many cows, a group of cows
(*b*) *many cow/meat, *a group of cow/meat

more and *lot* require only an argument that is {−**sg**}:

(39*a*) more cows, a lot of cows
(*b*) more meat, a lot of meat
(*c*) *more cow, *a lot of cow

(where (*c*) are viable only on a mass interpretation); *much* and *quantity* require an argument that is {−**sg**, −**pl**}:

(40*a*) much meat, a quantity of meat
(*b*) *much cow(s), *a quantity of cow(s)

a(*n*) takes an argument which is {**sg**, −**pl**}:

(41*a*) a cow
(*b*) *a cows, *a meat

One behaves either like *many* or *a*(*n*), depending on whether its argument is {**δ**} or not:

(42*a*) one cow, *one of the cow
(*b*) *one cows, one of the cows
(*c*) *one meat, *one of the meat

and it is inherently singular, unlike *many*, *much*, and *more*, which simply receive, where appropriate, the number of their argument (via the schema roughly formulated and illustrated in (35)). Thus, the sequence *one of the/those* behaves like a *many*-type quantifier sequence.

Similarly, interposition of {**δ**} allows *much*, *more*, and *all* to occur superordinate to a {**sg**}: *much/more/all of the cow*. {**δ**} appears to function as a constraint modifier and (arguably) specifically reducer: *more* and *all* require a {−**sg**} argument, *more/all of the* is unrestricted; *much* requires {−**sg**, −**pl**}, *much of the* only {−**pl**}; *one* requires a {**sg**}, *one of the* {**pl**}. We can regard even this last as a case of reduction, given that the requirement that an argument be {**sg**} is the 'marked' possibility, associated only with inherently {**sg**} items. For some exemplification see e.g. Selkirk 1977: § 1. Selkirk, in fact, argues against a 'partitive' analysis of quantifier + noun sequences. But some of her arguments depend on the assumption that e.g. *the* + noun is not also a partitive construction, and thus are not germane to the present account. The others concern the availability of {**N**}s as distinct antecedents for relative clauses, which can, on the present account, be related to whether or not superjunction of **abl** occurs, and behaviour under 'Extraposition from NP', the constraints on which are problematical (Oehrle 1977), but may also be related to the aforementioned factor. I therefore do not pursue these here.

The distribution in (43), as well as illustrating the constraint-reducing role of **δ**:

(43*a*) *many committee/many of the committee
(*b*) *more committee/more of the committee
(*c*) *much (of the) committee
(*d*) one (of the) committee

supports the proposal that 'collective' nouns like *committee* can be {**sg, pl**}.

We can associate a different pattern, or rather alternative patterns, with a variety of {**N**} {**abl**} we have not so far considered, namely those of Thrane's (1980) 'generic' category—*variety*, *kind*, *sort*—for which I shall introduce the subcategorization feature γ for genus. These are associated either with the restriction that their **abl** argument not disagree with them in plurality, as in (44):

(44*a*) this kind of pig
(*b*) these kinds of pigs
(*c*) this kind of pork
(*d*) these kinds of pork

where *pork*, as neither {**pl**} nor {**sg**} is compatible with both *kind* and *kinds*, or with a limitation of the **abl** to {−**pl**}, as is the case in (44*a*, *c*, *d*) and in (45):

(45) these kinds of pig

Altogether, only a {**pl, sg**} argument is restricted as to the number of its superordinate generic. Colloquially, some of these {**abl,** γ} items have developed a third pattern, whereby *kind*, for example, lacks inherent number and is simply transparent to number spreading, as in *these kind of pigs*. For some discussion of this and related phenomena see Juul (1975: pt. I, ch. 2), wherein are also documented many complexities ignored in the preceding, such as the compatibility, in certain notional circumstances, of *every* with a {**pl**} subordinate (*every three weeks*, etc.).

A final consideration relating to *a*(*n*) introduces an interesting asymmetry in English. With plural nouns invocation of a subset need not be overtly expressed (by *some* etc.). Compare (46):

(46*a*) Men are untrustworthy.
(*b*) Men came towards me.

(46*a*) will typically be taken to refer ('generically') to the set of men; while (*b*) invokes a subset (or, at least, non-exhaustion of the membership of the set). We can therefore associate with (46*b*) the representation in (47), realized cumulatively (and in syncretism with simple { {**N**} {**pl**} } for (46*b*)) as *men*. Compare too partitive uses of 'mass' nouns, as in *Give me water* (and contrast French *des* versus *les* and *du* versus *le*). (*Le* and *les* introduce a different syncretism.)

(47)
$$\begin{array}{c} \{\mathbf{N}\} \\ \{\mathbf{abl}, \boldsymbol{\varepsilon}\} \\ | \\ \mathbf{abl} \\ | \\ \{\mathbf{N}\} \\ \{\mathbf{pl}\} \end{array}$$

One might also note, parenthetically, that prototypical 'mass' nouns, when numbered, also bring along a particular non-overt additional element of interpretation: *a pork* and *porks* are equivalent to (44*c*) and (*d*) respectively. It may be, then, that we should attribute to them, in this use, a complex categorial representation analogous to that suggested for plural nouns with a (covert) subset interpretation, specifically, in this case, (48):

(48)
$$\begin{array}{c} \{\mathbf{N}\} \\ \{\boldsymbol{\gamma}, \mathbf{sg/pl}\} \\ | \\ \mathbf{abl} \\ | \\ \{\mathbf{N}\} \end{array}$$

With singulars, on the other hand, a subset marker, or more exactly (Thorne 1982) 'member marker' is required, in the form of the indefinite article, even when a particular member is not invoked, i.e. when characterization by $\boldsymbol{\varepsilon}$ is not appropriate:

(49*a*) A man is untrustworthy.
(*b*) A man came towards me.

(Cf. e.g. Burton-Roberts (1976) on the 'generic indefinite article'.) We thus require a constraint of the character of (50):

(50)
$$\begin{array}{l} \{\mathbf{P}\} \\ \{\,\{\mathbf{N}\} \\ \quad \{\mathbf{sg}\}\,\} \end{array} \Rightarrow \begin{array}{l} \{\mathbf{P}\} \\ \{\,\{\mathbf{N}\} \\ \quad \{\mathbf{abl}, \boldsymbol{\varepsilon}, \boldsymbol{\tau}\{\,\{\mathbf{N}\} \\ \qquad\qquad\qquad \{\mathbf{sg}\}\,\}\,\} \end{array}$$

which requires that an argument of a predicate such as is specified on the left can appear only within a configuration such as that on the right, even though in some cases the additional structure of the latter is not semantically motivated. The same constraint accounts for the *a* with the singular of the variable-number genus ($\{\gamma\}$) markers (*kind*, *sort*) and quantifiers (*group*, *lot*, *quantity*), and also, parasitically, with *a few* and *a little*. And in English it extends to predicative position: cf. (3*b*).

(46*a*) and (49*a*) also reveal the semantic neutralization of number associated with 'genericness', something which is quite dramatically displayed in the formation of 'generic subsets' such as are expressed in the *many a* construction (... *many a slip* ...), containing on the one hand an item associated with a plural **abl** (recall (38)) and on the other the singular and singular-requiring *a*(*n*).

(50) encapsulates one aspect of the grammaticalization (relative desemanticization) associated with the formation of a subclass of articles. Similarly, the definite article need not indicate a context-dependent subset but may be used 'generically', as in, say, (51):

(51*a*) The Picts invented that.
(*b*) The window is a wonderful invention.

Indeed, the presence of *the* rules out a (47) interpretation for plurals; cf. (51*a*) and (52):

(52) Picts invented that.

(Cf. too the 'generic' use of *the* with 'mass' nouns like *air*, *flesh*: Christophersen 1939: 34–5.) And quite generally *the* can serve an anticipatory ('cataphoric') function with respect to a following subset description rather than itself recalling some subset established by the context, so that a phrase like (53):

(53) the people who built Stonehenge

may mark the first introduction of the subset of people being referred to. As such too it can even be used 'generically' in the singular:

(54) The man who drinks tea is untrustworthy.

Cf. (55):

(55) A man who drinks tea is untrustworthy.

In these cases *the* seems to function as an indicator that the phrase it heads is to be treated as an 'extended' name; whereas in its function of indicating context-dependence it makes of the phrase an 'extended' pronoun. Thus, the subclassification of *the* as a $\boldsymbol{\delta}$ element is not always warranted semantically.[4]

Say that the articles do indeed present a case of grammaticalization. (Christophersen (1939) provides many further suggestive examples; and extension of grammaticalization to the dual *a couple* is illustrated by Bolinger's (1980) delicate dissection of its syntax and semantics.) It seems to me that the adequate characterization of this (the phenomenon of grammaticalization) depends upon the assumption that a notional basis for syntactic categories is the norm, and that grammaticalizations are precisely departures from this norm. I have tried here to articulate this assumption as a restrictive theory of syntactic categories wherein the major word classes are distinguished by combinations of the notionally based categorial features **N** and **P,** which determines the major distributional properties of words; and subclasses are differentiated by further notional features, which again determine distributional properties. Such a theory severely constrains the kind and degree of linguistic variation we can expect to find, both among different languages and in the evolution of individual varieties. Certainly, as recognized above, we must allow for lexical exceptions, items which fail to behave as other members of the same notional class; and there is evidence of grammaticalization, the development by a class of semantically arbitrary syntactic properties. But these are parasitic upon classes which are defined by the strongly universal categorial features in combination with the notional subcategories selected by the particular language from a universal set.

In terms of such a framework, for instance, the catastrophic category changes, involving the innovation of syntactic categories such as 'modal' and 'quantifier', which Lightfoot (1979) envisages as characterizing the history of English cannot be entertained. There can be no such categorially distinct classes as 'modal' or 'quantifier': the former are categorially {**P**}, the latter {**N**}. The categories therefore cannot be innovated as such. Further, syntactic properties hold of notional classes: there therefore cannot be autonomous syntactic changes. It is thus reassuring that there are independent reasons for rejecting Lightfoot's accounts, in relation to both the analyses proposed for various stages of English and the kind of changes sug-

[4] *Those*, like *the*, but less so, is not always prototypically $\boldsymbol{\delta}$; it also is grammaticalized as a ('cataphoric') indicator of a following subset label, as in *those of the men who* ... or *those men who* ....: cf. the discussion of the articles below.

gested. It would be inappropriate to rehearse these here; and the modal case in particular has come under detailed scrutiny elsewhere (see e.g. Anderson 1976, 1978; Warner 1983; Allan 1984; Plank 1984a). (And Anderson forthcoming a offers an account of the grammaticalization of the modals compatible with the assumptions defended here.) But given the focus in the above discussion on the structure of noun phrases, some concluding remarks on Lightfoot's proposals concerning the history of quantifiers may be in order.

Perhaps what is most curious about these is Lightfoot's failure to establish a class of 'quantifiers' for Present-day English, given his concern to support the view that English has innovated just such a class. He lists various positions, occurrence in which differentiates 'quantifiers' from other words, though not all of the individual positions are unique to such; and he cites various putative members of this class of 'quantifiers' ('items such as *all*, *any*, *both*, *each*, *either*, *every*, *few*, *more*, *none*, *some*'). But the majority of these fail to satisfy some of the positional criteria, particularly the more crucial (because most distinctive), such as occurrence as a pre-determiner (*ALL the peaches*); and, as we have already observed, the putative 'quantifier' *every* shares with its fellows only the highly non-distinctive prenominal position. This is unsurprising given the variety of subcategories to which we have found it appropriate to assign *all*, *many*, *some*, *every*, etc. The details of positional behaviour result from the interplay of these subcategories, rather than directly reflecting gross once-and-for-all word-class divisions. Paradoxically (given the general orientation of the book), Lightfoot seems to have in mind a notional grouping rather than one directly reflected in the syntax. It is certainly difficult to imagine how a language learner could acquire the concept 'quantifier' on the basis of Lightfoot's criteria, without help of semantics (but, then, there is no reason to suppose that he should be without such help).

The same equation of word class with the putative sharing of a battery of positional possibilities also bedevils the discussion of Old English, in which, Lightfoot argues, the ancestors of the 'quantifiers' belonged to the word class 'adjective'. And the quest for positional equivalences between 'pre-quantifiers' and other 'adjectives' has an air of desperation about it. For instance, Lightfoot proposes that the two groups share the possibility of occurrence in pre-determiner position on the basis of this being available to some 'pre-quantifiers' and a tiny and untypical set of 'adjectives', including possessives and some cardinals (whose distribution in Present-day English, as we have seen, is much more like that of 'quantifiers' such as *many* than that of adjectives). The major relevant change involved in the history of English is the increase in positional restrictions as far as 'adjectives' and some 'quantifiers' (such as *some*) are concerned. To what extent and how this is associated with the decline of inflexional morphology remains uncertain, but worthy of further investigation. The notion that English has innovated a word class 'quantifier', it would appear, does not.

2

Some General Properties of Reference-tracking Systems

Bernard Comrie

1. Introduction

In this contribution, I intend to set out on a search for general principles underlying reference-tracking systems, that is the devices used in different languages to keep track of the various entities referred to in a discourse.[1] It is thus intended as a contribution to the general problem area of coreference. Clearly, one of the important characteristics of a coherent discourse is that the hearer should be able to retrieve from the form of the message information as to which entity is being referred to at each point in the discourse, and to this end languages have a number of means of indicating, for instance, whether one noun phrase is coreferential with some other noun phrase, and if so with which noun phrase it is coreferential. Hitherto, work on coreference has tended to proceed in two quite distinct directions, with little connection between them. On the one hand, formal syntacticians have studied the formal constraints on various devices that indicate coreference, such as reflexivization and pronominalization; in general, however, they have not been concerned with the discourse function of these constructions, essentially taking for granted that speakers and hearers use quite general strategies of information-encoding and information-processing so

[1] This material is based in part upon work supported by the National Science Foundation under Grant No. BNS-8504293 ('A description of the Wiyaw language of Papua New Guinea').

The following abbreviations are used: Abs: absolutive, Antipass: antipassive, Class: classifier, Cnj: conjunctive, Dat: dative, Dec: declarative, Dir: direct, DO: direct object, DS: different subject, Erg: ergative, Fem: feminine, Fut: future, Masc: masculine, Obv: obviative, Pl: plural, Pres: present, Prox: proximate, Real: realis, SS: same subject, Su: subject, Top: topic.

that, given the formal constraints on anaphora in the language in question, discourses are constructed in such a way that anaphoric relations are readily retrievable (without the discourse becoming otiose through undue specificity) and are interpreted in terms of the variants permitted by the grammar of the language plus general assumptions on plausibility of interpretations, etc. At the other extreme, those working from a discourse perspective have tended to be interested precisely in the way in which anaphoric relations are marked and retrieved in discourse, which often means paying less attention to the formal syntactic details of anaphoric devices (these details only infrequently being of practical importance) while paying more attention to how speakers and hearers manipulate ambiguities that are not resolved by the syntax of the language in question.

I hope that the present paper will steer a middle course between these two extremes. I believe that both approaches have taught us much that is valuable about anaphora in its broadest sense, and I will indeed be delighted if this paper can serve to bridge some of the gaps that have tended to grow between the two approaches. One outward sign of the intermediate position adopted is that I switch freely between terminology associated more closely with formal syntax (e.g. coreference) and terminology more closely associated with work on discourse (e.g. reference tracking). In section 2 I list a number of reference-tracking devices, which then serve as illustrative material for the discussion of parameters in reference tracking in section 3.

2. Reference-tracking devices

In this section, I will examine a selection from among the devices available in natural language to keep track of referents in discourse. I emphasize that this is a selection, not an exhaustive survey, of such devices. The particular choice is determined in part by my own interests, in part by the degree of interest shown in these devices in recent work. My indebtedness to the survey of reference-tracking devices in Foley and Van Valin (1984: 321–74) will, incidentally, be readily appreciated. In principle, any syntactic process that is sensitive to coreference can serve as a reference-tracking device, so that the operation of Equi in an English sentence like (1) enables retrieval of the information that the subject of the infinitive is coreferential with that of the main verb:

(1) Arthur decided to leave.

The devices considered below are a selection from those that are particularly salient in terms of reference tracking in discourse.

2.1. Gender/class indexing

In languages that have a gender/class system, it is often possible for the referent of a noun phrase to be tracked without resorting to explicit repetition of the noun phrase in question, simply by using some morphological form that explicitly encodes the gender/class of the noun phrase in question—always assuming, of course, that there are no potentially conflicting referents belonging to the same gender/class. A simple example is provided by English, with the masculine/feminine gender opposition in the third-person singular pronoun:

(2) Beryl went to the cinema with Charles. It was the first time he had been able to persuade her to go out with him.

Since the only two referents in the discourse are Beryl and Charles, and given that *Beryl* is a girl's name and Beryl must therefore be taken up with a feminine pronoun, and that *Charles* is a boy's name and Charles must therefore be taken up with a masculine pronoun, it is clear that the pronouns *he* and *him* in the second sentence must refer back to Charles, while the pronoun *her* must refer back to Beryl, i.e. the interpretation is '. . . Charles had been able to persuade Beryl to go out with Charles'. The gender/class system of English is, of course, rather minimal, permitting in the third person a distinction between singular and plural, and within the former a distinction between (roughly) human and non-human, the human category being further divided into male and female. Many other languages have much richer systems, permitting in particular finer discrimination among inanimate nouns because of their assignment to different classes; the Bantu languages, such as Swahili, provide a good illustration of such richer gender/class systems.

Two brief notes are in order before leaving the initial presentation of gender/class indexing. First, I use the term 'indexing' rather than 'agreement' simply to avoid any commitment to the existence of a specific rule or set of rules of agreement, whereby one morphological form would be determined strictly by reference to some property of another item. Even if we take the second sentence of (2) in isolation, repeated as (3) below, then there is a sense in which the masculine pronouns still serve to index some referent from the set of male human individuals, the feminine pronoun some referent from the set of female human individuals, even in the absence of any other noun phrase with which they can agree:

(3) It was the first time he had been able to persuade her to go out with him.

Secondly, gender/class should be interpreted in a very broad sense, roughly encompassing all of what are traditionally grouped together as agreement parameters, thus including, for instance, person and number in addition to gender or class in their narrow interpretations.

2.2. Reflexive pronouns

Especially in the formal literature on coreference, reflexive pronouns are perhaps the classic instance of a reference-tracking device, in particular of a device indicating coreference (whence, under appropriate circumstances, the appearance of a non-reflexive pronoun may force an interpretation of non-coreference). Again, simple examples from English will serve as illustrations:

(4) Daphne poisoned herself.

(5) Daphne poisoned her.

In (4), the reflexive pronoun *herself* indicates unequivocally that the person poisoned is the same as the poisoner, i.e. is Daphne. Sentence (5) in Modern Standard English is just as unequivocal in indicating that the victim was some female human individual other than the poisoner, i.e. other than Daphne.

2.3. Switch reference and switch function

One device that is widespread across the languages of the world, though as it turns out rather rare in European languages, for keeping track of referents is switch reference. In a classical switch-reference system, and I will restrict attention to such systems here, a given sentence will normally contain one independent clause (i.e. a clause that could stand as an independent sentence in its own right), plus optionally a number of dependent clauses (i.e. clauses that could not stand as independent sentences in their own right); the verb of each dependent clause is marked with either a same-subject inflection or a different-subject inflection, the former indicating that the subject of the dependent verb is coreferential with the subject of the clause on which it is dependent, the different-subject inflection indicating that the two subjects are non-coreferential. The following examples are from Harway (Wiyaw), a non-Austronesian language of Papua New Guinea, spoken in the south-west of Madang Province:

(6) Ha döyw nwg^{w}-ön, bör dw-a.
child rat see-SS run go:Pres:3sg-Dec
'The child saw the rat and he ran away.'

(7) Ha döyw nwg^{w}-mön, bör dw-a.
child rat see-DS run go:Pres:3sg-Dec
'The child saw the rat and it ran away.'

The same-subject suffix *-ön* on the dependent verb in (6) indicates that the subjects of the two clauses must be coreferential; since the subject of the dependent clause is explicitly given as 'the child', the subject of the clause on which it is dependent must also be interpreted as 'the child'. Conversely, in (7) the different-subject suffix *-mön* indicates that the subject of the clause 'ran away' cannot be the same as that of the dependent clause, i.e. cannot be 'the child'. Since the only other available referent in the discourse is 'the rat', the interpretation most plausibly assigned is that the rat ran away, although in principle the subject of the second clause could be any entity indexible by a third-person singular verb form other than the child.

For a recent collection of studies on switch reference, both as a general linguistic phenomenon and in a variety of languages, reference may be made to Haiman and Munro (1983).

Somewhat akin to switch reference is the notion of switch function, a term introduced, I believe, by Foley and Van Valin (1984: 354-60). The classic illustration is from Dyirbal, an Aboriginal language of northern Queensland described in detail in Dixon (1972). In general, in Dyirbal one argument of a non-initial clause in a sentence may be omitted if coreferential with one argument of the initial clause, provided both the argument omitted in this way and the argument with which it is coreferential occupy a specific grammatical relation. This grammatical relation has been referred to in various ways in the literature: topic (Dixon 1972), subject (Comrie 1978), pivot (Dixon 1979); I shall use 'pivot' here as the most neutral term. The pivot of an intransitive clause is the single argument required by the valency of the verb; the pivot of a transitive clause in Dyirbal is its patient (not its agent). Thus in (8), the pivot of the second, intransitive clause has been omitted under coreference with the pivot of the first, transitive clause:

(8) Bala-n jugumbil ba-nggu-l yara-nggu
Class:Abs-Fem woman:Abs Class-Erg-Masc man-Erg
balga-n, bani-nyu.
hit-Real come:here-Real
'The man hit the woman and she came here.'

Since the pivot of a transitive clause is its patient, the omitted pivot of the second, intransitive clause must be interpreted as coreferential with the patient of the initial, transitive clause, i.e. as 'the woman'.

If, however, the verb of the non-initial clause takes the suffix *-ngurra* (which precludes the appearance of realis or irrealis markers), then the pivot omitted from the second clause must be interpreted as coreferential with the agent of the initial transitive clause, and not with its pivot, as in (9):

(9) Bala-n jugumbil ba-nggu-l yara-nggu balga-n, bani-ngurra.
'The man hit the woman and he came here.'

The suffix *-ngurra* can thus be viewed as indicating a switch in function, from non-pivot (more specifically, agent) in the initial clause to pivot in the second clause.[2]

[2] I differ from Foley and Van Valin in not considering the antipassive, as in (i), to be an instance of switch-function marking. In the antipassive voice, a lexically transitive predicate shows up as intransitive, with the agent as the only argument required by the valency of the verb (though the patient may also appear, in an oblique case). In the antipassive, the agent is thus the pivot, so that in a sentence like (i) both the coreferential noun phrase in the first clause and the omitted noun phrase of the second clause have the same function—that of pivot:

(i) Bayi yara bani-nyu, ba-gu-n
Class:Abs:Masc man:Abs come:here-Real Class-Dat-Fem
jumbil-gu balgal-nga-nyu.
woman-Dat hit-Antipass-Real
'The man came here and he hit the woman.'

Once one recognizes the shift in grammatical relations in the antipassive (relative to the unmarked voice), the generalization concerning omissibility under coreference of pivots given in the main text for the basic voice carries over unchanged to the antipassive.

2.4. Obviation

The last of the reference-tracking devices I wish to consider in this paper is obviation, found in its classical form in the Algonquian languages. In, for instance, Plains Cree, in a given discourse segment one animate entity is selected as being of prime importance, and the noun phrase referring to this entity is placed morphologically in the proximate form; any reference to the entity selected as proximate within the discourse segment must be by means of proximate morphology. All other animate entities are referred to by noun phrases in the obviative form; any reference to such other referents must be by means of obviative morphology.[3] The proximate/obviative distinction applies not only to the noun phrase itself, but also to any pronouns referring to it, and also to verb morphology indexing the referent of the noun phrase in question. The system is easiest to follow in a discourse with only two participants. In the following discourse segment, from a Plains Cree text (Bloomfield 1930), the Cree is selected as the proximate entity, therefore all proximate morphology refers to the Cree, while obviative morphology refers to the other participant, namely the Blackfoot. (For a more detailed commentary, see Foley and Van Valin (1984: 333–8); note that in direct verb forms, the suffixal person-number morphology indexes the subject/agent.)

(10) Mēkw ē-pimohtē-t ispatināw wāpaht-am,
while Cnj-walk-3Prox hill see-3Prox
ē-āmaciwē-yit ayīsiyiniw-a, nāpēw-a.
Cnj-climb-3Obv person-Obv man-Obv
Ēkwa kitāpam-ē-w kitāpākan
and:then observe-Dir-3Prox spy glass
ē-kanawāpākanēhikē-yit ayīsiyiniw-a
Cnj look:through:spy:glass-3Obv person-Obv

[3] I am being deliberately non-committal on two points, both of which appear to me to remain unresolved even among specialists in Algonquian languages (and on which it is conceivable that individual Algonquian languages may differ somewhat). The first is what factors determine where one discourse segment ends and another begins; it is, however, important to note that, at least in some Algonquian languages (including Plains Cree), a discourse segment may include more than one sentence. The second is what factors determine which entity is chosen as the proximate entity of a given discourse segment. While these are important questions, the answer to them does not affect the points that I wish to make in the text.

ē-nanātawāpam-ā-yit. Kiskēyim-ē-w ayahciyiniw-a.
Cnj-look:for-Dir-3Obv know-Dir-3Prox Blackfoot-Obv
Ēkwa o-paskisikan pihtāsō-w; mōstkīstaw-ē-w
and:then 3Prox-gun load-3Prox attack-Dir-3Prox
ē-pimisini-yit.
Cnj-lie-3Obv
'While he (the Cree) was walking he saw a hill on which someone (the Blackfoot), a man, was climbing. And then he (the Cree) observed him (the Blackfoot), as he (the Blackfoot) was looking through a spy glass, as he (the Blackfoot) was looking for people. He (the Cree) knew him (the Blackfoot) for a Blackfoot. And then he (the Cree) loaded his gun and he (the Cree) attacked him (the Blackfoot) as he (the Blackfoot) lay down.'

Although obviation may strike the non-Algonquianist as a particularly exotic phenomenon, somewhat similar devices are found in languages closer to home. In Spanish, for instance, if a story contains reference to two or three main characters whom it is not wished to name explicitly, then it is possible to distinguish them by assigning the noun phrase *fulano* to the first mentioned, *sutano* to the second mentioned, and *mengano* to the third mentioned; then whenever, for instance, *fulano* recurs in the story, reference is necessarily back to the first-mentioned participant. Somewhat similarly in English, three male participants can be arbitrarily designated as *Tom*, *Dick*, and *Harry*, in order of appearance. These Spanish and English reference-tracking devices, however, differ from obviation in having no grammatical repercussions (like proximate versus obviative morphology in Algonquian languages).

3. Reference-tracking parameters

In this section I will try to show that crucial insight into the relation among various reference-tracking devices can be gained by classifying them in terms of two binary features: inherent versus assigned, and local versus global, of which the second feature is gradient rather than all-or-none. Of course, I am not claiming that these two features exhaust the classification of reference-tracking devices, even allowing that the gradient nature of the local/global distinction permits in principle an infinite number of such devices. Rather, I am claiming that these two parameters are crucial to any classification of reference-tracking devices.

3.1. Inherent versus assigned[4]

By claiming that a reference-tracking feature is inherent to a noun phrase, I mean that the noun phrase in question has this particular feature value irrespective of the syntactic or discourse position in which it occurs. Of the four reference-tracking devices considered in section 2, only gender/class indexing is inherent in this sense. In English, for instance, the noun phrase *Charles* is male human singular, and this is independent of the particular way in which this noun phrase occurs in a particular discourse; likewise, the noun phrase *Beryl* is female human singular. In Swahili, the noun phrase *mtu* 'person' belongs to class I, while the noun phrase *kitu* 'thing' belongs to class VII. Note that it is not important how the feature in question is inherent in the noun phrase, for instance whether it is lexically determined (as is usually assumed, at least for most inanimate nouns, in Swahili) or whether it is determined by properties of the referent (as in English, in terms of humanness and sex); all that is important is that the feature be inherent rather than assignable on the basis of syntactic or discourse function. Moreover, the notion of inherence does not preclude that there may be some amount of leeway in the feature determination: in English, for instance, a male baby can be felicitously referred to either as *it* or as *he*; but whatever determines this choice, it is not syntactic or discourse function, so that the range of feature values is still determined inherently.

By contrast, the other reference-tracking devices mentioned in section 2 all make use of an assigned feature. I will illustrate this in detail with reflexive pronouns, in contrast to gender/class indexing, with briefer consideration of switch reference (and switch function) and obviation. Imagine the following two situations. In the first, Beryl and Charles share a house, taking turns in the cooking. Now consider the following two sentences:

(11) He poisoned her.

(12) She poisoned him.

[4] The inherent/assigned distinction is introduced by Foley and Van Valin (1984: 333), specifically to distinguish between gender/class systems (in the traditional sense) and obviation.

It is clear that, given this scenario, the pronoun *he/him* can only refer to Charles, while the pronoun *she/her* can only refer to Beryl. Changing their syntactic function from subject to object, for instance, does nothing to change this. The second situation is that Daphne and Edna share a house, taking turns in cooking:

(13) Daphne poisoned herself.

(14) Edna poisoned herself.

(15) Daphne poisoned her.

(16) Edna poisoned her.

Neither the reflexive *herself* nor the non-reflexive *her* is capable of distinguishing inherently between Daphne and Edna, since the pronouns are both female human singular, as are both of the referents. Thus, *Daphne* is a possible antecedent for *herself*, as in (13), but so too is *Edna*, as in (14); likewise for *her*. Yet, given the scenario set out above, (13)–(16) are just as unambiguous as (11)–(12). But this time the reference is determined not by inherent features of the noun phrases, but rather by their syntactic position in a particular sentence, very roughly as follows: the reflexive pronoun in English must be interpreted as coreferential with a noun phrase that precedes it within the same clause. Thus in (13) *herself* will be interpreted as coreferential with *Daphne*, the only noun phrase preceding within this one-clause sentence, while in (14), by the same principle, *herself* is interpreted as coreferential with *Edna*.

With switch reference, the same-subject marker imposes an interpretation of coreference between the subjects of dependent and independent clauses (while the different-subject marker excludes this interpretation), but again this is not the result of any inherent feature of the noun phrases in question, since in principle any noun phrase can occupy the subject position. If we change around subject and object in the first clause of (6) to give (17), then it is 'the rat', rather than 'the child' that serves as antecedent to the same-subject marking:

(17) Döyw ha nwg^{w}-ön, bör dw-a.
rat child see-SS run go:Pres:3sg-Dec
'The rat saw the child and it ran away.'

The same is true of switch function, as we can see by changing the syntactic functions of 'the man' and 'the woman' in (8):

(18) Bayi yara ba-nggu-n jugumbi-ru
Class:Abs:Masc man:Abs Class-Erg-Fem woman-Erg
bala-n, bani-nyu.
hit-Real come:here-Real
'The woman hit the man and he came here.'

And similarly with obviation. In example (10), one can simply assign proximate status to the Blackfoot and obviative status to the Cree and end up with a perfectly well-formed discourse, in fact one identical in truth value to (10) (though presumably differing from it in discourse perspective). By contrast, assigning masculine gender to *Beryl* and feminine gender to *Charles* in (2) will produce nonsense (or, equivalently, a discourse that cannot be interpreted literally).

3.2. Local versus global

A local reference-tracking device is one that applies only within a narrowly circumscribed stretch of text (for instance, within a clause, or within a sentence, or within a stretch in which only one potential antecedent is mentioned), while a global device is one that can extend in principle throughout an entire text. In fact, it will be necessary to recognize degrees of locality/globality, as will become clear in the ensuing discussion. It will also be necessary to recognize different kinds of locality, in terms of the kinds of properties that delimit the locality.

My recognition of locality/globality as a crucial parameter stems from acquaintance with work on discourse anaphora by Michael Bamberg. In particular, Bamberg (1986) contrasts the different strategies resorted to by children and adults in using a pronoun like *he* in English in a story where there is more than one potential antecedent (in the story as a whole) for the pronoun. Adults tend to use the pronoun *he* to refer back to the last-mentioned potential antecedent; this is thus a local strategy, since its application is delimited by the preceding occurrence of a potential referent. Children, on the other hand, tend to assign the pronoun *he* to one of the referents early in the story, and to retain *he* throughout as referring to this entity, even if there are intervening instances of other potential referents; this is thus a global strategy—some entity is identified as *he* for the totality of the discourse. Let us now examine the devices listed in section 2 in the light of this parameter.

Gender/class is clearly a global device, and this would indeed be true of any inherent feature: since the feature value is inherent, it cannot be changed, in particular it cannot be changed in mid-discourse, therefore it necessarily holds globally throughout the whole of a discourse. Thus, in a story about Beryl and Charles, and with no other human referents, it would be possible, after the initial mention of Beryl and Charles, to use only forms of the pronouns *he* and *she* with unequivocal reference, even if the story were to grow to novel length.

This observation might seem to conflict with that made in the preceding paragraph, where it was noted that adults use pronouns in English locally, while children use them globally. But the contradiction is only apparent. Gender/class as a reference-tracking device works only where the discourse contains only one potential referent in each gender/class. This was the case in the Beryl-and-Charles story just mentioned. Where there is more than one potential referent in the same gender/class, then gender/class is not usable as a reference-tracking device to distinguish between these referents, and this is the situation to which I referred in citing Bamberg's work: the question that arose here is, given two (or more) potential referents in the same gender/class (e.g. the *he* gender/class in English), how do we distinguish between them? And clearly, whatever the answer is, it is not 'by means of the gender/class system'.

By contrast, reflexive pronouns are a classic instance of a local strategy, as can be seen in sentence (19):

(19) Daphne poisoned herself, and then Edna poisoned herself.

In English, the antecedent-reflexive relation cannot cross over a clause boundary, and therefore the end of the first clause, marked by a comma, in (19) represents the furthest extent within which *Daphne* can be antecedent for a reflexive pronoun; the pronoun *herself* in the second clause must therefore have an antecedent in its own clause, the only candidate being *Edna*. The precise restriction on locality is somewhat different in different languages; in Japanese, for instance, a reflexive pronoun can have its antecedent in another clause, as in (20):

(20)	Taroo	wa	[zibun	ga	ik-u	to]	it-ta.
	Tarō	Top	self	Su	go-Nonpast	that	say-Past

'Tarō said that he (lit.: himself) would go.'

Probably in all languages the antecedent-reflexive relation can hold only within the sentence (in the traditional sense of 'sentence', i.e. not 'clause'), and certainly it is heavily constrained locally in all languages for which I am aware of analyses.

Switch reference is likewise a local reference-tracking device, since it relies on a relation between two clauses, one of which is directly dependent on the other. Indeed, one can construct chains of such dependencies in which the different-subject marker indicates a change in subject referent between each pair of clauses, as in the following Harway example, discussing a conflict between a group of people and a cuscus (a variety of marsupial):

(21) Nöbö mö nög sö w-mön, kñm nög bö
man woman vine above go-DS cuscus vine below
h-mön, ödör ab-mön, pn bör-öŋ-a.
come-DS cut throw-DS descend fall-Past:35g-Dec
'The people climbed the vine above, the cuscus climbed the vine below, they (the people) cut the vine and threw it down, he (the cuscus) fell down.'

Of course, dependency does not necessarily imply strict adjacency, so it is possible for switch reference apparently to 'jump over' a clause, as in Harway example (22):

(22) An ap mag wr-ön, yön-aŋ, nm-n-ŋ-a.
we food heat-SS cook-Cnj:Sg eat-Fut-1Pl-Dec
'We will heat the food and, when it is cooked, we will eat it.'

The verb *wr* in the first clause is transitive, and the same-subject marker relates this clause directly to the final clause. The intervening clause contains the intransitive verb *yön*, whose subject is clearly 'the food'; Harway conjunctive verb forms carry no information as to same or different subject, but are essentially restricted to dependent clauses. In this example, therefore, both dependent clauses are directly dependent on the final clause.[5] But what is crucial is that there must be a relation of syntactic dependency between two clauses in a classical switch-reference system, and this imposes a restriction of locality on the operation of the system.[6]

[5] One could, incidentally, have *yön-mön*, rather than *yön-aŋ*, in the second clause, with the same dependency relations between clauses. In either case, *wr-ön* could be replaced by *wr-mön*, with the first clause being directly dependent on the second.

[6] The use of the qualifier 'classical' does indeed mean that there are phenomena similar in many respects to classical switch reference but with at least looser constraints on locality. I hope to discuss these in greater detail at a later date.

Obviation, by contrast, is a good example of a global reference-tracking device. Within a discourse segment—and a discourse segment can in principle be indefinitely long—the assignment of proximate reference to a particular referent is made once and for all, and no matter what kinds of syntactic boundaries intervene or what kinds of other referents are mentioned between the initial introduction of the proximate referent and any particular piece of proximate morphology, that proximate morphology will always refer back to the proximate referent introduced at the beginning of the discourse segment. In principle, then, one could compose an indefinitely long story involving only two participants in which one participant is always identified by proximate morphology, the other by obviative morphology—somewhat similar to the Beryl-and-Charles story introduced in section 3.1, but with this significant difference: in the Beryl-and-Charles story in English, one must distinguish the participants by using male human pronouns for Charles and female human pronouns for Beryl (the gender feature is inherent), while in a Plains Cree discourse one can choose the perspective, making either Beryl or Charles the proximate referent (the proximate feature is assigned).

Before leaving the discussion of the locality/globality parameter, it is worth pointing out that there are, in a sense, two kinds of locality, namely syntactic locality and discourse locality. Syntactic locality is locality imposed by a syntactic constraint, as for instance the antecedent-reflexive relation (at least in its classic form). Thus in English, the locality constraint is essentially to within the clause; in Japanese, it is to within the sentence. (In both languages there are other restrictions, but since my main interest here is in the principle, I will ignore these other factors.) If, within the syntactic domain, there is more than one potential antecedent, then it will not be possible unequivocally to make assignments of coreference, as in the following Japanese example:

(23) Ziroo wa Saburoo ga zibun o but-ta to it-ta.
Jirō Top Saburō Su self DO hit-Past that say-Past
'Jirō$_i$ said that Saburō$_j$ hit him$_i$/himself$_j$.'

Ziroo is subject of the main clause, *Saburoo* subject of the subordinate clause. The reflexive pronoun can be interpreted as coreferential with either the subject of its own clause (*Saburoo*) or with the subject of the main clause (*Ziroo*).

The example discussed at the beginning of section 3, namely adults' use of the pronoun *he* in a discourse where there are several potential referents, is rather an instance of discourse locality. If we take the generalization to be, roughly, that the pronoun *he* refers to the last-mentioned potential antecedent, then it is clear that the notion of 'last-mentioned' is not definable syntactically; rather it is a topological property of the discourse as a whole.

4. Conclusions

In my contribution to this volume, I have suggested the following classification of reference-tracking devices. First, there are inherent (and therefore also global) strategies, like gender/class indexing. Secondly, there are local assigned-reference strategies, like the use of reflexive pronouns, and also switch reference. Thirdly, there are global assigned-reference strategies, like obviation. While I have concentrated on syntactic manifestations of locality versus globality, there is clearly also room for a distinction within this parameter between syntactic locality and discourse locality, and in either case locality versus globality is a matter of degree rather than an all-or-none distinction. The use of a particular form in a particular discourse may involve the interplay of different parameters. For instance, the use of *he* in English is constrained, initially, by an inherent global strategy, in that the referent must be compatible with the features 'human, male' required by the pronoun *he*. But if more than one referent in the discourse satisfies this criterion, then the choice among these syntactically potential antecedents involves the parameter of discourse locality—with children tending to opt for globality, adults for locality.

3

An Approach to the Description of Gender Systems*

Greville G. Corbett

1. Introduction

In several of the more familiar languages, the gender pattern is straightforward and the way in which the system is analysed is taken as self-evident. In other languages, linguists may present the pattern as though it were equally uncontroversial, but we find that similar situations are described differently by those working on different language families. This causes problems, particularly for those involved in typology. In contrast there are a few languages in which the number of genders has been the subject of interminable dispute.

The purpose of this paper is to develop a consistent approach to gender. After a brief discussion of terminology (section 2), we move on to the central notion of 'agreement class' (section 3). Then, in section 4, we investigate how the nouns in an agreement class may make up a 'controller gender'. Controller genders must be distinguished from 'target genders', and this distinction allows us to solve one of the perennial problems in the study of gender, namely the

* This article is based on research funded by the Economic and Social Research Council (ESRC), reference number C00232218. This support is gratefully acknowledged. Versions of the paper were read at the Spring Meeting of the Linguistics Association of Great Britain, University of East Anglia, Apr. 1986; at the Taylor Institution, Oxford, May 1986; at the Graduate Faculty Seminar in Linguistics, University of Sussex, May 1986; and at the Typology Seminar, School of Oriental and African Studies, University of London, May 1986. I would like to thank those present for helpful discussion. I am also very grateful to Professor Bernd Heine, Professor Dee Ann Holisky, Dr Ewan Klein, Dr Graham Mallinson, Professor F. R. Palmer, Professor Rebecca Posner, Professor Malathi Rao, Professor Roland Sussex and two anonymous referees for their comments, and to Doug Arnold and Dr Louisa Sadler for editorial suggestions. This does not mean, of course, that they agree with the views expressed here.

number of genders in Romanian, and to describe other complex systems in a consistent way. For all its advantages, the agreement-class approach runs into what may be termed the 'maximalist problem', where more agreement classes are identified than the intuitively satisfying number of genders in a given language. Principled reasons are proposed for determining which types of agreement class should be recognized as genders (section 5). Zaliznjak's original insight is considerably extended as a result of analysing a wide range of languages. We shall see that, in many cases, deciding the number of genders in a language is a genuinely difficult problem. In some instances we reach solutions similar to traditional ones but we are able to put these traditional solutions on a sounder theoretical base.

2. Terms

The use of terms in this area has become confused (see the discussion at the end of *Classification nominale* 1967: 391–7). There seems little point in trying to maintain a strict distinction between 'gender' and 'noun class' since comparable systems are described as genders in one language family and as noun classes in another. For example, there are several points of similarity between Tamil and Karata; Tamil is said to have three genders, since it is a Dravidian language, while Karata is described as having three noun classes, because it is a North-east Caucasian language (Andi subgroup).[1] We shall follow the widely accepted view that the existence of gender can be demonstrated only by agreement evidence. (The point is that, for instance, the presence of class markers on nouns, as prefixes or suffixes, does not of itself indicate that a language has genders/noun classes; if we accepted that it had, then we could equally claim that

[1] Certain attempts to distinguish gender and noun class depend largely on a contrast between Indo-European and Bantu languages (part of the Bantoid subgroup of Benue-Congo, within Niger-Congo, which is the major part of Niger-Kordofanian). These attempts prove less convincing when Dravidian languages and languages of the Caucasus are taken into account. An alternative approach, however, is that adopted in the UNITYP project, in which gender and noun class are seen as 'focal instances' on a 'scale of classificatory techniques' (as in Serzisko 1982a, for example). A discussion of different approaches can be found in De Wolf (1971: 26–46). He uses gender as a higher level term than noun class (thus a singular and plural noun class may form a gender) but he does not consider agreement to be a prerequisite.

English had a gender comprising all nouns ending in *-tion*.) The view we are following is implicit in most work on gender, and it is stated explicitly in, for example, Fodor (1959: 2), Greenberg (1978b: 50), and Heine (1982: 190). The fact that agreement is the defining factor reinforces the point that gender and noun classes should not be distinguished, but at the same time allows us, like Dixon (1982: 213–18), to separate them from nominal classifiers (in languages like Thai), which we shall not consider here.

3. Agreement classes

The approach based on agreement classes is usually associated with the name of Zaliznjak (1964); the approach is partly foreshadowed by Schenker (1955). Gladkij (1969, 1973a, 1973b) gives a more formal, mathematical treatment and reaches results similar to those of Zaliznjak; Kibrik (1972) uses the method in an interesting account of Archi. In a series of papers and in a section of his book, Marcus (1962, 1963, 1967: 115–55, 1970), following ideas of Revzin, also proposed a formal definition of gender, but this works less well than that of Gladkij. His notion of 'class of distribution' proves too wide, and leads to the postulation of large numbers of genders—eight or possibly more for Romanian (1967: 151). By treating, for example, the difference between proper and common nouns as a question of gender, he moves away from the central, well-established problems of gender. Most seriously, it is not clear that there is necessarily any upper limit to the number of genders to be found in a given language. Nevertheless, his contribution to the study of gender has been considerable; several scholars working on Indo-European languages have adopted his approach, probably the most recent being Cosmas (1981, 1982).

Let us now return to Zalinjak and the agreement-class approach. An agreement class may be defined as follows (this definition is a reworking of the idea found in Zaliznjak (1964: 30):

> An agreement class is a set of nouns such that any two members of that set have the property that whenever
>
> (i) they stand in the same morphosyntactic form, and
> (ii) they occur in the same agreement domain, and
> (iii) they have the same lexical item as agreement target, then
>
> their targets have the same morphological realization.

The intuitive content of the definition is that two nouns are in the same agreement class provided that given the same conditions they will take the same agreement form. The three numbered clauses of the definition spell out what is involved in 'the same conditions'. Being in 'the same morphosyntactic form' (clause (i)), or the same 'grammatical' form, means that the nouns have the same specifications for all relevant syntactic features. The features most commonly involved are number and case. We rely on the notions of number and case being given (Gladkij, on the other hand, defines case); this is reasonable since they are simpler notions, which can often be justified simply on morphological evidence, without reference to agreement. It must be stressed that identity of morphosyntactic form does not imply morphological identity. Two nouns may both be specified as, say, accusative singular, and yet differ morphologically; for example, Russian *mat'-ϕ* 'mother' and *sestr-u* 'sister'. Such nouns have different morphological features in their lexical entries, indicating that they belong to different declensional paradigms. Moreover, two morphosyntactic forms may have a single morphological realization; for example, Russian *okno* 'window' may be the nominative singular or the accusative singular.

Clause (ii) requires that the nouns occur in the same agreement domain. This means that the configuration in which agreement applies must be identical in each case: it might be the agreement of modifiers with the head of a noun phrase, subject–verb agreement, and so on.

Clause (iii) requires that the lexical item which stands as the agreeing element or target must be the same. The point is that not all lexical items have the same agreement possibilities. It would not do to use in one instance an adjective which distinguished gender and in the other an adjective which did not. Of course, we are interested in items which have the largest number of forms, and by specifying that identity must be found 'whenever' these conditions are met, we include the case of the most differentiated target.

The definition depends on the notion of agreement, which we understand to be a matching of features between controller and target. (The reference to matching excludes government where, for example, a verb may require a particular case on a noun phrase but is not itself in that case.) As is generally, but not universally, accepted, the agreement relation covers anaphoric pronouns, whose agreement features depend on features of the controller. Our definition of agreement class requires two additions. For technical reasons we should add a clause that the nouns in question must share at least one grammatical form. This is to cover the limiting case in which two defective nouns could never stand in the same grammatical form and so the conditions would be filled vacuously. The second addition, which is found in Zaliznjak's definition, is that the target may take not only the same morphological realization but also the same set of stylistically variant forms. This is to cover the situation in which a given combination of syntactic features may have alternative realizations (e.g. Russian adjectives mark the feature set instrumental singular feminine with *-oj* or, archaically and poetically, with *-oju*).

Let us first consider French, as a straightforward illustration of the basic notion of agreement classes.

(1) un grand garçon — cf. *une grande garçon
a big boy

(2) un grand jardin — cf. *une grande jardin
a big garden

(3) une grande femme — cf. *un grand femme
a big woman

(4) une grande fleur — cf. *un grand fleur
a big flower

In these examples we have ensured that the nouns being tested occur in identical conditions: they stand in the same morphosyntactic form (the relevant feature specification is singular), in the same agreement domain (agreement of modifiers within the noun phrase), and the lexical items involved as agreement targets are identical. The nouns *garçon* and *jardin* require the article and the attributive adjective to stand in the same form ((1) and (2)). If we consider other possible agreement targets, or if we change to the plural, we still find that the agreements required by *garçon* and *jardin* are identical. They therefore belong to the same agreement class. Similarly, the nouns *femme* and *fleur*, while differing from *garçon* and *jardin*, require the same agreements as each other ((3) and (4)). They belong to the second agreement class. There are many thousands of nouns in each of these two classes, which are the traditional masculine and feminine genders.

Zaliznjak was concerned with a more difficult case—Russian.

Before looking at Russian, let us see what the notion of agreement class can contribute to one of the established conundrums of gender, the Romanian system.

4. Controller genders and target genders

As mentioned above, the literature on gender in Romanian is extensive; it includes contributions by Jakobson (1959), major Romanian linguists such as Graur (1937), Rosetti (1965: 83–92, 1983: 382–404), and notably Marcus (1967: 115–55), and many more; for further references see R. A. Hall (1965: 421–2), Marcus (1967: 153–5), Wienold (1967: 75, 170), Luxt (1970: 88–9), Windisch (1973), Priestly (1983), and Mallinson (1984: 450–1).

Consider the following data (from Mallinson 1984: 441) concerning the nouns *bărbat* 'man', *fată* 'girl', and *scaun* 'chair'.

(5) bărbatul e bun
man-the is good

(6) scaunul e bun
chair-the is good

(7) fata e bună
girl-the is good

Note that the definite article is postposed; in nouns like *fată* its effect is to change the quality of the final vowel (mainly by lowering) to *fata*. The evidence so far demonstrates the existence of two agreement classes, one including nouns like *bărbat* and *scaun* and the other comprising nouns like *fată*. There is a second case (genitive-dative), but in the singular *bărbat* and *scaun* again take identical agreements while *fată* differs. But the situation is more complex, as emerges when we consider the same phrases in the plural:

(8) bărbatii sînt buni
men-the are good

(9) scaunele sînt bune
chairs-the are good

(10) fetele sînt bune
girls-the are good

If we had only the data of (8)–(10), then we would postulate two agreement classes—one for nouns like *bărbat* and one for nouns like *scaun* and *fată* (the oblique case in the plural shows the same pattern, separating *bărbat* from the other two). The argument, which has gone on for decades, is whether we have two genders or three. The problem is that nouns like *scaun* have no agreement forms which are used uniquely for them. In terms of agreement classes, however, the situation is clear: we must set up three classes as follows:

I. nouns taking ϕ in singular and *i* in plural (*bărbat*)
II. nouns taking ϕ in singular and *e* in plural (*scaun*)
III. nouns taking *ă* in a singular and *e* in plural (*fată*)

Thus we have an unambiguous answer: there are three agreement classes, and there is no reason not to recognize each as a gender. However, this analysis is exactly what we would obtain for Latin, Tamil, or German, even though in each of these languages, intuitively, the situation is rather different. All of them have some agreement forms which are unique to each gender. The point is that the agreement-class approach leads us to the number of sets into which nouns are to be divided or, in a feature-based approach, to the number of different feature specifications which are required on nouns to enable gender agreement to operate correctly. It is certainly the case that *bărbat*, *scaun*, and *fată* (and the hundreds of other nouns in each class) must be labelled differently. Nevertheless the morphology of agreeing forms (targets) is simpler than is implied by the statement that Romanian has three genders. We should therefore differentiate *controller genders*, (the genders into which nouns are divided) from *target genders*, the genders which are marked on adjectives, verbs, and so on (depending on the language).

The distinction is illustrated in Table 3.1. It can be seen that Romanian has two target genders in both singular and plural, but three controller genders (indicated by the lines). I is usually called masculine, II is the feminine, and III is the disputed class sometimes called 'neuter', sometimes 'ambigeneric'; the latter is perhaps the better term, provided it is used not to imply that there is no distinct

TABLE 3.1. *The gender system of Romanian*

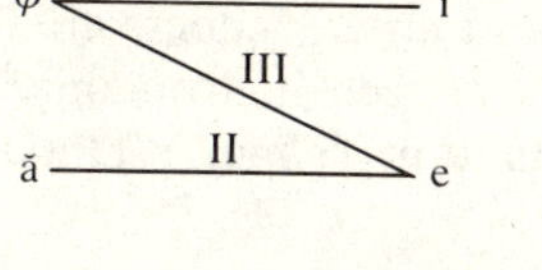

gender but rather that the situation is different from the more common Indo-European three-gender system.

Diagrams like that above can be labelled in various ways; the alternatives deserve brief consideration. The first controller gender is designated ϕ on the basis of adjectives like *bun* 'good'. However, not all adjectives take this form: *aspru* 'rough' has *-u*, as shown by comparison with *aspră* corresponding to *bună*. We have chosen to give a typical allomorph for each target gender. This method avoids the danger of premature naming of genders; on the other hand, problems can arise when the typical forms chosen suggests similarities which are not general through the system. (Taking Latin adjectives, we might suppose that the feminine singular *-a* is equivalent to the neuter plural *-a*; however, not all adjectives have identical forms in these two positions.) A way of avoiding the latter problem is to list all the allomorphs, but this can become unwieldy. Since it is hardly practical to keep referring to strings of allomorphs, names tend to be preferred. Let us consider French again in this form (Table 3.2).

TABLE 3.2. *The gender system of French*

singular		plural
masculine	masculine	masculine
feminine	feminine	feminine

In a language of this type, it is natural to use the same labels for the classes into which nouns are divided (controller genders) and the sets of agreeing forms (target genders). It is when this usage is carried over into more complex systems that difficulties arise. Indeed, although the distinction between controller and target genders may seem an obvious one, there are numerous examples in the literature of the number of genders being given for a particular language, in cases where the situation is complex, without any indication as to what is meant. It is true that there are many languages where the number of controller and target genders are the same, but mismatches of the type we have seen in Romanian are not uncommon. Another example is found in Telugu, a Dravidian language (South

TABLE 3.3. *Verbal agreement forms in Telugu*

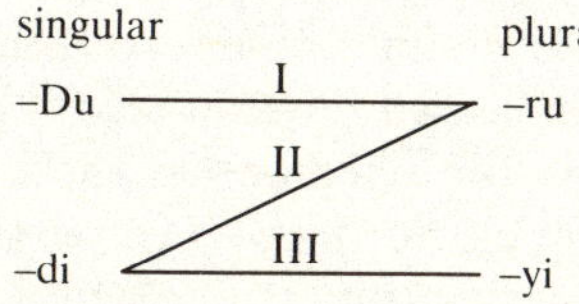

Central Group). Table 3.3 gives the verb-agreement forms (Malathi Rao, personal communication).[2]

Again there are three controller genders and two target genders (in both singular and plural). However, I is masculine, II feminine, and III irrational or neuter. The comparison between Romanian and Telugu illustrates the point made in the introduction that similar situations are described differently in different geographical traditions; while there has been interminable debate about Romanian, there has, to my knowledge, been no such debate about the status of the third (controller) gender of Telugu. However, unlike Romanian where the personal pronouns follow the same pattern as the other agreement targets, in Telugu the pronouns are more complex. There is a set which corresponds closely to the verb agreements (see Table 3.4). These are not the only forms. Besides

TABLE 3.4. *Telugu personal pronouns*

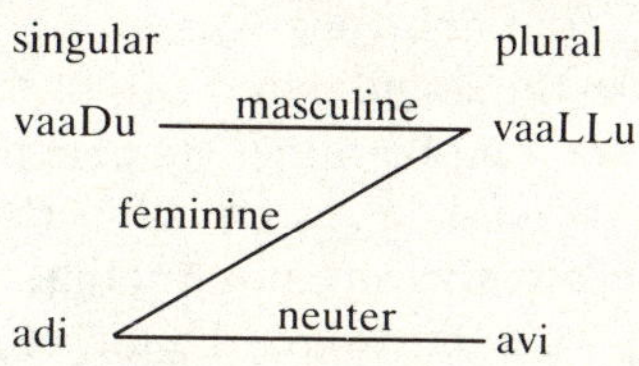

vaaDu, which is an informal form for referring to a man or a boy, there is also *atanu* (partly formal) and *aayana* (formal) for referring to an adult. Telugu uses the plural to show respect (when referring to someone who merits respect, not just in direct address); *atanu* can take plural agreement and *aayana* must do so in Koosta Telugu (in some other dialects *aayana* can take a singular). The use of the plural

[2] I am most grateful to Malathi Rao for the data on Telugu; her Koosta dialect varies slightly from that described in Krishnamurti and Sarma (1968), where the transliteration scheme is also somewhat different.

to show respect requires a complication of the grammar, but it does not affect our account of the gender system, nor does the existence of additional masculine pronouns. When we turn to the pronoun *adi* the picture changes; *adi* is used for reference to neuters (animals and things) and sometimes for reference to girls. For reference to a woman, there is a different form *aaviDa* (partly formal or formal) which can take singular or plural agreement. It is not used for inanimates. The existence of this pronoun means that pronoun targets distinguish feminines from neuters. This confirms the analysis which claims three controller genders (cf. section 5.2); it also breaks the parallelism with Romanian.

A more complex system is found in Lak, a North-east Caucasian language (Lak-Dargva group). Agreement is marked on some attributives, verbs, adverbials, and pronouns, as illustrated in the next example:

(11) k'i-*j*-a ars ša-*w*-a *ϕ*-ušar (Xajdakov 1980: 206)
two son at home be
'Two sons are at home.'

The italicized elements all mark agreement with the Class I noun *ars* 'son'.

The pattern of typical markers is given in Table 3.5 (from Kibrik 1979: 4; the forms like -*j*- found in numerals are not included). By convention, forms before the slash are prefixal, those after are infixal or suffixal. There are four controller genders in Lak. Then there are three target genders in the singular and two in the plural. (In view of the warning about representing target genders by typical markers, it should be said that the table gives typical verb agreement markers which undergo numerous alternations, but that these alternations do not provide grounds for subdividing the target genders as given.) It

TABLE 3.5. *The gender system of Lak*

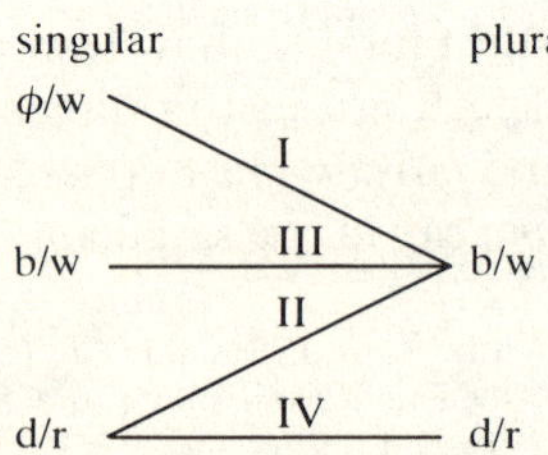

is noteworthy that there are only three different sets of forms (*ϕ/w*, *b/w*, and *d/r*) covering eight theoretical forms.

We have established the value of distinguishing the notions 'controller gender' and 'target gender', in our analysis of complex gender systems. The distinction leads to other fruitful lines of enquiry, as we shall see in the sections which follow.

4.1. The relation of gender and number

As far as controller genders are concerned, gender and number are typically independent: a noun has a particular gender, irrespective of the number it stands in. Gender is inherent to the noun and is in a sense prior to the number in which it occurs in a given sentence. (There are occasional exceptions which must be labelled as such in the lexical entry of the nouns involved; see section 5.3 for some examples.) Target genders, on the other hand, may be found in the realizations of feature bundles and so may vary according to the other features involved, most notably number. And there are interesting areas to investigate in these interactions. In particular, there are the patterns of matching between singular and plural.

The most straightforward system is that in which each singular target gender matches one plural gender and vice versa. Gender in one number determines gender in the other and vice versa: there is a one-to-one mapping of the target genders in one number on to the target genders in the other. We call such systems 'parallel' systems. French can serve as an example of this type (see Table 3.6).

TABLE 3.6. *Target genders in French*

singular		plural
masculine	———	masculine
feminine	———	feminine

Then there are 'convergent' systems, in which gender in one number determines gender in the other, but not vice versa: there is a many-to-one mapping of target genders in one number on to target genders in the other. (Parallel and convergent systems taken together are what Heine terms 'paired systems', 1982: 196–7.)

A clear example of a convergent system is found in German (see Table 3.7). In Tamil, a Dravidian language, three singular target

TABLE 3.7. *Target genders in German*

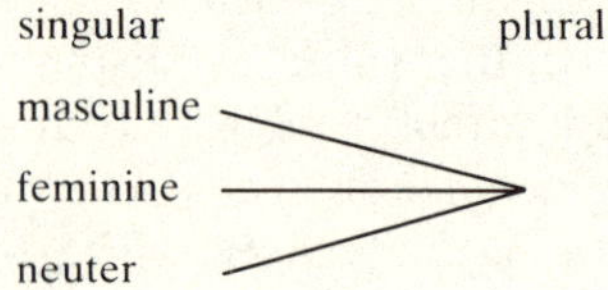

TABLE 3.8. *Target genders in Tamil*

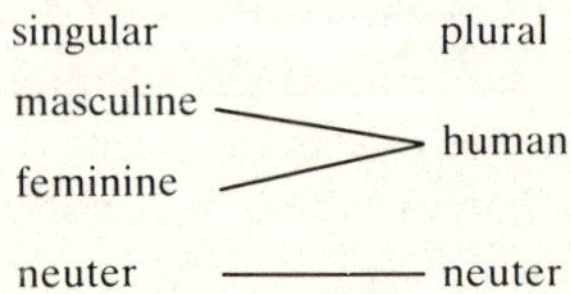

genders correspond to two plural genders (Table 3.8). An identical system is found, as mentioned earlier, in the North-east Caucasian language Karata (Magomedbekova 1967: 324–5, 327).

In ChiBemba, a Bantu language, (data from Givón 1972: 14–17) there are considerably more target genders. The numbers given in Table 3.9 are the traditional Bantu noun-class numbers. We omit here the locative genders, which are discussed in relation to another Bantu language in section 4.3.

TABLE 3.9. *Target genders in ChiBemba*

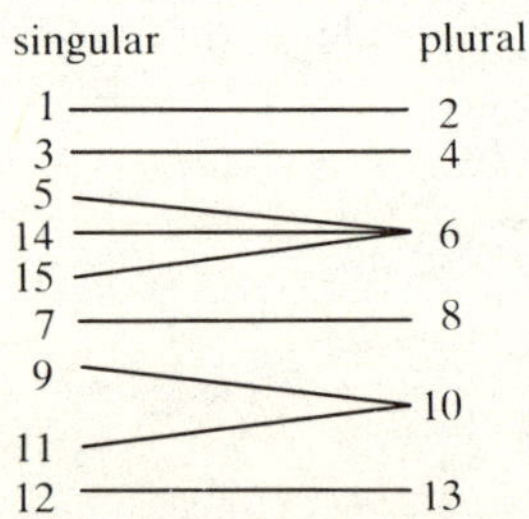

The third possibility is what Heine calls a 'crossed' system (1982: 197). In such a system, gender in neither number determines the gender in the other; there is what some would call a many-to-many mapping between the target genders in the different numbers. Examples are Romanian (Table 3.1), Telugu (Table 3.3), and Lak (given again for convenience as Table 3.10).

TABLE 3.10. *The gender system of Lak*

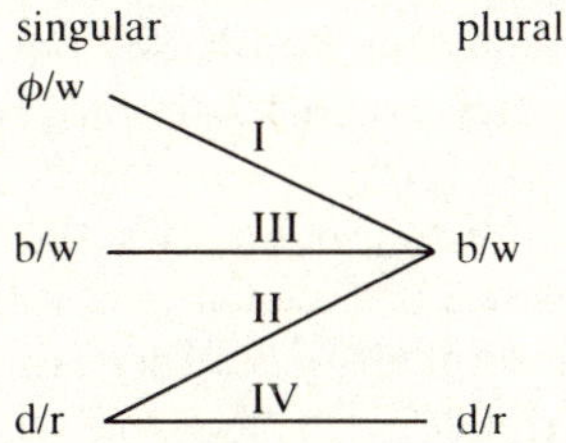

Here we see a system with four agreement classes, but with three target genders in the singular and two in the plural. The fact that we find such systems, as well as convergent systems like those above, with more singular target genders than plural, but not the converse (with more plural than singular genders), is, of course, a reflection of Greenberg's universal number 37: 'A language never has more gender categories in nonsingular numbers than in the singular' (1966: 112). If we adopted just the agreement-class approach, there would be no way in which to state Greenberg's universal, since differences caused by change in number lead to the setting up of additional agreement classes. In terms of agreement classes, Table 3.10 simply provides evidence for four classes. Clearly then Greenberg's universal must be stated in terms of target genders.[3] The Lak data also suggest how, once controller and target genders are distinguished, we can approach the question of syncretism of target genders; we also have the framework for an account of the associated question of polarity, notably in Cushitic languages (see Serzisko 1982b).

Before leaving the question of gender and number we consider languages with more than two numbers. For simplicity we have discussed languages with only singular and plural. When we turn to fuller number systems, we find that the types established, 'parallel',

[3] Though this is not required for Greenberg's universal, we should consider the justification for linking particular target genders in the singular with others in the plural. In languages like French, the point may seem too obvious for discussion; but there are instances where the analysis is not so clear-cut, and in any event, we must recognize that it is a matter of analysis, not a fact. To justify associating particular singular and plural target genders (and target genders in different agreement targets, such as attributive modifiers and predicate verbs), we need the notion of 'consistent agreement pattern'. This concept is discussed in section 5.5; it gives a principled basis for associating particular agreement forms.

'convergent', and 'crossed', hold between each pair of numbers, rather than of the system as a whole. This can be seen from the gender system of Slovenian, a South Slavonic language (we omit here two subgenders, which are just as in Slovenian's closest relative Serbo-Croat, described in section 5.1) (see Table 3.11). We can see that the feminine and neuter share forms in the dual only. Thus there is a relation of convergence between singular and dual and between plural and dual, but of parallelism between singular and plural. (See Corbett and Hayward 1987 for an analysis of a four-number system.)

TABLE 3.11. *The gender system of Slovenian*

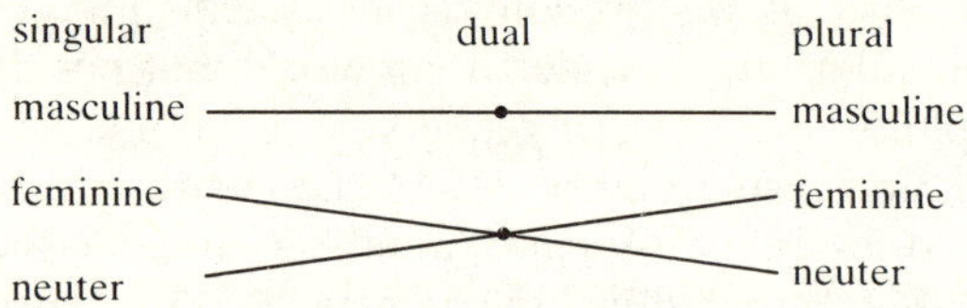

4.2. Relation to semantics

The semantic aspect of gender is most evident in controller genders; the way in which nouns are assigned to genders (assignment systems) is a well-established area of research with a correspondingly large literature. There is always a semantic core to gender systems, but the degree of semantic justification can vary from almost complete to much less than that. Thus in Dravidian languages such as Tamil and Telugu it is normally sufficient to know the meaning of a noun in order to assign it to a gender (see e.g. Asher 1985: 136–7). In many other instances, in Indo-European languages like French and German, in Bantu languages like Swahili and Chichewa, and in a large proportion of the languages of the Caucasus like Lak, many nouns can be assigned to a gender according to their meaning (typically those denoting humans) but many cannot.

It is much less frequently observed that the question of semantic justification can also be pursued with regard to target genders. If the controller genders of a language are based solely on semantics, then the appearance of a particular gender agreement form will provide unambiguous information. Thus a feminine agreement form in Tamil implies that a female human is referred to at some point, while a feminine agreement form in French or German does not necessarily do so. When we turn to convergent and crossed systems, we find that the syncretic forms may have varying degrees of semantic justification. Compare Lak (Table 3.10) with Archi (Kibrik 1972) (Table 3.12). The plural target-gender forms of Lak have no direct semantic correspondence. In Archi, their semantics are clear, once the controller genders are given: Class I comprises male humans, God, and other spiritual beings considered male, II is similarly for females, III is for most animals and some inanimates, and IV includes the remainder (some animals and the remaining inanimates). Thus the target gender *b/ib* in the plural implies reference to humans, while *ϕ/ib* is for non-humans. (For other examples see Xajdakov 1980.)

TABLE 3.12. *The gender system of Archi*

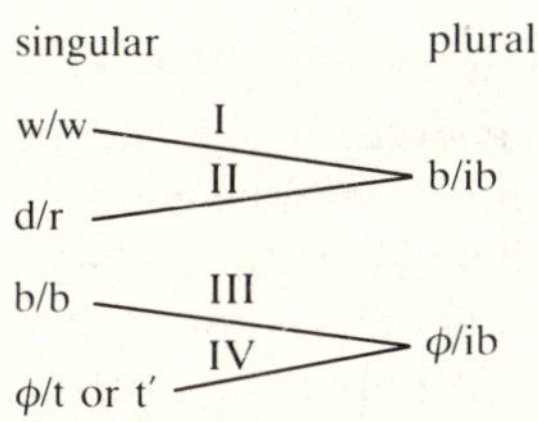

4.3. The relation of controller genders to target genders

In many languages, as noted earlier, there is a straightforward one-to-one relation between the two types of gender. We have also seen several examples of languages in which the number of controller genders exceeds the number of target-gender forms distinguished in either number. For example, Romanian has three controller genders, but only two target-gender forms in both singular and plural.

It is also possible to find languages in which the number of target genders exceeds the number of controller genders, if we include within the target genders what we shall term 'non-lexical genders'. These are of two types; the first, the neutral gender, is a target-gender form which cannot have a noun phrase headed by a noun as its controller. A good example is found in the Surselvan dialect of Romansh (Haiman 1974: 130–4). The agreement-class approach leads us to postulate two genders; one takes the ending *-s* on predicative adjectives and participles (masculine), sometimes with a change of root vowel, while the other takes *-a* (feminine). There is, however, a third agreement marker, namely *ϕ*; this occurs with controllers which are not specified for gender and number: sentential subjects, the demonstrative pronoun *quei* 'that', and the impersonal pronoun *igl*. For example:

(12) Sgarscheivla ei la paupradad
Wretched (Fem) is the poverty

(13) In urezi ei sesalzaus
A storm is arisen (Masc)

(14) Igl ei sesalzau in urezi
There is arisen (Neutral) a storm

The form which is found in (14) cannot occur with a noun phrase headed by a noun as controller; we term this target gender the 'neutral' gender.

The second type of non-lexical gender (and so the second way in which target genders may exceed controller genders) involves 'minor target genders'. These differ from the neutral gender in that they can have a nominal controller. They differ from ordinary target-gender forms in that there are no nouns regularly assigned to a corresponding controller gender.[4] Examples would be the locative genders of Bantu; consider the following example from Chichewa, a Bantu language spoken in Malawi:

(15) munyumba mu-kutentha
in house is hot
'It is hot in the house.'

[4] Greenberg (1978b: 53) and Heine (1982: 198) both use the term 'minor gender' in this sense, and further examples are given in Greenberg (1978b: 79). The term 'minor gender' has also been used to signify simply an agreement class with few nouns in it (e.g. by De Wolf (1971: 42 and Watters (1980: 135). An alternative term for an agreement class with few members is 'minority gender' (Voorhoeve 1980: 68). We shall suggest in section 5.3 that the status of classes with few members depends on the agreements they take; the particular cases analysed by Watters and Voorhoeve are inquorate genders in our terms, while some classes with few members are recognized as genders (as we shall see in the case of Lelemi).

The potential for confusion over the different uses of the term 'minor gender' is not unduly serious since Greenberg's use can be seen as relating to target genders (minor genders are, in our approach, target-gender forms with no nouns regularly assigned to a corresponding controller gender) while De Wolf's use involves controller genders (minor genders are agreement classes with relatively few members). To be unambiguous we can use the terms 'minor target gender' and 'minor controller gender'.

Nyumba 'house' belong to gender 9/10 in the traditional Bantuist numbering and would normally take the prefixed agreement forms *i* (singular) and *zi* (plural). However, in (15) it has the prefix *mu*, meaning 'in', and the verb takes the same prefix *mu* as an agreement marker. No other gender has this marker so we could treat it as a separate target-gender form. But there are no nouns which must take *mu* as their agreement form; apart from semantic restrictions, any noun could take the prefix *mu* and become part of this locative gender. Thus the agreement form *mu* represents a minor target gender; such genders are clearly rather different from the more familiar genders.

Thus far the agreement-class approach appears to give useful results, provided it is recognized that it gives an analysis of one side of the problem, the controller genders, and that it must therefore be supplemented by the notion of target genders.

5. The maximalist problem

A problem which arises with the agreement-classes approach is that the number of classes may be considerably larger than the traditional (and often intuitively satisfying) number of genders generally accepted for a given language. Zaliznjak and Gladkij were both aware of the problem and addressed it directly. Some later investigators carefully establish agreement classes but take the analysis no further; in some cases the agreement classes are claimed to be genders. Dalewska-Greń and Feleszko (1984) find fifteen agreement classes in Serbo-Croat and thirteen in Polish. Quirk, Greenbaum, Leech, and Svartvik (1984: 314) propose nine gender classes for English. While the value of identifying all the classes of noun which differ in their agreement possibilities should not be underestimated, the raw analyses which result tend to be unsatisfactory for two reasons: first, they miss generalizations (some of which are captured in more traditional accounts); and second, they make similar systems appear more different than they really are.

We shall, therefore, investigate how the number of agreement classes may be reduced, in principled ways, to give a lower number of genders. Again we shall find the notion of controller and target genders helpful.

5.1. Subgenders

The notion of subgenders is useful and intuitively clear, though it proves difficult to formalize. Consider the data from Serbo-Croat given in Table 3.13. Serbo-Croat has seven cases, but the cases not given do not provide further distinctions. (More agreement classes can be set up on different evidence, as in Dalewska-Greń and Feleszko 1984, but these are more marginal; similar agreement classes will be considered later in the paper.) The accusative singular gives evidence for four agreement classes. We could simply say that there are four genders in Serbo-Croat. Given appropriate agreement rules this solution would work, but it appears unsatisfactory. The alternative is to treat the agreement class including nouns like *student* and that including nouns like *zakon* as subgenders of a single main gender. We would then recognize three genders (as is the tradition in Serbo-Croat grammars): masculine being divided into masculine animate (*student*) and masculine inanimate (*zakon*).[5]

TABLE 3.13. *Gender agreement in Serbo-Croat*

	ovaj student 'this student'	zakon 'law'	škola 'school'	vino 'wine'
Singular				
Nominative	ovaj student	ovaj zakon	ova škola	ovo vino
Accusative	ovog studenta	ovaj zakon	ovu školu	ovo vino
Genitive	ovog studenta	ovog zakona	ove škole	ovog vina
Plural				
Nominative	ovi studenti	ovi zakoni	ove škole	ova vina
Accusative	ove studente	ove zakone	ove škole	ova vina
Genitive	ovih studenātā	ovih zakonā	ovih školā	ovih vinā

The intuition we wish to capture is that the difference between the behaviour of words like *student* and *zakon* is less significant than that between both of them and those like *škola* or *vino*. Serbo-Croat provides a particularly clear case for a subgender; it proves difficult to give a definition which will cover more complex cases as well. The following is an attempt to specify when agreement classes can be analysed as subgenders rather than as full genders:

[5] There is a considerable literature on the place and development of animacy in Slavonic; see e.g. Hjelmslev (1956) and Huntley (1980).

> Subgenders are agreement classes which control minimally different sets of agreements, that is, agreements differing for a small proportion of the morphosyntactic forms of the controller (typically a single one), not including the most basic form (usually the nominative singular).

This definition fits the Serbo-Croat data well. The agreement classes represented by *student* and *zakon* differ in the accusative singular only, that is, in one morphosyntactic form out of fourteen, if we consider only attributive agreement (though it should be said that syncretisms reduce the number of independent morphological forms to less than fourteen for any given declensional type). If we apply the same procedure to Romanian, we find that masculine and ambigeneric (and also feminine and ambigeneric) nouns take different agreements in two forms out of four; this is not 'minimally different'. It follows that subgenders will be found only in languages with relatively complex inflectional systems. Note that a minimal difference cannot include the nominative singular; the most basic nominal form is traditionally (and with good reason) considered to provide sufficient evidence to justify a separate gender. Returning to the Serbo-Croat data, we have already said that the use of subgenders allows us to reflect more accurately the relative similarity of *student* and *zakon* as opposed to the others. In particular, some rules can refer to the feature [+masculine] without any account of the feature [+/−animate]. There is a second advantage, which is that the assignment rules are rather different for genders and subgenders. For the main genders there is a semantic rule (basically males are masculine, females feminine); the remaining nouns (not referring to sex-differentiable beings) are assigned according to morphology (the declensional class). On the other hand, the distinction between animates and inanimates is, with a very few exceptions, purely semantic.

Table 3.13 reveals a further peculiarity of the subgenders in Serbo-Croat, namely that the agreement forms involved are not independent but syncretic.[6] The question arises as to how we should count the

[6] It should be said that a syntactic analysis, which would involve changing the case of the whole noun phrase, would be inadequate, as is shown by masculine nouns ending in *-a*, which themselves take the accusative in *-u*:

(i) vidim ovog gazdu
(I) see this boss

Guzdu is unambiguously accusative; the attributive modifier *ovog* is masculine and is accusative-genitive.

target genders of Serbo-Croat. For this we require the notion of 'dependent target gender'.

> A dependent target gender is a target gender consisting of a set of morphological realizations which mark agreement with members of a given agreement class by an opposition involving only syncretism (and no independent form).

The sets of morphological realizations which mark accusative singular masculine in Serbo-Croat fit this definition. As was illustrated in Table 3.13, when, say, the determiner *ovaj* 'this' is in agreement with an accusative singular masculine inanimate noun like *zakon* 'law', its morphological realization is the same as for the nominative singular. This is a systematic syncretism; other agreeing elements take a different ending from *ovaj*, but always the same as for the nominative. No target has an independent form for this feature specification. Similarly, the corresponding forms which agree with animates are syncretic with the genitive. The opposition animate/inanimate is marked only by syncretism and so both sets of morphological realizations, those for animate and those for inanimate, constitute dependent target genders. We can then say that Serbo-Croat has three controller genders, one of which has two subgenders, three (independent) target genders (singular and plural mark the same distinctions), plus two dependent target genders. This situation is presented graphically in Table 3.14.

TABLE 3.14. *The gender system of Serbo-Croat*

singular		plural
masculine	animate inanimate	masculine
feminine	——	feminine
neuter	——	neuter

Let us now examine Russian, the language which both Zaliznjak and Gladkij analysed. The singular yields the same distinctions as Serbo-Croat: masculine, feminine, and neuter, with two subgenders in the masculine—animate and inanimate. However, while Serbo-Croat differentiates masculine, feminine, and neuter in the plural, Russian has lost this distinction and replaced it by animacy, as shown in Table 3.15.

In some examples there are changes of stress, but this need not concern us here. We find three controller genders, each with two

TABLE 3.15. *Gender agreement in Russian*

	ètot student 'this student'	dub 'oak'	sestra 'sister'	sosna 'pine'	čudovišče 'monster'	okno 'window'
Singular						
Nominative	ètot student	ètot dub	èta sestra	èta sosna	èto čudovišče	èto okno
Accusative	ètogo studenta	ètot dub	ètu sestru	ètu sosnu	èto čudovišče	èto okno
Genitive	ètogo studenta	ètogo duba	ètoj sestry	ètoj sosny	ètogo čudovišča	ètogo okna
Plural						
Nominative	èti studenty	èti duby	èti sestry	èti sosny	èti čudovišča	èti okna
Accusative	ètix studentov	èti duby	ètix sester	èti sosny	ètix čudovišč	èti okna
Genitive	ètix studentov	ètix dubov	ètix sester	ètix sosen	ètix čudovišč	ètix okon

TABLE 3.16. *Genders and subgenders in Russian*

masculine	animate	student
	inanimate	dub
feminine	animate	sestra
	inanimate	sosna
neuter	animate	čudovišče
	inanimate	okno

subgenders (Table 3.16). This is the solution favoured by both Zaliznjak and Gladkij (though terms vary and both also deal with problems of number, which we will address in section 5.4). Zaliznjak (1964: 28) considers that setting up two layers of features is an analysis which should and can be argued for, but that it does not reflect an objective division of nouns in the way that agreement classes do. Gladkij (1973b: 193–4) argues that: 'if two case-number forms coincide for a given noun, and if they have the same segments in agreement with them . . . these forms should, in a definition of gender, "fuse" into a single form'. He then includes this idea in his formal definition. Unfortunately, the idea is flawed, since there are nouns which are clearly masculine animate but whose case-number forms do not coincide:

(16) Nominative moj djadja 'my uncle'
Accusative mojego djadju
Genitive mojego djadi

Our definition, which is fully in the spirit of Zaliznjak's agreement-class approach, appears adequate here. For the feminine and neuter, the two agreement classes for each (animate and inanimate) differ only in one form out of twelve (excluding syncretism), namely the accusative plural. For the masculine, there is a difference in the accusative singular (as in Serbo-Croat) and the accusative plural. Since it is the same case in both instances and the syncretism is the same, it is reasonable to accept the two agreement classes as minimally different.[7]

[7] There is a little evidence showing that neuter animates are beginning to take animate agreements (that is, identical to the genitive) in the singular as an alternative to the inanimate forms described (Ickovič 1980: 88). They are thus becoming less like feminines and more like masculines. The change represents a further stage in the integration of animacy into the gender system.

Given that the type of syncretism found with the animacy features is always the same in Russian, and that it has a role elsewhere in the grammar (see Corbett 1981), the subgender analysis is clearly superior to one recognizing six genders. A six-gender scheme would allow agreements for animate masculines to be completely different from other animates, whereas in all examples it is syncretism of accusative and genitive agreeing forms which is involved. Russian also provides the justification for the last part of our definition. If the agreement form for the accusative singular is analysed as equal to nominative or genitive, depending on subgender, then the only remaining difference between masculine and neuter is the agreements with the nominative singular. According to our definition, this fact prevents their being reanalysed as subgenders of a non-feminine gender. We can thus retain the traditional three genders (Zaliznjak and Gladkij were also keen to retain the insights of the grammatical tradition as far as possible). The system is shown in Table 3.17. Russian then has three controller genders, each with two subgenders. It has three target genders, plus two dependent target genders.

TABLE 3.17. *The gender system of Russian*

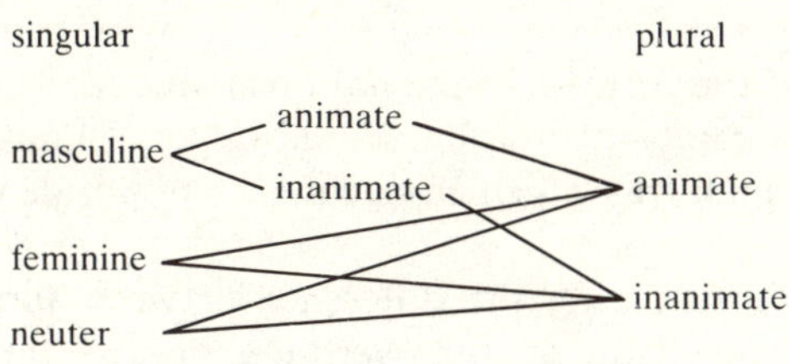

5.2. Overdifferentiated targets

We continue with other methods which, like the use of subgenders, allow us to restrict the number of agreement classes which are recognized as genders. In 'maximalist' analyses, which produce large numbers of agreement classes, marginal targets may be included. Zaliznjak (1964: 30) discusses briefly Russian collective numerals such as *dvoe* 'two', which can be used with some nouns but certainly not all. He does not use them to set up further agreement classes, rightly I believe, since the use of *dvoe* rather than *dva* 'two' can be considered a matter of co-occurrence restrictions rather than a question of agreement.[8] Several examples of such items being used greatly to complicate gender patterns can be found in the literature.

There are, however, more serious problems with apparent agreement targets which permit more distinctions than do typical targets in the language: we term such targets 'overdifferentiated' (using a term of Bloomfield 1933: 223–4). A dramatic example is found in a group of closely related Dravidian languages: Kolami (Emeneau 1955: 56), Ollari (Bhattacharya 1957: 19), Parji (Burrow and Bhattacharya 1953: 9–10), and Naiki (Emeneau 1955: 141). Each has two genders, basically male human and other. Yet some lower numerals (2, 3, and 4 in Kolami) have forms for female human additionally, as the following Kolami data show:

(17) iddar ma·sur
two men

(18) i·ral pillakul
two women

(19) indiŋ siḍl
two buffaloes

I would argue that we should maintain the traditional account that these languages have two genders (as demonstrated by verb agreement and the forms of personal pronouns) and that the three exceptional numerals (overdifferentiated targets) should be labelled as having special forms which co-occur with nouns denoting female humans.

It is worth considering the difference between subgenders and agreement classes induced by overdifferentiated targets. In the former case, agreement classes are separated by a distinction which is widely and consistently marked, but only for a small proportion of

[8] A related problem is Polish *dwa* 'two' (a normal numeral with no collective meaning), which distinguishes feminine gender from others in the plural; other attributive modifiers do not do so. Schenker (1955) bases a good deal of his analysis on *dwa*, while Zaliznjak, considering the similar case of *oba* 'both' in Russian, dismisses it in a footnote (1964: 31), saying that the feminine forms are being lost. The fact that such forms are being lost (speakers have some problems with Polish *dwa* as well) confirms their marginal status. When a small number of targets (particularly if they are in some other way unusual—*dwa* and *oba* both have syntactic quirks) serves to establish agreement classes in excess of those found on the basis of typical targets, these additional agreement classes will not be recognized as genders. Rather the overdifferentiated targets should be marked lexically.

the morphosyntactic forms of the controller. The distinction is therefore not so significant as that between the main genders. In the Serbo-Croat case almost all agreeing attributive modifiers (as well as the relative pronoun) make the animate–inanimate distinction,[9] but as we saw this distinction is found only in the accusative case. In Kolami, however, it is not a whole target type (like attributive modifiers or agreeing predicates) which is involved, nor is it a whole word class (such as all numerals). There are just three irregular numerals, and these should be lexically marked as such.[10]

We can now approach the gender system of English. It might be argued that the personal and reflexive pronouns of English are overdifferentiated and that therefore English has no gender system. But personal pronouns are central to the syntax in a way which the numerals 2, 3, and 4 are not. They are the basis of a separate target type. And given that pronominal systems which mark gender typically repeat gender systems found elsewhere, either in the same language (e.g. in the verb) or in gender systems in other languages, it seems more reasonable to accept gender systems based on the personal pronouns. In addition, those languages which have gender reflected both in pronouns and elsewhere (verbs or attributive modifiers) typically require similar machinery to account for the appropriate forms of each. It may be significant that pronouns may be used by native speakers to ask about gender, as in the following Russian example (the gender of *kofe* is changing):

(20) Kofe, èto on, da?
coffee that (is) he yes
'"Coffee" is masculine, isn't it?'

More important is the fact that our definition of agreement class depends of course on a definition of agreement. This has caused considerable controversy, but most recent attempts to define

[9] An exception would be the numeral *dva* 'two', which distinguishes only feminine from non-feminine and so is underdifferentiated.

[10] We can therefore distinguish three cases: (i) agreement classes are induced for a sizable proportion of the morphosyntactic forms of the controller but only by a particular target type (e.g. attributive modifiers): separate genders; (ii) agreement classes are induced by a particular target type but only for a small proportion of the morphosyntactic forms of the controller: subgenders; (iii) agreement classes are induced by a small number of targets (not a complete target type or word class): overdifferentiated target.

agreement include personal pronouns as a possible target. For this reason, we should recognize English (and similar languages such as Zande) as having a gender system; however, to make clear that it is not a system which penetrates the syntax to the extent of the gender system of, say, Romanian or Serbo-Croat, we will refer to systems like that of English as 'pronominal gender systems'.

5.3. Inquorate genders

Inquorate genders are the controller counterpart to overdifferentiated targets. While the latter might artificially raise the number of genders on the basis of a small number of targets, inquorate genders are those postulated on the basis of an insufficient number of nouns, which should be lexically marked as exceptions.

For example, it was stated above that Lak has four genders. Yet there is a single noun which does not fit into the four genders, namely *q̄at̄a* 'house'. Žirkov (1955: 21) immediately dismisses the idea of a fifth gender. There is in fact an easy solution: this noun can be labelled as class III in the singular and class IV in the plural. Similarly in Archi (Kibrik 1972: 126), there are two nouns which do not fit into the four main classes (there are also common-gender nouns of a type to be dealt with under section 5.5.1). These two nouns can be marked as class III (singular) and class I/II (plural). Even in French, which everyone 'knows' has two genders, there are three nouns (*amour* 'love', *délice* 'delight', and *orgue* 'organ') which are masculine in the singular and feminine in the plural. These too should be marked as lexical exceptions (in any case they are not straightforward singular–plural pairs). The situation is different from Romanian where there are thousands of nouns which take the same agreements.

While these cases may appear uncontroversial, it is worth pointing out that if the first published analysis takes a different approach, the existence of a larger number of genders can be perpetuated through the literature. For example, it is regularly stated that Tsova-Tush, formerly called Bats, which is a North-central Caucasian or Nakh language, has eight genders. This view can be found, for example, in the grammar by Dešeriev (1953). Tsova-Tush has an apparently complex crossed system; the eight genders may be represented as in Table 3.18.

TABLE 3.18. *Gender in Tsova-Tush*

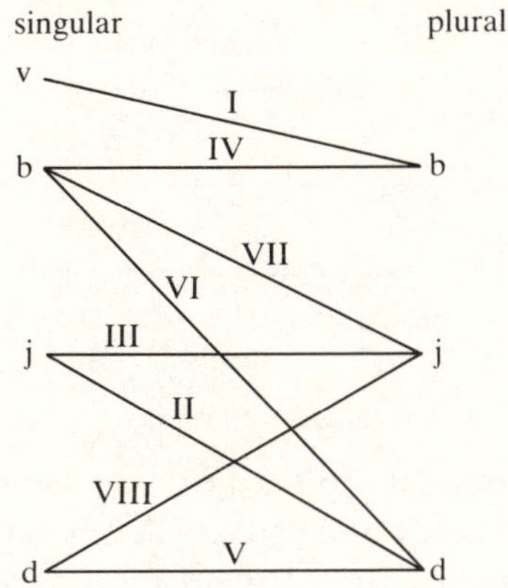

However, the membership of the classes is unequal.[11] Class VIII (*d–j*) contains only three nouns, 'lip', 'ear', and 'hand'; we should label them as [V singular/III plural]. Class IV is also small: it has only one native word, meaning 'a knit shoe', together with the word for 'boot', a borrowing from Russian. These should be labelled: [VI singular/I plural]. There are also some singularia tantum which Dešeriev treats as class IV, but these could equally well be treated as class VI. Class VI is the largest class: it appears to be absorbing the last remnants of class IV, which would leave the plural marker *b* as a marker exclusively for class I (male human).

The most interesting class for our purposes is class VII (*b–j*), which consists of the words for 'wing' (of a bird), 'mouth', 'lung', 'leg', 'arm', 'fist', 'finger', 'nail' (of finger), 'eye', and 'throat, gorge'. We find ten nouns in all (Dešeriev lists two others which now appear to have moved into class III). Like class VIII, class VII is strong on body parts, particularly paired body parts. There appear to be good grounds for declaring class VII 'inquorate'; that is to say, we should mark the nouns listed as lexcial exceptions and not recognize a class VII. The system would then be as in Table 3.19 (with the original class numbers retained, but with the layout

[11] Information on class membership is given in Dešeriev (1953: 138–45). This has been revised and updated in the light of data kindly provided by Dee Ann Holisky based on her fieldwork in Zemo-Alvani, on lecture notes from a course by Rusudan Gagua, and on Kadagidze and Kadagidze (1984).

TABLE 3.19. *Gender in Tsova-Tush* (*excluding inquorate genders*)

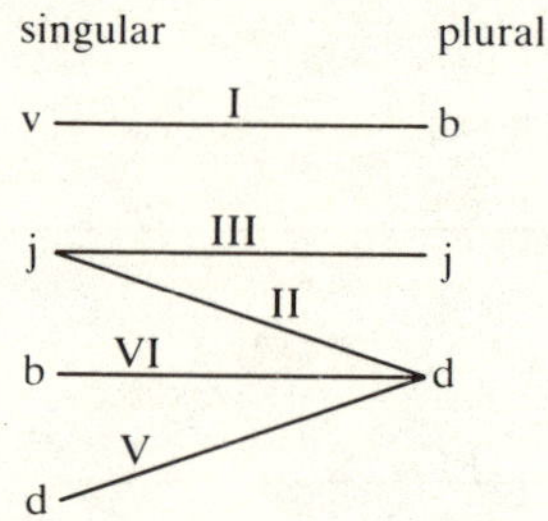

rearranged). This leaves the interesting question as to when a gender becomes quorate. There can be no simple answer: we should look to evidence such as productivity, changes affecting the class of nouns as a whole (rather than individual members), and so on. But it is important that when the number of nouns in a agreement class is known to be small, this should be stated, particularly if it is claimed that the agreement class should be recognized as a gender.[12]

It is important to note, however, that in all the cases discussed the nouns could be given an exceptional marker (for an unusual pairing of singular and plural target-gender forms) which would allow the agreement rules to assign the required markers. It does not follow that any agreement class with a small number of members is necessarily inquorate, since it may not be possible to give all the nouns an irregular marker in this way.

Let us consider the very interesting case of Lelemi (a Togo Remnant language, in turn part of Niger-Kordofanian, spoken in the Volta region of Ghana by 14,900 people at the 1960 census). Heine (1982: 197–8) presents it as an example of a complicated crossed system. There is more information in Heine (1968: 114–15) and it is that source which we shall follow. There is evidence for ten agreement classes, which Heine labels I–X (see Table 3.20).

Agreement classes II and VIII normally both take the plural agreement marker *á*-, but class II has the optional alternative *lɛ́*- for the demonstrative pronoun −*mɛ̌* 'this' only. We should mark this

[12] Voorhoeve (1968: 587) adopts the useful convention of indicating classes with few members by broken lines in representations like Table 3.20. Unfortunately the broken line, like the star, has a different meaning in synchronic and diachronic description; De Wolf (1971: 49) uses a broken line to indicate an innovative pairing while a solid line indicates one retained from the parent language.

TABLE 3.20. *Agreement classes in Lelemi*

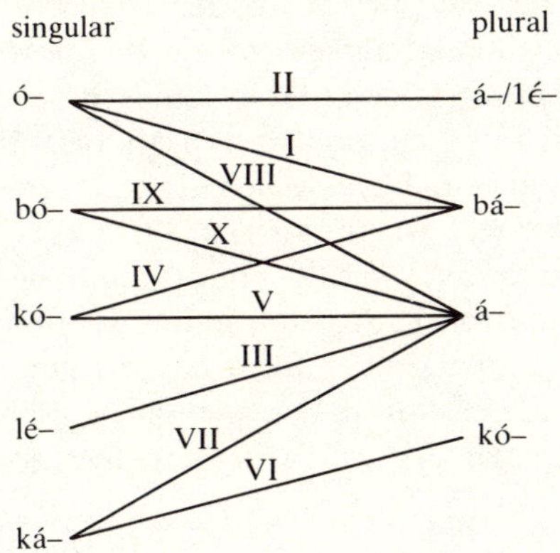

pronoun as overdifferentiated and so not recognize VIII as a separate gender. When we look at the examples given both in the section on Lelemi and in the general word list (Heine 1968: 212–57), it is clear that the agreement classes shown in Table 3.21 account for most of the nouns.

TABLE 3.21. *Main agreement classes in Lelemi*

Agreement class	Agreements	
	Singular	Plural
I	ó-	bá-
II	ó-	á-
III	lé-	á-
V	kó-	á-
VI	ká-	kó-

Provided they are as uncommon as appears to be the case, the nouns in agreement classes IV (*kó-bá-*) and VII (*ká/á-*) could be lexically marked (as V singular and I plural and as VI singular and III plural respectively). What then of the remaining classes IX and X? Heine gives just one example in IX (agreements *bó-/bá-*), and two examples in X (agreements *bó-/á-*). Let us assume the worst case, that there are no other nouns in either agreement class. We would like to treat them as inquorate. However, unlike the cases considered so far, there is no exceptional marker available, since no other gender has *bó-* for singular agreement. Furthermore, we cannot look to an irregularity in a particular target, since there are seven possible agreement targets in Lelemi and it appears that all seven take the marker *bó-*. Thus although we do not need to recognize Heine's IV, VII, and VII as genders, we must accept IX and X. These agreement classes are not inquorate, since the nouns cannot be lexically marked as exceptional, and they are not induced by overdifferentiated targets since the target gender form *bó-* is found throughout the agreement system. Lelemi has a genuinely complicated gender system, including genders which contain few nouns yet are not inquorate.

5.4. Defective nouns

There are many instances of nouns which lack forms for certain morphosyntactic specifications; most commonly they have no singular or no plural. Intuitively, where in all the morphosyntactic forms available these nouns take the same agreements as normal nouns (in the forms they share), then they are of the same gender. Thus Russian *razgovorčivost'* 'talkativeness' is found only in the singular. Its agreements are the same as those of the feminine inanimate noun *sosna* 'pine', when singular. We can therefore label *razgovorčivost'* as feminine inanimate. There can similarly be nouns which have no singular. In languages like Russian where gender distinctions are not found in the plural, there is a slight complication (this is considered in detail by Zaliznjak (1964: 32–40), who introduces an additional gender class, which is something we shall avoid). The noun *nožnicy* 'scissors' occurs only in the plural; its agreements match those of *duby* 'oaks' (masculine inanimate), *sosny* 'pines' (feminine inanimate), and *okna* 'windows' (neuter inanimate) in Table 3.14. Since Russian distinguishes animacy but not the main genders in the plural, it is sufficient that *nožnicy* be marked as plural and inanimate. There are insufficient grounds for creating an extra gender. This much follows from the definition of agreement class given in section 3. Whenever nouns like *nožnicy* meet the conditions of the definition; they will be found to be in the same agreement class as inanimate plural nouns. The best solution is therefore to have them underspecified in this way (that is, as inanimate, but with no specification as to main gender). If, however, in a particular theory it was necessary for every noun to have a gender feature, then *nožnicy* could be assigned arbitrarily to any gender, or preferably it could be assigned to the feminine since its morphology is like that of a feminine noun in the plural (other nouns would be masculine or neuter accordingly). Peculiarities of the syntactic behaviour of such nouns, notably with quantifiers, are a problem of number rather than of gender, and so need not concern us. Thus the fact that nouns lack forms for particular morphosyntactic specifications does not give rise to new gender categories.

5.5. Consistent agreement patterns

The question of differences in targets has already been mentioned. In some languages all targets mark the same distinctions so that we may take any one target type and use it to establish the agreement classes. In other languages different targets make a greater or lesser number of distinctions; we noted examples of animacy being reflected in attributive modifiers but not in the predicate. In such cases we include the target type which marks more distinctions. In both instances we must establish 'consistent agreement patterns'. This is usually done without comment, but it crucially determines the analysis of the gender systems.

Russian can again serve as an example. We established three main target-gender forms. For an attributive adjective we have the nominative singular endings *-yj*, *-aja*, and *-oe*. The past tense verb has three singular endings: *ϕ*, *a*, *o*. The relative pronoun has the same endings as the attributive adjective, and the personal pronouns are *on*, *ona*, and *ono*. For the vast majority of nouns, the agreements are as in Table 3.22. (This is of course a simplified table; the full version would include the other cases, the plural number, and

TABLE 3.22. *Agreement patterns in Russian*

Attributive adjective	Predicate	Relative pronoun	Personal pronoun	Traditional gender
yj	ϕ	yj	on	masculine
aja	a	aja	ona	feminine
oe	o	oe	ono	neuter

therefore the animate and inanimate subgenders.) The question is how this analysis is done, given that there are nouns which take other combinations of agreements. For example, *vrač* in the meaning 'female doctor' can occur in the following constructions:

(21) novyj (Masc) vrač

(22) novaja (Fem) vrač
new doctor

Examples like (21) are more common than (22). In the predicate, the feminine is somewhat more common:

(23) vrač rabotal (Masc)

(24) vrač rabotala (Fem)
doctor worked

The relative pronoun is usually feminine and the personal pronoun is almost always feminine.

How then is the table constructed? In this case there are phonological clues (*-a* in the feminines, for example) but this is not always a reliable indicator. There are two important factors. The first is that, as mentioned earlier, the vast majority of nouns which take *−yj* also take *-ϕ* and *on*; the second point is that these are nouns for which we can give absolute rules—they always take the same agreements. Each horizontal line of Table 3.22 represents a 'consistent agreement pattern', which we define as follows:

> A consistent agreement pattern is a set of target-gender forms such that:
> (i) the agreement class it induces is as large as possible;
> (ii) agreement rules relating to this agreement class will be simple and exceptionless.

Bear in mind that the number of target genders in the singular may not be the same as that in the plural and that different targets may distinguish different numbers of target genders. However, when different targets make the same number of distinctions, then forms which occur within the same consistent agreement patterns are realizations of the same target gender. The notion of consistent agreement pattern gives us a principled way of capturing the intuition that, for example, a feminine marker on an attributive modifier is 'the same as' a feminine marker on a verb, even if they are phonologically different. A point often overlooked is that it is insufficient to require that a particular type of agreement, say feminine, should occur with one and the same noun, since there are examples like Russian *vrač* 'doctor', which can take different agreements at the same time:

(25) naš vrač prišla
our (Masc) doctor came (Fem)

It is the notion of consistent agreement pattern which allows us to differentiate the agreements in (25), and so to give an account of nouns like *vrač*.[13] Of course, the majority of nouns will belong to agreement classes which have a consistent agreement pattern and which are recognized as genders or subgenders. But we must now consider those which do not. We shall distinguish between nouns which take all the agreements of more than one consistent agreement pattern and those which have fewer possibilities than that. An example from the pronominal gender system of English will make the distinction clear. We find three consistent agreement patterns (see Table 3.23). The word *baby* can occur with all the forms of all

TABLE 3.23. *Gender in English*

who	he	(masculine)
who	she	(feminine)
which	it	(neuter)

three patterns. *Ship* on the other hand may take the neuter agreement pattern:

(26) The Canberra, which has just docked, is a fine ship. It sails again on Friday.

[13] It is perhaps worth spelling out why the notion of consistent agreement pattern is necessary, since it might appear to duplicate apparatus already given. In particular, we must consider whether agreement patterns which are not consistent are simply those which induce agreement classes which are inquorate genders. Unfortunately things are not that simple. The notion of inquorate gender is necessary for cases like Tsova-Tush (section 5.3) where there would otherwise be no principled reason for choosing between possible singular–plural pairings. (We were able to exclude some since the classes involved were small and the nouns could be marked as lexical exceptions.) But nouns like *vrač* in Russian are too numerous to be simply labelled an inquorate gender. Given their ability to take two types of agreement, and especially the variability involved, we need the notion of consistent agreement pattern to ensure that such nouns do not form the basis of genders, rather than the more straightforward ones.

Ship (and other expressions denoting ships) can also take the personal pronoun *she*, but not the relative *who*:

(27) I sailed on the Canberra. She's a fine ship.

(28) *The Canberra, who is a fine ship . . .

Thus *ship* takes agreements from two consistent agreement patterns but does not take all the forms of both.[14] We shall consider these two types of noun in turn.

5.5.1. Double and multiple gender nouns

These are nouns, like English *baby*, which can take all the agreements of more than one consistent pattern. Thus the Lak noun *ħakin* 'doctor' can take the pattern associated with class I, class II, or class III, depending on whether the doctor is a man, an older woman, or a younger woman (Xajdakov 1963: 50). Such nouns are often called nouns of common gender. This term is useful, as long as it does not imply the existence of a new gender. (After all, when we find verbs which govern the accusative or the dative, we neither postulate a new archicase accusative-dative, nor do we set up a special class of verbs—those governing accusative or dative.) Clearly nouns like *ħakin* and *baby* must be specially marked in some way. One possibility is to treat them as homonyms: $baby_1$ (feminine), $baby_2$ (masculine), $baby_3$ (neuter). This is the solution adopted by Zaliznjak (1964: 27). The alternative is to label them as having more than one gender, just as we label certain verbs as permitting more than one complement type.

The notion of double or multiple gender is wider than common gender. Common-gender nouns take different agreements for semantic reasons; other nouns may take alternative agreements without any semantic motivation and so still have double gender. For example, in Babanki (one of the Ring languages, which form part of the Western Grassfields group within Bantu, spoken in north-west Cameroon), there are several nouns which can take the agreements either of gender 3/13 or of gender 5/13. This forms part of a more general change in which the target-gender form labelled class 3 is supplanting class 5 (Hyman 1980: 231–3, 236). Other languages may show double gender with borrowings which do not fit into the established gender system, and so are not unambiguously

[14] For further discussion of 'boat nouns' see Malone (1985).

assigned to a gender by the prevailing assignment rules. Such genuine examples of double gender are to be distinguished from those where related nouns are morphologically distinct; the difference in morphology determines the different genders and two separate lexical items are involved.

5.5.2. Hybrid nouns

These are nouns which neither simply take the agreements of one consistent agreement pattern nor belong to two or more genders. A good example is the German word *Mädchen* 'girl'. It can take agreements exactly as a neuter noun. It may also take the feminine personal pronoun *sie*; but it cannot take the other agreements of the consistent agreement pattern associated with feminine nouns. Examples of this type typically arise when assignment rules are in conflict; in this case, nouns referring to females are usually feminine in German, but nouns formed with *-chen* are normally neuter. Such nouns must be lexically marked.

A more complex example is Russian *vrač* 'doctor', which was mentioned earlier. When *vrač* refers to a male doctor, then it takes the consistent agreement pattern associated with masculine animate nouns. When it refers to a female doctor it takes both masculine and feminine patterns as follows:

attributive modifiers	usually masculine, feminine possible
predicate	both possible
relative pronoun	normally feminine, masculine rare
personal pronoun	almost always feminine

The agreement required is variable for four different types of target. Thus *vrač* referring to a female is a 'hybrid' noun as it does not take consistently feminine agreements, nor consistently masculine agreements, nor both. Again this results from a conflict of the assignment rules, since it is female (and so should be feminine) yet its declensional class is such that it should be masculine. Taking *vrač* as a whole, it is a curious composite with one half being masculine, apparently half of a double gender noun while the other half is a hybrid noun.

There are several nouns like *vrač*. However, the frequency with which they take the different agreements varies. The Panov survey of nearly 4,000 speakers (see Corbett 1983: 32 for details and source) produced the data presented in Table 3.24.

TABLE 3.24. *Agreement with* vrač *and similar nouns in Russian*

	Attributive modifiers (% of informants favouring feminine agreement)	Predicate agreement (% of informants favouring feminine agreement)
vrač '(female) doctor'	16.9 (N = 3,835)[a]	51.7 (N = 3,806)[a]
buxgalter '(female) accountant'	25.5 (N = 3,835)[a]	—[b]
upravdom '(female) house manager'	—[b]	60.7 (N = 3,806)[a]

[a] N indicates the total number of informants.
[b] — indicates a combination not included in the survey.

It is evident that *vrač* and *buxgalter* do not take exactly the same agreements; no more, we must assume, do other nouns of the same type. This fact leads to an explosion in the number of agreement classes (Zaliznjak does not discuss nouns of this type). Naturally we do not wish to propose a separate gender for each noun; rather they must be lexically marked as masculine and feminine, with an indication as to the relative weight of the two features.[15] This solution puts the high degree of idiosyncratic variability into the lexicon, where it belongs. Nevertheless, there are generalizations to

[15] The position tentatively adopted here is that hybrids cannot form a full gender, but must be marked as lexical exceptions. An alternative would be to abstract away from the frequency of particular agreements and to allow a consistent agreement pattern to include alternatives for one or more targets. Since in the latter solution the nouns involved would still have to be lexically marked to allow for differences in frequency of the different forms of agreement, the first solution appears preferable.

There are more complex hybrids than Russian *vrač*. Serbo-Croat has a group of nouns like *gazda* 'master' which are consistently masculine in the singular, but can take masculine or feminine agreements in the plural. These nouns demonstrate that the notion 'consistent agreement pattern' cannot be restricted to establishing connections between different target positions but may also be required to establish connections within target positions. Thus masculine nouns in Serbo-Croat take one set of agreement forms and feminines another; hybrids like *gazda* take the same agreements as the masculines when singular, and the same as masculines or feminines when plural (provided the agreement target is an attributive modifier, a predicate, or a relative pronoun, but not a personal pronoun: data in Corbett 1983: 14–17; further examples in Corbett forthcoming).

be made concerning the behaviour of hybrid nouns: a set of such generalizations are grouped under the constraints of the Agreement Hierarchy (Corbett 1979, 1983: 8–41). It is also worth noting that hybrid nouns are one route for change in the gender system. (An alternative is for anomalous nouns to lead to a change in the semantics of the gender system, as has happened in Konkani, see Miranda 1975.)

6. Conclusion

We have seen that in establishing the number of genders in a particular language, Zaliznjak's approach, based on the notion of agreement class, is a useful starting-point. It is important to recognize, however, that this approach leads us towards controller genders; the other side of the coin is the system of different forms of the agreeing elements: we term these forms target genders.

In some languages there are numerous agreement classes: following Zaliznjak we do not recognize every agreement class as a gender. Some are subgenders—a notion we have made more precise. Other agreement classes are based on overdifferentiated targets and so are not accepted as genders; nor indeed are inquorate genders. Nouns belonging to the latter require a feature in their lexical entry, to mark their irregularity, as do defective nouns and nouns with double or multiple gender and hybrid nouns.

Thus, to find how many genders a language has, we begin with agreement classes but eliminate as many as possible. This minimalist position has been justified at each point. It is interesting to note that in many cases it leads us to traditional analyses; like Zaliznjak we have tried to improve the foundations of some shaky edifices.

4

Subject and Object in Universal Grammar

R. M. W. Dixon

1. Introduction

This paper deals with the ways in which the semantic roles, or arguments, of a verb (such as agent, patient, instrument; donor, gift, recipient) are mapped on to syntactic relations (such as subject and object). Particular attention is paid to verbs that have alternate syntactic frames; these generally involve the possibility of mapping either of two semantic roles on to object relation (e.g. *he gave the book to Mary*, *he gave Mary the book*).

Data from a fair sample of languages has been surveyed for this contribution to linguistic typology. (About two dozen linguists each completed a questionnaire on alternate syntactic frames for a language they had close familiarity with.) Tentative conclusions are put forward about those means available to human languages for alternate syntactic coding of a semantic role: (i) the use of different lexemes; (ii) productive syntactic processes; and (iii) alternative syntactic frames for a constant verb form.

My approach is meaning-based. The prime function of language is to convey meaning from speaker to hearer (phonological and grammatical systems exist as the mechanisms by which this is achieved). By adopting a semantics-prior approach we are able to explain many grammatical phenomena that appear arbitrary and without explanation within an approach that accords priority to syntax. (Further details of and justification for this approach will be found in Dixon forthcoming.)

2. Semantics and syntax

Each language has thousands of words. These can be grouped into SEMANTIC TYPES, reflecting common factors of meaning. There are terms describing KIN relations, such as 'mother', 'brother', 'wife'; those referring to HUMANS, such as 'woman', 'doctor', 'seer'; to other ANIMATES; to other THINGS such as 'sun' and 'moon', 'star' and 'water' and 'fire'; to COLOURS such as 'black', 'white', 'red'; to DIMENSIONAL descriptions such as 'big', 'short', 'wide'; to PHYSICAL PROPERTIES such as 'hot', 'heavy', 'wet'; to HUMAN PROPENSITIES such as 'jealous', 'rude', 'clever'; to descriptions of MOTION such as 'walk', 'jump', 'fetch'; to descriptions of LIKING such as 'love', 'prefer', 'abhor'; and so on.

Something of the order of 30 semantic types are needed, and these correspond quite closely between different languages. That is to say, every language will need a type COLOUR, although its size may vary—from two terms in some languages to a score or more in others. Every language has a set of GIVING words—usually one general term that closely translates English *give* and a number of hyponyms of this. But the semantic nature of the hyponyms varies from language to language; in English we have *present*, *donate*, *bequeath*, *lend*, etc., while in other languages GIVING terms may reflect sociocultural responsibilities relating to kinship ties, or the like.

Turning now to grammar, every language classifies its words into a number of word classes (or parts of speech). Each word class has identificatory syntactic and/or morphological properties within that language (although these do differ from language to language). In Latin, nouns inflect for case and number; in English, a noun can occur after an article, with nothing having to follow the noun. Word classes are identified between languages—and given the same name—because of their semantic similarity.

Each grammatical class is, effectively, a grouping together of a number of semantic types. All languages have a class Noun, which includes HUMANS, ANIMATES, THINGS, and usually also KIN. All languages have a Verb class, which includes MOTION, GIVING, and other types. Most languages have a separate, large Adjective class, including DIMENSION, COLOUR, PHYSICAL PROPERTY, and HUMAN PROPENSITY. In some languages there is a smaller Adjective class, including DIMENSION and COLOUR, but not PHYSICAL PROPERTY (which is then usually associated with the Verb class) or HUMAN PROPENSITY (which is then often put into the Noun class). In some languages there is no separate Adjective class at all, with typical adjectival types being grouped with MOTION, GIVING, and others into a larger-than-usual Verb class. A few semantic types vary in their class membership from language to language—LIKING words are classed as verbs in some languages, as adjectives in others, and even as nouns in a few languages. (There is more discussion and exemplification of this in Dixon 1982: 1–62.)

The Noun class has a fair degree of semantic homogeneity—HUMANS, ANIMATES, THINGS can all be touched and drawn. (There are usually a few abstract nouns, such as *beauty* and *idea* in English; these vary from language to language and always make up just a small proportion of the total set of nouns.)

The Verb class does not show the same degree of semantic homogeneity. We know that *swim*, *carry*, *cut*, *give*, *see*, *tell*, and *enjoy* are similar grammatically; they all inflect for tense, which is the major criterion for Verb in English. But their meanings are quite diverse. What is there in common to someone propelling themself through the water, someone transporting an object on some part of their body, the surface of an object being affected by a sharp-bladed implement, or the ownership of an object being transferred? They do all involve some sort of motion—we could say, an action. But now add to these someone's eyes receiving a sensory impression of something, someone conveying a message to someone else, and the happy state that a human mind is in when it receives agreeable sensations. Is there any element of meaning that they all share, save that what is being described may extend for a period of time (but is not permanent)?

There are a number of distinct semantic types associated with the class Verb and each should be considered separately, if we aim to gain any understanding of how language works. That is, we must investigate the properties of MOTION verbs, of GIVING verbs, of LIKING verbs, and so on, in English, before attempting to reach inductive generalizations about all verbs in English. And we must undertake intensive study of the verbs in a wide sample of individual languages before generalizing further, striking out for general properties of verbs in all languages.

A verb is the centre of a clause and it presupposes a number of participants—one, two, or three, depending on the verb and the semantic type concerned. For each semantic type the participants have different roles and should be accorded different labels. Table 4.1 lists the roles for each type in alphabetical order (the italics will be explained in section 3).

Some MOTION verbs are intransitive—that is, they involve just one role, the thing that is moving. Others are transitive, with the second role being the person that causes the thing to move (compare *the dog*

TABLE 4.1.

Type	Roles
GIVING	*donor*, gift, recipient
TELLING	addressee, news, *speaker*
ATTENTION (e.g. 'see')	impression, *perceiver*
LIKING	*experiencer*, stimulus
AFFECT (e.g. 'hit')	*agent*, instrument, patient
MOTION	(*causer*), thing-moving

came in / I brought the dog in; *the stone rolled down the hill / I rolled the stone down the hill*).

It is important always to bear in mind that different types do have, from a semantic point of view, distinct roles. Later work—spanning a representative sample of human languages—may suggest a certain amount of identification and conflation, but this must not be presupposed in advance.

Consider one instance. In English, German, and a number of other languages, the major TELLING verbs have very similar syntax to GIVING verbs—*give a book to the girl / give the girl a book*, *tell a story to the boy / tell the boy a story*. However, it is invalid to conclude that TELLING is a semantic subtype of GIVING ('giving an item of news') on the basis of syntactic parallelism in some languages. From the point of view of meaning, TELLING and GIVING deal with different kinds of activity, and they must be retained as separate semantic types, each with its own set of roles. (We show in section 4.3 that in some languages these two types have rather different syntactic possibilities.)

Preliminary research suggests that there may in total be about twenty semantic types associated with the grammatical class Verb. Each has its own set of semantic roles so there may, in all, be forty or fifty role labels.

Turning now to syntax, we find that each language has a much more limited set of syntactic relations—things like subject, object, indirect object, beneficiary, instrument. It is most useful to recognize three basic core relations:

S intransitive subject
A transitive subject
O transitive object

There are two kinds of verb, according to the number of roles they require. Intransitive verbs take a single role and, whatever the semantic type, this is always mapped on to S at the syntactic level. Thus, for *laugh*, *cry*, *die*, and *yawn* from the CORPOREAL type, *jump* from MOTION, *sit* from REST, *speak* from TELLING, the sole semantic role does in each case correspond to syntactic relation S.

Transitive verbs require two or more semantic roles; one will be mapped onto A and one of the others onto O. Which semantic role corresponds to which of the two core transitive syntactic relations, A and O, is the main topic of this paper.

Each language has some mechanism(s) for marking syntactic relations. It may be by case inflection (e.g. nominative for S and A, accusative for O; or absolutive for S and O, ergative for A), or by grammatical particles, or by prepositions or postpositions. As in English, it may be by the order in which constituents appear—S and A before the verb, O immediately after it. Or it may be at least partly by cross-referencing within the verb, one series of pronominal prefixes indexing S and A, and another O, for instance.

In some languages there may be several different kinds of realization for a given syntactic relation (conditioned, at least partly, by semantic type). Thus Nichols (1983: 248) states that there is a unified category of subject in North-east Caucasian languages even though 'it is nominative if the verb is intransitive, ergative if the verb is transitive, dative if it is an inverse verb of perception, genitive if it denotes possession, and so on'.

Conversely, there are languages that can have the same marker for two different syntactic functions. Hock (1985) describes how in Sanskrit two constituents in a clause may both receive accusative case. However, only one of them is in object function: this *must* have accusative marking and can be passivized; for the other constituent another case (dative, ablative, instrumental, etc.) can be substituted for accusative and passivization is not possible. A similar situation prevails in the Australian language Martuthunira (Dench 1983, 1987): with the verb 'to throw', that which is thrown must take accusative case (and can passivize) whereas what it is thrown at can be in accusative or locative; other verbs of this type include 'cook', 'carry' and 'leave'.

A lot of attention has been focused on Bantu languages, in which two noun phrases, without any case marking, may follow the verb. Either of them can be direct object, in which circumstance this NP will immediately follow the verb; it is then passivizable, and cliticizable (Hyman and Duranti 1982; see also Gary and Keenan 1977, Duranti and Byarushengo 1977; and Dryer 1983 on the slightly different situation in Kinyarwanda). The two NPs have the same (zero) marking and while either *can be* object only one NP *is* in object role, in a particular clause. (Alternate syntactic frames of this sort are discussed in section 4.3 below.)

A verb will have one, or sometimes two, assignments of syntactic relations to semantic roles. Each language also has a number of syntactic processes (or transformations) that shift constituents between roles, and are marked by a special morpheme attached to or associated with the verb. Passive will typically move underlying O into derived S function, and simultaneously shift A into a non-core function (that can be deleted). One syntactic process in Indonesian promotes a benefactive NP into O function, at the same time marking the verb with affix *-kan* (Chung 1976, Givón 1984b: 161).

There are two reasons why we do not take subject and object as basic relations but prefer instead to work in terms of S, A, and O. One is that ergative languages group S and O, while accusative languages group S and A. The other is the difference between underlying (or deep) and derived (or surface) function assignment (after the syntactic processes mentioned in the last paragraph have applied), and the fact that some languages work with different groupings of the core roles at these two syntactic levels.

At the deep level (which is closest to semantics) every language identifies S and A functions—we can refer to the conjunction of S and A as 'subject'. But at the surface syntactic level some languages use S and A as the 'pivot' for syntactic operations such as coordination, relativization, deletion under coreferentiality, and pronominalization, whereas other languages employ an S/O pivot, or a combination of S/A and S/O pivots (see Dixon 1979: 101–30).

In summary we have, for verbs:

About 20 SEMANTIC TYPES, each with 1–3 semantic roles (40–50 roles in all)	mapped onto ⟹	Perhaps 6–10 SYNTACTIC RELATIONS (S, A, O, and other, peripheral, relations), each with specific marking (case inflections, prepositions, word-order, cross-referencing. (Deep) SUBJECT is conjunction of S and A; (deep) OBJECT is O—at this level.
		syntactic processes apply ⇓ reassigning relations
		(Surface) PIVOT is S/A, or S/O, or a combination of these.

The semantic types and their associated semantic roles may well be universal. Core syntactic relations S, A, and O are also probably universal (a possible exception concerns Philippine languages, where some experts say 'subject' can be recognized, but not 'object'—Paul Schachter, personal comment, and Gil 1984). Peripheral syntactic relations show a fair amount of variation from one language to another.

In the remainder of this paper we investigate the way in which the various semantic roles are mapped onto syntactic relations—particularly the core relations S, A, and O—investigating how much universality and how much variation there is.

3. Subject and object

If a verb has a single semantic role it will be mapped on to S. There is thus no common semantic factor to constituents identified as S. (Some languages mark a volitional S, which controls the activity, in the same way as A; and a non-volitional S by the same marking as O. These have been called 'active' or 'split-S' languages—see Klimov 1974, Dixon 1979: 80–5, Durie 1987.)

If a verb has two or more semantic roles one will be mapped on to A and another onto O. Which role should be A and which O for verbs of GIVING, which for verbs of ATTENTION, which for verbs of AFFECT? We will divide this question into two parts, looking first at A, and then at O.

It has always seemed to me a remarkable universal property of languages that they identify precisely the same semantic roles as A—those which were italicized in Table 4.1. What is there in common to the participant who transfers ownership of some object, for 'give', to the participant who receives (often involuntarily) a sense-impression, for 'see' and 'hear', and the participant who inflicts an injury, for 'hit' and 'cut'?

I discussed this question at some length in a long paper on 'Ergativity' (Dixon 1979: 101–9) and concluded that the participant whose role potentially initiates or controls the activity is identified as A. There is a fullish discussion of difficult cases in the 1979 paper, to which the reader is referred; additional research over the past ten years has not caused me to want to modify or add to this treatment of A. (As already mentioned, 'subject' is the conjunction of A and S. We have noted that although an S controls or initiates the activity for some verbs—e.g. 'walk', 'sit', 'speak', 'smile'—it certainly does not so do for other verbs—e.g. 'break', 'die', 'grow'.)

The O role presents greater difficulties. Every (or almost every) language has a grammatical category of transitive direct object, although of course it is marked in different ways in different grammars—in Latin O must bear accusative case, in English it immediately follows the verb, in Dyirbal it is marked by absolutive case (if a noun) or by accusative case (if a pronoun). The question we must face is: which semantic roles are mapped on to O, and why?

For a two-role verb the matter is straightforward. That role which is *not* identified as A (on the grounds that it could initiate or control the activity) is taken as O. Thus, in all of *the woman watched that boy*, *the teacher likes that boy*, *father fetched that boy*, it is *that boy* which is O (the semantic roles are 'impression', 'stimulus', and 'thing-moving' respectively).

Difficulty arises when we turn to three-role verbs, such as those in the GIVING, TELLING, and AFFECT types. Languages agree in identifying 'donor', 'speaker', and 'agent' as A. Which of the other two roles is assigned to O? For GIVING, is it the 'gift' that is taken to be O, or is it the 'recipient'?

In English two constructions are possible for most verbs of GIVING, and they cover both these possibilities—*John gave a dog to the boy* and *John gave the boy a dog*. Similarly for TELLING the 'news' can be O, or the 'addressee' can be—*John told the result to the boys*, *John told the boys the result*. And for AFFECT it is the 'patient' which is most often in O relation, as in *John hit the vase with his stick*, but it can be the 'instrument', as in *John hit his stick on the table*.

We can refer to these as 'alternate syntactic frames'. (It does not seem very useful to look for reasons for considering one of these frames as more basic, with some transformation like 'dative shift' deriving the other. They are, simply, alternative syntactic codings of a set of semantic roles.)

Most languages have some alternate syntactic frames, for a certain number of three-role verbs; English is unusual in the number of verbs for which it has alternate frames.

In the next section we consider the wider question of role alternation, before looking in more detail at different kinds of syntactic frames, in 4.3. But first it is necessary to insert a caveat: there are some languages which do not show any alternate syntactic frames, for two quite different sorts of reason.

Firstly, languages which have extensive cross-referencing of subject and object in the verb may seldom or never include more than two free NPs in a clause; many American Indian languages are of this type. Margaret Langdon (personal communication) reports that the Yuman language Diegueño would not be likely to include three pieces of 'new information' in a clause. (There may be three overtly marked arguments, since there is obligatory pronominal marking of core constituents within the verb, but not three independent NPs.) Theoretically one should be able to say, 'my new neighbour showed this book to the policeman', but in practice a sequence of two or three clauses would be used, e.g. 'there's this new neighbour who wrote a book and showed it to the policeman'. Plainly, languages of this character would not be likely to have alternate syntactic frames for three-role verbs.

The other type of exception concerns languages that make use of serial verbs. An extreme case is to use two verbs, in serial construction, where other languages would employ a single three-role verb, e.g. *he cut the meat with a knife* would be translated into Vagala (Ghana) by 'he take knife cut meat' (Foley and Van Valin 1984: 189, after Pike 1967: 4). Many serial-verb languages do have three-role verbs that can take three NPs, but only in *one* syntactic frame; where languages like English show a second frame, a serial verb construction must be used. Consider the English sentences *Mary dug sweet potatoes from the ground* and *Mary dug the ground for sweet potatoes* translated into Chinese. The first can be rendered by a verb with three NPs (see Li and Thompson 1981: 463 ff. for *bǎ*, which immediately precedes a direct object in certain circumstances):

(1) Mǎlí cóng dì-shang bǎ báishǔ wā-chūlái
Mary From earth-At sweet potato dig-out

However, the alternative construction for *dig* in English is achieved in Chinese by a serial verb construction:

(2) Mǎlì wā dì zhǎo báishǔ
Mary dig ground look for sweet potato

(Chinese data from Hilary Chappell.)

4. Alternate syntactic coding of semantic roles

In order to study the mechanisms languages have for alternate syntactic coding of semantic roles, I circulated a short questionnaire. A great deal of what follows is based on the twenty-odd responses to this. (Full details are given under acknowledgements at the end of the paper.)

There appear to be three possibilities (one or more of which may occur in any particular language):

(i) there may be two or more lexemes, with almost identical semantic content but different semantic role/syntactic relation identifications, e.g. *John robbed Mary of her savings* / *John stole Mary's savings from her*;

(ii) there may be a syntactic process that alters the syntactic mapping of semantic roles, with a specific morpheme (often, an affix to the verb) marking this. For example in Dyirbal an instrumental NP may be switched to O function, with the original O moving into indirect object slot (marked by dative case), and the verb must then take a derivational affix *-ma-*. Thus, from:

(3)	[bayi	barrgan]$_O$	[baŋgul	yara–ŋgu]$_A$
	Masc+Abs	wallaby+Abs	Masc+Erg	man–Erg

balga – n	[baŋgu	yugu – ŋgu]
hit – Past	It+Inst	stick – Inst

'The man is hitting the wallaby with a stick.'

can be derived:

(4)	[bala	yugu]$_O$	[baŋgul	yara – ŋgu]$_A$
	It+Abs	stick+Abs	Masc+Erg	man – Erg

balgal – ma – n	[bagul	barrgan – gu]
hit – Deriv – Past	Masc+Dat	wallaby – Dat

'The man is hitting the wallaby with a stick'(with an overtone of the sense: 'the man is using a stick to hit the wallaby').

(iii) there may be alternate syntactic frames available involving exactly the same lexeme, without any derivational marking on the verb. To the examples already given from English, involving *give*, *tell*, *hit*, and *dig*, we can add *rub*, as in *John rubbed the cloth over the table* / *John rubbed the table with the cloth*.

Note that for each of (i), (ii), and (iii) the same set of semantic roles is present in each of the alternate sentences.

There is relatively little alternation relating to subject slots (S and A). We do have pairs of verbs such as *like/please* and *lend/borrow*, under (i), and passive could perhaps be included under (ii) (although the original A is severely demoted, and often omitted from the passive clause). Alternate syntactic frames, (iii), almost never involve A or S. English does have the verbs *rent* and *hire*, each of which is its own converse with respect to A and a peripheral syntactic relation (e.g. *Mary rented a car from John*, *John rented a car to Mary*) and also alternations like *John hit me with his stick* / *John's stick hit me* (where the second alternative disowns John's responsibility for the blow). But I know of no true alternate syntactic frames—of type (iii)—involving A or S for any other language.

Most alternations, of all three types, involve O. We have mentioned that, for a three-role verb, one role will be assigned A status. Either of the others can be O. We may now ask what *motivates* the assignment of the O syntactic role.

The answer appears to be that the non-A role which is *most salient* to the way the speaker wishes to describe an activity is placed in O function. It is well known that subject is more likely to be definite and individuated than object, and that a passive may be used where this would not be the case e.g. *my little brother was hit by a falling tree*, in preference to *a falling tree hit my little brother*. In similar fashion, if there are two non-A NPs, then that which is definite and individuated should if possible be in the O slot: *I told that marvellous new joke to some people last night* is more felicitous than *I told some people that marvellous new joke last night*, and *I told my very best friend a joke* (*to cheer him up*) is surely better than *I told a joke to my very best friend* (*to cheer him up*).

Give is generally considered to be equally at home with either 'gift' or 'recipient' as O. There are, however, restrictions in the case where the recipient is only vaguely specified. Parallel to *John gave all his money to the Royal Canberra Hospital* we can say *John gave the Royal Canberra Hospital all his money*, since the 'recipient' is quite specific. But consider *John gave all his money to good causes*. The alternate construction, *John gave good causes all his money*, sounds distinctly odd, mainly because *good causes* is not a definite, individuated recipient.

Discourse considerations appear to be another factor in deciding which non-A role to put in O function (see Givón 1984b: 153 ff.). There is a preference for an established topic to be placed in a core syntactic role, such as O. Compare *John picked out a stick and hit it against the table to test its strength* (where the 'instrument' role is O of *hit*) with *John hunted down the wallaby and hit it with a stick to kill it* (where the 'patient' is O for *hit*). This surely interrelates with what was said above about *salience*—a discourse topic is likely to be definite and individuated, and should be accorded a central syntactic role in every clause in which it appears (whereas the NP *a stick*, in the last sentence quoted, is very much an extra, peripheral feature, occurring in just one clause). The example given earlier, *I told my very best friend a joke to cheer him up*, exemplifies the same point, only here the O NP *my very best friend* begins a topic chain (rather than continuing one).

We now consider, in turn, the three ways of achieving syntactic role alternation.

4.1. Alternate lexemes

Most languages have a number of pairs of lexemes which share essentially the same meaning and the same semantic roles, but have these mapped on to syntactic relations in different ways. Of course the syntactic role assignment does have semantic implications. We mentioned that the A NP refers to that participant who could control or initiate the activity. A modifying verb like *try* can only relate to the potentially controlling A participant.

Consider the exchange of a piece of merchandise for a sum of money, describable by *sell* or *buy*. Suppose Mary has ten dollars, which is the value of John's book. If she is the one who attempts to finalize a transaction then we must use *buy*, with 'recipient' in syntactic role A: *Mary tried to buy the book from John for $10*; whereas if John is the one who is eager for the sale to take place then *sell* is the appropriate verb, with 'seller' (a particular instance of the 'donor' semantic role, which applies for all verbs of GIVING) as A: *John tried to sell the book to Mary for $10*.

Only a few semantic types show pairs of lexical converses, with respect to A and some other syntactic relation. For the GIVING type there are *lend/borrow* in addition to *buy/sell* (and *hire*, *rent* is each its own converse). For *give* itself there is no exact converse, although *receive* comes close. Then we also have *like* and *please*, to which similar comments apply—compare *John tried to please Mary*, and *Mary tried to like John*. (*Fear* and *frighten* are another pair where A and O cross-correspond.)

We mentioned in section 2 that the LIKING type relates to different word classes in different languages. In English it belongs to the Verb class but either the 'stimulus' or the 'experiencer' can be coded as A. Why does LIKING have this property, when for other types only one semantic role may be A (e.g. 'speaker' for TELLING, 'perceiver' for ATTENTION)?

The reason becomes apparent on comparing LIKING and AFFECT (a most important type, which belongs to the Verb class in every language) at both the semantic and syntactic levels. First, let us compare semantic roles between these two types. The 'agent' of AFFECT must be a human or higher animate whereas the 'patient' can be anything (*John cut the meat/tree*, but not **the meat/tree cut John*). Similarly, the 'experiencer' for LIKING must be a human or higher animate, whereas the 'stimulus' can be anything (*John liked the dance/sunset*, but not **the dance/sunset liked John*). On the grounds of semantic congruence between 'agent' and 'experiencer', and between 'patient' and 'stimulus', there is one set of LIKING verbs (*like*, *hate*, *enjoy*, *prefer*, etc.) for which 'experiencer' is A, parallel to the 'agent' of AFFECT.

However, when the syntax of AFFECT and LIKING verbs is compared, a different sort of congruence emerges. For AFFECT the 'agent' is normally A, but there is an alternative construction with 'instrument' as head of the A NP and the 'agent' a possessor to it. Compare:

(5) John hit Bill with his stick (when he was swinging it).

(6) John's stick hit Bill (when he was swinging it).

Now consider the parallel construction pair:

(7) Mary pleased Sandra with her dancing.

(8) Mary's dancing pleased Sandra.

It is the 'stimulus' role in (7)–(8) which corresponds to the 'agent' in (5)–(6). Because of this, there is a second set of LIKING verbs (*please*, *satisfy*, *annoy*, *surprise*, etc.) for which the 'stimulus' is A, parallel to the 'agent' of AFFECT verbs.

English has some lexemes which differ in the assignment of semantic roles to O and to a peripheral function, marked by a preposition. There is the *rob/steal* pair mentioned earlier, and also *John reported the accident to the police / John told the police about the accident* (although here *report* does have a more specific meaning than the general verb *tell*).

Eskimo is particularly rich in pairs of verbs that have very similar meanings but assign different semantic roles to O, e.g. *cikir-* 'to give', which has 'recipient' as O (marked with absolutive case) and 'gift' in instrumental case, and *tune-* 'give, sell, exchange, trade', which has 'gift' as O and 'recipient' in allative case. (Data from Tony Woodbury, who also mentioned other pairs for 'supply', 'show', and 'tell'.)

Tawala, an Austronesian language spoken in Milne Bay, Papua New Guinea (data from Bryan Ezard), has two verbs corresponding to the English *dig*. 'John dug the ground for yams' would be rendered through the verb *taw-i*, with 'ground' as O and 'yams' in benefactive case, while 'John dug yams from the ground' would use *lukepa-ya*, with 'yams' as O and 'ground' in locative case. Tawala also has two verbs 'to sweep', one used in 'John swept leaves from the place', and the other in 'John swept the place of leaves'.

Dyirbal has a number of pairs of 'alternate O' verb lexemes. Suppose that a liquid is being poured on to something. If the speaker decides that the most salient role is that of the liquid (he is effectively describing what the actor does with the liquid) then the verb *buŋga-* 'empty out, capsize, lay (egg)' would be used, as in:

(9)	[balan	bana]O	[baŋgul	yara – ŋgu]A
	Fem+Abs	water+Abs	Masc+Erg	man – Erg

buŋga – n	[bagu	jiya – gu]
empty – Past	It+Dat	chair – Dat

'The man emptied out the water on to the chair.'

If, however, the thing that is made wet is focused upon, a different verb must be used, *jilŋga-* 'pour on to, empty on to', as in:

(10)

[bala	jiya]$_O$	[baŋgul	yara – ŋgu]$_A$
It+Abs	chair+Abs	Masc+Erg	man–Erg

jilŋga – n	[baŋgun	bana – ŋgu]
pour on to – Past	Fem+Inst	water – Inst

'The man emptied out water onto the chair' (lit.: 'the man emptied out on to the chair, with water').

4.2. Syntactic processes that switch functions

Most languages have some productive or semi-productive syntactic processes that switch the syntactic functions assigned to semantic roles; these must be explicitly marked, usually by a morpheme attached to the verb.

Prefixes and preverbs in the Slavic languages and Hungarian often have an ostensive aspectual and directional (e.g. 'away', 'up') meaning, but they can also engender role switching. This can be illustrated with *pogružil* and *zagruzil*, two forms of the verb 'to load' in Russian (data from Ju. Apresjan):

(11) on pogružil meški na mašinu
he + Nom load bags + Acc on car
'He loaded the bags into the car.'

(12) on zagružil mašinu meskami
he + Nom load car + Acc bag + Inst
'He loaded the car with bags.'

In Hungarian the verb *ajándékoz* 'give a present' places the 'gift' in accusative and the 'recipient' in dative case; but with the completive prefix *meg-* (i.e. *megajándékoz*) 'recipient' is transferred to accusative and 'gift' to instrumental case (data from Robert Hetzron).

In Fijian a transitive verb is marked by an explicit transitive suffix. Many (perhaps one-quarter) of verbs have a choice of two suffixes. In some instances the suffix alternation has entirely semantic effect e.g. *samu-ta* 'hit with a club', *samu-la'ina* 'hit many times with a club'; but in most cases it engenders a rearrangement of syntactic functions. There is just one verb where this alternation involves A, i.e. *voli-a* 'buy', *voli-ta'ina* 'sell'; for all the rest the alternation involves O and a peripheral syntactic relation. Thus, with *qoli-* 'fish with a net':

(13) au aa qoli – va [a i'a]$_O$ [i+na lawa yai]
I+A Past fish – Tr_1 [Art fish]$_O$ [Prep+Art net This]
'I caught fish with this net.'

(14) au aa qoli – va'ina [a lawa yai]$_O$ [i+na i'a]
I+A Past fish – Tr_2 [Art net This]$_O$ [Prep+Art fish]
'I fished-with this net for fish.'

There are also verbs such as *lua-* 'vomit (on)', where one transitive form, *lua-ca*, has as O 'what the vomit falls on to', and another transitive form, *lua-ra'ina*, has as O 'what is vomited up'. (A full account is in Dixon 1988.)

We have already mentioned the productive process in Indonesian which moves the beneficiary into O function, and adds a suffix *-kan* to the verb; and the process in Dyirbal whereby a transitive verb is suffixed with *-ma-*, the original instrumental NP goes into O slot, and the original O receives dative case marking (the A is unchanged). (See also Rude 1982 for an account of the variety of promotion-to-object processes in Nez Perce. For a similar process in Kinyarwanda see Givón 1984a: 177–8, based on Kimenyi 1976.)

It is of course often the case that syntactic role alternation which is shown in one way in one language may be realized in quite a different manner in another language. Alternate lexeme pairs such as *buy* and *sell* in English (and in many other languages) correspond to a single verb with two different suffixes in Fijian. There are two lexemes 'to dig' in Tawala and two lexemes 'to give' in Eskimo, where English has a single lexeme with alternate syntactic frames.

Now Dyirbal is like English in having a fair number of verbs with alternate syntactic frames (and no overt marking of this on the verb). But there is also the instrument-to-object syntactic derivation marked by *-ma-*; this *must* be used wherever it would be appropriate, e.g. to continue a 'topic chain' which has the instrumental NP in (S or O) topic function (see example (254) in Dixon 1972: 96).

In English a verb like *plait* or *weave* or *knit* can occur in two frames—for one the O is the material used, and for the other it is the object made e.g. *I knitted the wool into a sweater*, and *I knitted a sweater with the wool.* The Dyirbal verb *bunya-* 'to plait' must have the thing made in O function, and the material used in instrumental case:

(15) [bala jawun / It+Abs dilly bag+Abs]$_O$ [baŋgul yara-ŋgu / Masc+Erg man-Erg]$_A$ bunya-n / plait-Past

[baŋgu mangi-ŋgu / It+Inst vine-Inst]

'The man plaited a dilly-bag with the vines.'

An alternative frame can be obtained, as described above, by adding *-ma-* to the verb:

(16) [bala mangi / It+Abs vine+Abs]$_O$ [baŋgul yara-ŋgu / Masc+Erg man-Erg]$_A$ bunyal-ma-n / plait-Deriv-Past

[bagu jawun-gu / It+Dat dilly bag-Dat]

'The man plaited the vines into a dilly-bag.'

Thus Dyirbal uses mechanism (ii) for something that is achieved by mechanism (iii) in English.

4.3. Alternate syntactic frames

Almost all grammars and dictionaries—of both obscure and well-known languages—pay little or no attention to the question of alternate syntactic frames. There is a tendency to notice that a particular verb occurs with its semantic role coded in *one* way syntactically and to leave it at that, without enquiring whether there are *other* possible codings.

It was only when, after completing a grammar of Dyirbal, I began to work on a dictionary of that language (something which is still forthcoming), analysing the multiplicity of examples that had accumulated for common verbs, that I became aware how many verbs had alternate case frames. For instance:

(17) [ŋaja] [bala yugu] gunba-n
[I+A]$_A$ [It+Abs tree+Abs]$_O$ cut-Past

[bagul jambun-gu]
[Masc+Dat grub-Dat]

'I chopped the tree for grubs (which burrow in its bark)'.

(18) [ŋaja] [bayi jambun] gunba-n
[I+A]$_A$ [Masc+Abs grub+Abs]$_O$ cut-Past

[baŋum yugu-ŋunu]
[There+Abl tree-Abl]

'I chopped grubs from the tree.'

The same verb is used in both (17) and (18), and the A noun phrase does not alter. But the O NP from (17) is in ablative case in (18), and the O from (18) is in dative case in (17).

It appeared striking that, for a high proportion of the Dyirbal verbs which have alternate case frames, there are also alternate frames available for the corresponding English verb, as in the translations of (17) and (18) (English prepositions 'for' and 'from' correspond to dative and ablative cases in Dyirbal, in these constructions).

A study of a wide variety of other languages (by perusing the limited literature available, and through a circulated questionnaire) showed that almost all have a sprinkling of alternate case frames, but nothing like the number shown by Dyirbal or by English.

However, the methods of constructing alternate case frames are by no means exactly parallel between English and Dyirbal. This can be illustrated with *give* and *tell*, two verbs that use almost exactly the same case frames in English:

(19*a*) John gave the book to Mary.
(*b*) John gave Mary the book.

(20*a*) John told the news to Mary.
(*b*) John told Mary the news.

In (19*a*), (20*a*) *the book/news* is O NP with *Mary* being marked by preposition *to*. In (19*b*), (20*b*) *Mary* is in O slot, with *the book/news* being now a post-object NP without any prepositional marking (grammars of English differ on the syntactic status they assign to *the book/news* in (19*b*), (20*b*)).

The alternate frames in Dyirbal are, for *wuga-* 'give':

(21*a*)
[bala bugu] [baŋgul Jani – ŋgu]
[It+Abs book+Abs]$_O$ [Masc+Erg John – Erg]$_A$

wuga – n [baŋun Marri – ŋu]
give – Past [Fem+Gen Mary – Gen]

'John gave the book to Mary.'

(*b*)
[balan Marri] [baŋgul Jani – ŋgu]
[Fem+Abs Mary+Abs]$_O$ [Masc+Erg John – Erg]$_A$

wuga – n [baŋgu bugu – ŋgu]
give – Past [It+Inst book – Inst]

'John gave Mary the book.'

In (21*a*) the 'gift', *bala bugu*, is O with the 'recipient', *Marri*, in genitive case; in (21*b*) the 'recipient' is in O relation and the 'gift' in instrumental case. (There is also a less-used alternation, with 'gift' as O and 'recipient' in dative case—see Dixon 1972: 300.)

For *buwa-* 'tell' the frames are rather different—either the 'news' or the 'addressee' may be O, and whichever of these semantic roles is not O will receive dative case marking:

(22*a*)
[bala wanda] [baŋgul Jani – ŋgu]
[It+Abs message+Abs]$_O$ [Masc+Erg John – Erg]$_A$

buwa – nyu [bagun Marri – gu]
tell – Past [Fem+Dat Mary – Dat]

John told the message to Mary.

(*b*) [balan Marri]$_O$ [baŋgul Jani – ŋgu]$_A$
[Fem+Abs Mary+Abs]$_O$ [Masc+Erg John – Erg]$_A$

buwa – nyu [bagu wanda – gu]
tell – Past [It+Dat message – Dat]

'John told Mary the message.'

We thus see that although both English and Dyirbal have alternate syntactic frames for 'give' and for 'tell', allowing either of the non-A semantic roles to be O, the frames are not parallel between the two languages. English treats *give* and *tell* (and also *show*) in the same way; Dyirbal has different pairs of constructions for the two semantic types (SHOWING is in Dyirbal coded in exactly the same ways as TELLING).

Close examination of verbs that take alternate syntactic frames shows that they fall into two subclasses:

(i) 'give', 'tell', 'show' and their hyponyms have alternate frames in relatively *few* languages; where they do, there is little semantic difference between the frames;

(ii) *every* language I have investigated (which freely allows a clause to include three NPs) has alternate case frames for some verbs out of 'weave', 'dig', 'cover', 'shake', 'sweep', and similar items; here there is a more definite semantic difference between the two frames.

We now discuss these subclasses, one at a time. (See also the data and discussion in Givón 1984b and Faltz 1978; and the insightful discussion of Amharic in Hetzron 1970.)

4.3.1. GIVING, TELLING, *and* SHOWING

In most languages that I have investigated, the O NPs for verbs from these types are 'gift', 'news', or 'thing shown', with the person to whom it is given, told, or shown marked by dative case, or a preposition, or something similar. This applies to Thai, Burmese, Russian, Polish, Hindi, Telugu (Dravidian), Abkhaz (North-west Caucasian), as well as Austronesian languages such as Acehnese, Fijian, and Paamese, and Australian languages such as Warlpiri, and Kalkatungu. In these languages there is only one syntactic frame available for verbs in the three types.

A smaller group of languages have a single syntactic frame but with the O slot reserved for 'recipient', 'addressee', or 'person to whom shown', and with the 'gift'/'news'/'thing shown' coded into a peripheral relation. The Uto-Aztecan language Huichol (Comrie 1981: 61–4, 1982), the Austronesian language Tawala (data from B. Ezard), and the Australian language Nakkara (Eather forthcoming) are of this type.

It is unusual to find a language that does not treat 'give', 'tell', and 'show' in a parallel manner for object identification. This does happen in the Austronesian language Gilbertese (data from S. P. Harrison), which has the 'recipient' of 'give' and the 'addressee' of 'tell' as O, but the 'thing shown' as O for 'show'. (This is related to the fact that *kaota* 'to show' is the causative of *oti* 'be revealed, clear'.)

Then there is another fairly small set of languages that have two syntactic frames for all of 'give', 'show', and 'tell', allowing both non-A roles to be O. Besides English and Dyirbal, the Austronesian language Banjarese (Sari 1984) behaves in this way, as do those Bantu languages which allow two NPs to follow the verb, in either order—the one that immediately follows is generally the object (see references in section 2 above). The Australian language Yidiny has only one syntactic frame for 'give' and 'show' (with 'gift' and 'thing shown' as O) but alternate frames have been recorded for 'tell'.

The semantic difference between alternate frames, such as (19*a*, *b*), (20*a*, *b*) in English and (21*a*, *b*), (22*a*, *b*) in Dyirbal, relates mainly to the general semantic characteristics of the O syntactic role. We mentioned above that a direct object in English should be definite and individuated, which accounts for the infelicitous nature of *John gave good causes all his money*. When we examine a cross-section of verbs from the GIVING type in English we find that some are like *give* in occurring in two syntactic frames (*lend*, *rent*, *sell*, *pay*, for instance) but that others (such as *donate*, *bequeath*) differ. The meaning of *donate* and *bequeath* focuses particularly on the 'gift'; this is the role that is most salient, in these varieties of giving, and it must be coded as O.

Dyirbal has a variety of verbs of GIVING. *Wuga-* 'give' and *bila-* 'send, give by taking over' can occur in both the frames illustrated in (21*a*, *b*). (Although if the gift is 'meat', then the (21*a*) frame is preferred, with 'gift' as O. This may be because when a hunter brings home an animal, each of his relatives has the right to receive a certain portion, according to the nature of the kinship link, and it is this portion of meat which has the most salient role.) *Munyja-* 'share out' most often has 'gift' in O slot, as in (21*a*), while *gibi-* 'provide food for relatives' (e.g. a boy feeding his potential mother-in-law so that he will be recognized as an adequate provider and allowed to claim her daughter in marriage) prefers frame (21*b*), with the 'recipient' as O—although both of these verbs can occur in either frame. There is also a verb *wudi-* 'don't give, refuse to give' that is only used in frame (21*b*); that is, the recipient—or rather, the person who did not receive anything—must be in O slot.

There are similar degrees of preference or exclusion among verbs from the other types, in Dyirbal. Both the general verb *buwa-* 'tell' and the more specific *jinga-* 'tell some particular piece of news, or a story' occur in frames (22*a*) and (22*b*). But *buwa-* is most commonly heard in (22*b*), with 'addressee' as O, while the preferred frame for *jinga-* is (22*a*), with 'news' being recognized as particularly salient, and thus coded as O.

Two verbs in Dyirbal correspond to *show* in English. *Nyula-* 'show something to someone by taking them over to it, and pointing it out' shows a preference for frame (22*a*), although it does also occur in (22*b*), while *jumba-* 'show something to someone by holding it up' is restricted to (22*a*) (where the 'thing shown' is O).

4.3.2. Other verbs

In a classic paper, Stephen Anderson (1971) discusses sentences like:

(23*a*) John sprayed the paint on the canvas.
(*b*) John sprayed the canvas with the paint.

(24*a*) John loaded the hay on the wagon.
(*b*) John loaded the wagon with the hay.

It has been suggested that in (23*a*) all the paint is used up, in (23*b*) all of the canvas is covered with paint, in (24*a*) all the hay is loaded, and in (24*b*) the wagon is completely filled with hay. (Anderson, following B. Hall 1965, omitted *the* from before *paint* in (23*a*, *b*). He had *the* before *hay* in (24*a*) but not in (24*b*). There is, of course, a preference for a direct object NP to be definite, whereas an instrumental NP need not be; but it is useful to have NPs in alternate syntactic frames being directly comparable, as they are in (23*a*, *b*), (24*a*, *b*).)

This exemplifies the point that—for verbs of types other than

GIVING, TELLING, SHOWING—there is usually a fairly major semantic difference between alternate syntactic frames. Consider:

(25*a*) John will dig yams from the ground there.
(*b*) John will dig the ground there for yams.

Sentence (25*a*) implies that John knows there are yams in that patch of ground (perhaps he planted them there) and it is a fact that if he digs he will get them. (25*b*), in contrast, suggests that he will dig the patch of ground hoping to find yams; the preposition *for* before *yams* indicates that this vegetable is the final goal of John's digging, but not that there is any certainty he will achieve this goal.

It is the object NP which is most salient, which is being focused on. In (25*a*) yams will be got, in (25*b*) the ground will be dug, in (24*a*) the hay will be loaded somewhere, in (24*b*) the wagon will be loaded up. There need not necessarily be a 'holistic' (i.e. 'all of') interpretation of the object NP. (See also Wierzbicka 1980: 70 ff.)

It is better to state the meaning-frame correspondence the other way round to that attempted by Anderson. We can say that *if* all of the paint is sprayed on to the canvas then it is felicitous to have *the paint* in O slot (but if *the paint* is in O slot it need not necessarily imply that all of the paint is used up). And *if* all of the canvas is covered then it is most felicitous to have *the canvas* in O slot (but if *the canvas* is in O slot it does not necessarily imply that all the canvas is covered).

Alamblak (Sepik district, Papua New Guinea) has alternate syntactic frames for 'rub', among other verbs, e.g.

(26*a*) na hëhrampan gëbrërnayanm yimar-n
I oil rub + I + 3Pl man-Loc
'I rubbed oil on the man.'

(*b*) na yimar gëbrërnayanr hëhrampa-e
I man rub + I + 3Sg oil-Inst
'I rubbed the man with oil.'

When Les Bruce, who elicited this material, enquired if 'dead man' could be substituted for 'man' in (26*b*), the Alamblak speaker responded: 'Do you have medicine you can rub on a dead man to bring him back to life?' The semantic role that is placed in the O syntactic slot in Alamblak must be salient to the extent that it is affected in an appropriate manner by the activity. With the medicinal action of rubbing oil on a person, to make him better, placing the 'person' in O slot implies that he was made better.

I know of no alternate syntactic frames (for a single verb lexeme, with no special marking) that involve syntactic role A, except for *rent* and *hire* in English. For (17)–(26), and all other examples gathered from a wide range of languages, A remains unchanged between the two construction types.

Languages that use alternate syntactic frames for GIVING, TELLING, and SHOWING have alternate frames—with a more significant meaning difference—for a range of verbs from other types. In Dyirbal I have recorded two or more distinct case frames for over thirty verbs, including *gida-* 'poke with stick into hollow log (to see if animal is there)', and *baya-* 'sing', as in:

(27*a*) [ŋaja / I+A]$_A$ [bala yugarri / It+Abs hollow log+Abs]$_O$ gida – n / poke – Past
[bagun gujila – gu / Fem+Dat bandicoot – Dat]
'I poked in the hollow log for a bandicoot.'

(*b*) [ŋaja / I+A]$_A$ [balan gujila / Fem+Abs bandicoot+Abs]$_O$ gida – n / poke – Past
[balay yugarri – ga / There+Loc hollow log – Loc]
'I poked at the bandicoot in the hollow log there.'

(28*a*) [ŋaja / I+A]$_A$ [bala gama / It+Abs song style+Abs]$_O$ baya – n / sing – Past
[bagul barrgan – gu / Masc+Dat wallaby – Dat]
'I sang a Gama-style song about a wallaby.'

(*b*) [ŋaja / I+A]$_A$ [bayi barrgan / Masc+Abs wallaby+Abs]$_O$ baya – n / sing – Past

[gama – ŋga / song style – Loc]

'I sang a song about a wallaby in the Gama style.'

With 'tell' and 'show' the NP which is not O is dative in both frames (see (22*a*, *b*)). With 'give' it is instrumental in one and genitive in the other (as in (21*a*, *b*)). For 'cut', in (17)/(18), the alternation is dative/ablative. In both (27*a*, *b*) and (28*a*, *b*) it is dative/locative. Other case combinations attested in alternate frames include locative/comitative, ablative/comitative, dative/comitative, and instrumental/dative.

Grammars of English sometimes list verbs from the GIVING, TELLING, and SHOWING types that have alternate frames (e.g. Quirk and Greenbaum 1973: 169, 370–1) but not those like *cut*, *dig*, *rub*, *load*. There is some discussion of the latter set in Givón 1984a: 169 ff. A full investigation of this topic, and the kinds of semantic alternation involved, should be a high priority for future research.

Most languages have a single frame for each of 'give', 'tell', 'show', and their hyponyms. But every language that I have investigated (except for those which find it difficult to permit three NPs in a clause) does have at least a sprinkling of alternate syntactic frames in other types. For Hindi, Yamuna Kachru supplied me with a list of 'alternate case frame' verbs that includes *koRnaa* 'to dig', *bharnaa* 'to fill', *laadnaa* 'to load', and *maarnaa* 'to hit'. Alternate case frames appear to be rarer in Dravidian languages, from South India, but Bh. Krishnamurti reports 'cover' in Telugu, e.g.:

(29*a*) kamala pillawaaNNi duppaTitoo kappindi
Kamala boy + Acc sheet + With cover + Past
'Kamala covered the toy with a sheet.'

(*b*) kamala pillawaaDimiida duppaTi kappindi
Kamala boy + On sheet + Acc cover + Past
'Kamala covered a sheet on the boy.'

Abkhaz has alternate frames for 'weave'; Kuniyanti for 'throw' (O alternating between what is thrown and what it is thrown at);

Warlpiri, Yolngu, and Burmese for 'dig'; Paamese for 'shake' (as in 'shake the dirt off the blanket', 'shake the blanket because of dirt' with Causal case on 'dirt'); Ewe for 'ask', 'search', and 'polish/rub'; and Tawala for 'shake' and 'cover'.

As mentioned in section 4.2, Fijian has many verbs with two transitive endings, each of which may encode a different semantic role as O. In addition, it does have some alternate frames for a single lexeme-plus-transitive-suffix—for 'ask', 'weave', 'dig', and 'shake' (but not for 'tell', 'give', or 'show').

The point to be made is that alternate syntactic frames are a recurrent feature of human languages. It would be fascinating to undertake a detailed cross-language comparison of the semantic differences engendered by these syntactic variations, and see if any generalizations are possible. But a prerequisite would be detailed descriptions of the phenomenon in individual languages; up until now grammars and dictionaries have scarcely mentioned the topic.

(One must also take care not to get too carried away. János Zsilka devoted much of his academic life to a study of alternate syntactic frames in Hungarian—see e.g. Zsilka 1967, 1973. Unfortunately, Zsilka's theoretical ideas affected his perception of the data; some of the sentences he quotes are at best only marginally acceptable to other speakers of Hungarian.)

5. Conclusion

We began by dividing the verbs of a language into semantic types, each of which has a number of semantic roles associated with it. These roles are then mapped on to the basic syntactic relations of the language.

There is remarkable agreement among languages about the roles identified as A (transitive subject). For types that have three semantic roles available (i.e. verbs that are trivalent) there are two non-A NPs, either of which could be marked as O (transitive object).

Often there is a need to mark one of these NPs as O in some circumstances and the other as O in other circumstances. Ways of achieving this are (i) to have two lexemes, which differ only in this particular, e.g. *rob/steal*; (ii) to have a productive syntactic process which shifts a non-O NP into O slot and moves the original O NP into a peripheral slot (still retaining it in the derived clause); or (iii) there can be two (or more) syntactic frames for one verb, with no marking of this save on the NPs, e.g. *cut the cake into pieces, cut pieces off the cake.*

If mechanism (i) or (ii) is available, this will always take precedence. We noted that Dyirbal has many alternate case frames, but there is also a syntactic process, under (ii), that puts an instrumental NP into O slot (and the original O into dative), illustrated in (3)/(4), (15)/(16); here the employment of alternate frames, of type (iii), is blocked.

Grammar thrives on system, on exact coding, which then allows for unambiguous decoding. To allow one verb to have two or more potential assignments of syntactic functions to its semantic roles is anarchic, going against the principles on which a grammar is based. But it is sometimes necessary (if no grammatically marked mechanism is available) in order to bring out needed semantic alternations and/or permit syntactic linkages needed for a certain discourse organization.

Alternate frames for verbs like 'give', 'show', and 'tell' involve a small (though discernible) semantic difference. It is unusual for languages to have alternate syntactic frames for these verbs (as English in fact does have). However, almost all languages (save those which seldom allow three NPs in a clause, either because they make much use of serial verbs, or else because they have considerable role cross-referencing in the verb) have some verbs with alternate frames for types like AFFECT (e.g. 'hit', 'cut', 'dig', 'rub'), or MOTION ('fill', 'shake', 'cover'), or verbs like 'sing' and 'teach'. There is then a real semantic difference between the alternate constructions; this probably varies from language to language, and is connected with the semantic import of the syntactic function 'direct object' in that language. A fuller study of the topic would doubtless throw more light on the nature of 'object' as a universal syntactic relation.

Acknowledgements

I owe a tremendous debt to the following colleagues and friends, who supplied data and/or talked over the topics dealt with in this paper or commented on a draft of it: Felix Ameka (Ewe), Barry Blake (Kalkatungu), David Bradley (Burmese), Les Bruce (Alamblak), Hilary Chappell (Mandarin Chinese), Ping Chen (Mandarin Chinese), Sandra Chung, Bernard Comrie, Terry Crowley (Paamese, spoken on Vanuatu), Probal Dasgupta, Valerij Dem'jankov (Russian), Alan Dench (Martuthunira), Tony Diller (Thai), Tamsin Donaldson (Ngiyambaa), Mark Durie (Acehnese), Bronwyn Eather (Nakkara), Bryan Ezard (Tawala), Bill Foley, Talmy Givón, Sheldon Harrison (Gilbertese), Robert Hetzron (Hungarian), B. G. and I. K. Hewitt (Abkhaz), Dee Ann Holisky (Tsova-Tush, or Bats), Paul Hopper, Larry Hyman, Yamuna Kachru (Hindi), Ed Keenan, Bh. Krishnamurti (Telugu), Margaret Langdon, Beth Levin, Bill McGregor (Kuniyanti), Marianne Mithin (Mohawk), Frances Morphy (Yolngu), Pam Munro, David Nash (Warlpiri), Johanna Nichols, Dave Perlmutter, Nirmala Sari (Banjarese), Paul Schachter, Tim Shopen, Bob Stockwell, K. V. Subbarao, Sandra Thompson, Anna Wierzbicka (Polish), David Wilkins, Tony Woodbury (Central Alaskan Yupik Eskimo) and David Zorc (Aklanon, spoken in the Philippines).

5

Competence and Performance in the Explanation of Language Universals

John A. Hawkins

1. Introduction

The major challenge facing any general linguistic theory is to extract the universals from the enormous range of variation exhibited by the 5,000 or so currently spoken languages. Whatever universal regularities there are must be discovered and described. More general principles underlying them must be inferred, and we must try to explain why natural languages obey these regularities and principles rather than others.

The kinds of explanations that are currently being pursued in this context can be divided into roughly two groups. There are those that view grammar as a self-contained (but perhaps ultimately innately determined) system and which explain universals in terms that are internal to the system itself without looking outside it (except to hypothesize some genetically transmitted human linguistic endowment). Other explanations appeal directly to aspects of linguistic performance. The relevant language universals are argued to reflect the communicative functions of language, or considerations of discourse, or they are seen as responses to the production and comprehension mechanisms of speakers using language in real time.

We might refer to the former group as 'competence explanations' and to the latter as 'performance explanations'. Performance explanations, like competence explanations, may appeal ultimately to certain innate predispositions in humans, for example when providing a processing explanation in terms of psychological difficulty or memory limitations, etc. Other performance explanations make no appeal to innateness (those that are properly labelled 'functional' since they reflect the various functions that humans use language for), just as some competence explanations make no such appeal. The true distinguishing characteristic between our two types of explanation is therefore whether the underlying explanatory principles that are proposed (apart from innateness) involve grammatical regularities alone, or grammar in conjunction with facts and principles pertaining to language use and language users. The use of the term competence at the descriptive level (as an account of the native speaker's grammatical knowledge of his/her language) should therefore be distinguished from the use of the same term at the explanatory level within the present context. A native speaker's (descriptive) competence grammar will be explained both in terms of (explanatory) competence principles alone, and in terms of (explanatory) performance principles, namely when the grammar encodes some response to communicative or processing needs of the type to be illustrated below.[1]

A priori, there is nothing remarkable about the proposal that language universals reflect both narrowly grammatical and user-based principles. The difficulty and the challenge lies, as we shall see, in attaining a satisfactory level of precision about what the ultimate competence and performance principles are in this context, and in

[1] At the level of innateness, it is not inconceivable that the human language faculty encodes grammatical universals that have evolved, in part at least, in response to performance (particularly processing) considerations, as Chomsky and Lasnik (1977) and Fodor (1983) point out. If this is so, the innate linguistic knowledge that guides the construction of a competence grammar in every human child may already be 'user-friendly' or heavily performance-based. Alternatively, the kinds of performance principles to be discussed in this paper may represent diachronically inherited properties of the languages of the world, and not of the innate language faculty, and may have simply evolved over time in response to universal performance needs. Yet a third possibility is that performance principles (again especially those having to do with processing) are part of some innate human endowment which is either unique to the processing of language or which may hold more generally across other cognitive and perceptual domains, but which is none the less separate from the innate language faculty and which has not influenced the class of grammars compatible with this latter (i.e. this is a modular view of innate human cognitive abilities). Whichever of these possibilities turns out to be correct (and so far we can merely enumerate the possibilities) our basic distinction between system-internal grammatical or competence principles and user-based performance explanations for language universals remains clear enough in principle, even though it is far from clear to what extent and in what form either set of principles is innate. By remaining non-committal about the nature and extent of innateness, we can still try to tease out and separate those general principles underlying universals that derive from language use from those that do not and that are system-internal, which we lable performance and competence explanations respectively.

understanding how they interact with one another to determine the surface forms and form-meaning mappings that we find across languages. It is this interaction between competence and performance principles that I shall be addressing in this paper. I begin with a brief summary of some examples of competence and performance explanations that are currently being offered for language universals, before presenting a more detailed discussion of some cross-language data involving *left–right asymmetries*, which I shall explain in terms of just such an interaction between competence and performance principles.

1.1. Some competence and performance explanations for language universals

Within Chomskyan generative grammar, the ultimate grammatical principles and atoms that explain the rules and data of all languages are the formal and substantive universals of the theory (cf. Chomsky 1965, and 1981/1982 for a more recent version). Formal universals are those that determine the form and shape of the grammar, e.g. the components, rule types, principles of rule interaction, or (in more recent versions) the various modules of the theory. Substantive universals refer to the contents of these rules or modules, e.g. the categories and bar levels of X-bar theory, the various distinctive features of phonology, etc. These principles and atoms of universal grammar are, in turn, claimed to be innately represented in the human species (cf. e.g. Chomsky 1968 for a particularly clear discussion). And it is these innate principles that structure and explain the child's rapid acquisition of language, despite (it is argued) insufficient data as input on the basis of which the highly complex grammar of the native language could be learned. To quote one recent formulation:

> . . . [explanatory principles of UG] should be linked to the problem of how the child attains a rich and structured system of rules—a grammar—on the basis of degenerate and deficient data. [The] concern is to look for and specify that a-priori knowledge, available to the language-learning child, which permits language acquisition to circumvent the impoverished stimulus. (Coopmans 1984: 55.)

I am sympathetic to this general line of reasoning. However, two cautions are in order. First, the kinds of assumptions made about both learnability and the set of data to which the learner is exposed (cf. further Wexler and Culicover 1980, Baker and McCarthy 1981) must be considered very tentative. The reasoning is almost entirely a priori, theory-internal, and syntactic rather than semantic, and there is little discussion of the kinds of learning strategies or operating principles for which psycholinguists such as Dan Slobin have argued, and of how these might influence assumptions made about innate knowledge. Given how little is known in general about the strategies and inferences that characterize language learning by the child, it would be unwise to draw hasty conclusions about just what the child can and cannot extrapolate from the positive evidence before him/her, and hence about the conclusiveness of the evidence for innate principles as a supplement to learning (cf. Bowerman 1983 for further discussion). And yet I would argue that it is highly plausible that there are some innately represented features of language in the human species, and that these do facilitate language acquisition. The question is: which features of language are so represented, and which universals are to receive an explanation in innateness terms?

Second, I am not convinced by what I consider to be a premature leap from universal grammar to innateness within many generative discussions. There are other types of causal factors that can be invoked to explain why languages are the way they are, and the reasoning from grammar to innateness typically ignores these. We can accept, therefore, that there are some innately given linguistic principles. The issue is: what are they precisely; and what is the relation between these biologically given principles of UG and other types of causal factors?

A second type of competence explanation for various universals can be found in the work of Keenan (1978, 1979), who proposes a number of principles of a semantic nature. The logic of his explanation is as follows: certain universal facts of grammatical form (morphology or syntax) are the way they are because of their corresponding semantic interpretations. The semantics renders the grammar predictable. The precise causal link between semantics and grammar takes slightly different forms in Keenan's different principles. A paradigm example is the Meaning–Form Dependency Principle (MFDP).

Keenan observes that the phenomenon of morphological agreement across languages obeys an interesting restriction. Consider adjectives and nouns within the noun phrase. If one of these categories agrees with the other, it is always the adjective that agrees with the noun (e.g. in number or gender), and never the reverse. In addition, adjectives exhibit a form of semantic agreement with their nouns. The precise interpretation of an adjective typically varies with the choice of head noun, whereas the precise interpretation of a noun does not usually depend on that of an accompanying adjective. Compare (1) and (2):

(1) flat tyre
flat beer
flat road

(2) flat road
dusty road
windy road

The interpretation assigned to *flat* in (1) differs radically in conjunction with *tyre* versus *beer* versus *road*. But the interpretation of *road* in (2) remains constant through the three examples.

More generally, Keenan argues that all function categories (which include adjectives) vary their precise interpretations depending on the choice of argument. And if there is morphological agreement between these categories, it is always the function category that agrees with the argument, rather than vice versa. The result is internal consistency within the grammar: a dependency in form (with the adjective looking to the noun for its agreement features) mirrors a dependency in meaning. That is, linguistic form mirrors meaning.

This small illustration of Keenan's principles will suffice in this context. I consider his semantic explanation for this universal of morphological agreement to be highly plausible and intuitive. And yet surface form (syntax and morphology) does not always mirror meaning in this way. For example, there is a mismatch between semantic and syntactic categories in Keenan's (1979) other major example involving cross-categorial word-order correlations. There is no uniform semantic basis underlying statistical word-order universals, and Keenan is forced to propose a Dissimilation Principle, whereby the top two pairs of function-argument categories in Table 5.1 are typically placed in the opposite order from the bottom two in one and the same language type. By contrast, a syntactic generalization in terms of head versus modifier status does accord with the

TABLE 5.1. *Head-modifier and function-argument predictions for statistical word-order correlations*

		Head-modifier (syntactic)	Function-argument (semantic)
(NP)	Adj + N	modifier + head	function + argument
(AdjP)	Adv + Adj	modifier + head	function + argument
(VP/S)	Obj + V	modifier + head	argument + function
(AdpP)	NP + Po	modifier + head	argument + function

Source: This table is adapted from data in Hawkins (1983, 1984).

statistical correlations and permits a single unifying generalization: a head of phrase either consistently precedes or follows its modifiers, with more than chance frequency (cf. Hawkins 1983, 1984, and also Zwicky 1985).

Moreover, numerous rules of syntax are not in any straightforward correspondence with semantic rules and representations, e.g. syntactic rules that rearrange arguments from their predicates, such as raisings, rules creating ambiguities, rules of deletion. And such rules have provided the motivation all along for considering syntax at least partially autonomous of semantics.

In short, grammatical form *sometimes* conserves and reflects properties of its associated semantics, but *sometimes* does not. The challenge before us is to understand better when we can invoke Keenan's principle and intuition, and when we cannot.

Contrasting with these competence explanations are various explanations that appeal to linguistic performance. Often a direct appeal is made to the communicative functions performed by language. If every grammar contains pronouns distinguishing at least three persons and two numbers (cf. Greenberg 1966: 96 and Ingram 1978), then an explanation involving the referential distinctions that speakers of all languages regularly need to draw is, a priori, highly plausible. Another paradigm example has recently been pointed out by Bernard Comrie (personal communication). Comrie observes that if a language has a reflexive/non-reflexive distinction on its first-person pronouns (*me-myself*), then it also has this distinction on second-person pronouns (*you-yourself*); if it has it on second-person pronouns, it also has it on third-person pronouns (*him*/*himself*, etc). That is, some languages have a reflexive/non-reflexive distinction on all three persons (English), or on the second and third only (Huichol), or just on the third (German, cf. *ihn/sich*). (Cf. also Faltz 1985: 120 for confirmation of this universal.)

Comrie proposes a functional explanation for this distribution. The third-person distinction is, he argues, the most functional and useful. The number of potential third-person referents is very large, and so the distinction between same and non-same referents (*he washed himself/him*) is one that it is useful to be able to capture clearly and quickly. The second-person distinction is slightly more useful than the first (*you washed yourself/you*), given the possibility of addressing more than one addressee. But the first-person distinction is almost totally useless, on account of the uniqueness of the speaker (*I washed myself/?me*).

This explanation appeals, ultimately, to the number of occasions on which a formal distinction is useful in performance. I find it highly plausible. And yet it raises a fundamental question. When can we appeal to such functional considerations in general, and when not? After all, one could imagine numerous potentially useful real-world distinctions being given formal expression in language, which do not actually receive it. For example, speakers regularly have occasion to refer deictically to objects on their left as opposed to their right side. Yet deictic systems across languages are not organized on this basis. Hence, although Comrie's explanation for his reflexive universal is very convincing, it is somewhat after the fact. If other similar functional motivations for the grammaticalization of real-world distinctions do not have the same effect, when can we appeal to a functional explanation and when not?

A second type of performance explanation for universals appeals to pragmatic aspects of meaning, i.e. to those which make crucial reference to the context of utterance (the speaker, the hearer, their shared knowledge and beliefs, the communicative task at hand, the place of utterance, the time of utterance). For example, it has been argued that ordering constraints on free-word-order languages are determined by pragmatic principles. Givón (1983) provides extensive text counts from diverse languages permitting subject + verb/verb subject and object + verb/verb + object alternations, and shows that the selection of the appropriate order reflects the degree of accessibility of the subject or object NP to the speaker and the hearer at the time of utterance. Thus, when an NP is recently mentioned in the text (or 'continuous'), the orders verb + subject and verb + object are highly preferred, thereby presenting the predicate before the already established NP. But when the NP is either referentially indefinite or not recently mentioned in the discourse (and hence 'discontinuous'), the orders subject + verb and object + verb are preferred. Givón reasons that these left–right orders instantiate a pragmatic principle which he paraphrases as: 'attend first to the most urgent task'. If the subject or object NP ('topic' in his terms) is not immediately accessible to speaker and hearer, establishing the reference is the most urgent task, prior to predicating something of this referent, whence subject + verb, etc. But if subject and object are immediately accessible through recent previous mention, the predicate becomes the most urgent information and is ordered first.

Another example of a left–right ordering reflecting the relative importance or urgency of the information conveyed can be seen in numeral systems across languages. Greenberg (1978c) points out that almost all languages express a complex additive numeral such as 10,253 in the (English) order ten thousand, two hundred, and fifty-three, with larger addends preceding smaller ones, as opposed to three, fifty, two hundred, and ten thousand (which is, in fact, the order in Malagasay). The advantage of the English order is that it provides immediate access to the most important addend, 10,000, which approximates to the final product, with every successive item giving a further specification. The opposite (Malagasay) order leaves the hearer in the dark till the very last item is reached. This explanation is confirmed by languages with mixed systems, such as Indo-European. The order smaller + larger addend occurs only with smaller sums (cf. German 'three and fifty' but 'ten thousand, two hundred, and fifty'), which involve no significant delay in the presentation of the higher addends.

By contrast, there are many left–right orders across languages that have no obvious pragmatic motivation of any of these kinds. Cross-categorial rules of head placement (cf. Table 5.1) have nothing to do with pragmatics. Nor does a language-particular rule such as the one that orders Tense + (Modal) + (have + en) + (be + ing) + (be + en) + Verb in English. So when can we invoke a pragmatic motivation for linear order, and when can we not?

A third type of performance explanation for language universals draws upon psycholinguistic principles of language processing, i.e. principles of comprehension and production that have been derived from controlled experiments on real-time language use. These explanations appeal ultimately to two major considerations: human beings are limited-capacity machines—there are, for example, real limitations on short-term memory, and such limitations are reflected in linguistic structure—and different linguistic structures may be associated with different degrees of processing difficulty.

One structural type which has been argued to involve considerable processing difficulty is centre embedding. Compare the ungrammatical centre-embedded question in English with its grammatical equivalents (involving clause-initial and clause-final embeddings):

(3*a*) *Who did *that Mary hit Bill* surprise?
(*b*) *That Mary hit Bill* surprised who?
(*c*) Who did it surprise *that Mary hit Bill*?

Dryer (1980) has found cross-linguistic support for the regular avoidance of centre embedding due to such processing difficulty (cf. section 3 below). For example, many SOV languages employ SV*O* order when the direct object is a sentential complement, replacing a clause-medial with a clause-final complement.

On the other hand, it is not invariably the case that structures that have been argued by psycholinguists to be difficult to process are systematically avoided across languages. Frazier and Rayner (1982), for example, argue that so-called 'temporary ambiguities' cause processing difficulty when the processor's initial decision about the structure of a string turns out to be incorrect, as in (4):

(4) *The guest expected to be late* arrived.

This sentence will be temporarily ambiguous in its left-to-right presentation: up until *arrived*, *expected to be late* can be parsed as a main clause VP or as a reduced relative (cf. *who was expected to be late*). The former interpretation will initially be preferred on account of general parsing principles (cf. section 2 below), but this preference will necessarily be revised as soon as *arrived* is encountered, resulting in a 'garden-path' effect. And yet temporary ambiguities of this sort, and even non-temporary or real ambiguities, are quite commonplace across languages (though Hawkins 1986 suggests that there may none the less be systematic differences between languages in their tolerance of such ambiguities, cf. particularly pp. 216–17).

What this means is that some sources of processing difficulty are regularly avoided by grammars (centre embeddings), whereas others are not (temporary ambiguities). Moreover, even when some type of processing difficulty is regularly avoided across languages, the avoidance is not exceptionless: centre embeddings *are* tolerated in Japanese, although frequently avoided even in this language. But these considerations pose a challenge similar to the one we encountered for our other explanations. What is the status of an explanation for certain linguistic facts of grammar in terms of processing difficulty, when other cases of putatively equal processing difficulty do not result in any avoidance of the structures in question, and when not all languages avoid a source of processing difficulty which is productively avoided elsewhere?

1.2. Preliminary conclusions

All of these critical considerations do *not* argue against the validity of each of these competence and performance explanations for language universals. Each of them *is* plausibly responsible (in part at least) for some area of linguistic data. But they are regularly insufficient as they stand. Semantic transparency is plausibly responsible for Keenan's MFDP data, yet there is considerable non-transparency or autonomy of linguistic form. Avoidance of centre embeddings on account of processing difficulty is plausibly what underlies many universals of complementation, yet languages tolerate other forms of processing difficulty, and some languages tolerate centre embeddings. Pragmatic principles of word order do have a lot of support, yet they account for only some word-order facts in some phrasal categories.

There is a twofold moral to all of this. First, we need to clarify the precise link between explanans and explanandum in these examples. What precisely is meant by semantic transparency, and why is it operative in some cases, but not in others? What precisely is it about centre embeddings that makes them difficult to process, in contrast to, say, temporary ambiguities?

Second, we must adopt a more interactive approach to description and explanation whereby principles of one type are not pursued in isolation from others, and we must clarify the logic of this interaction. The grammars of the world's languages represent a complex interaction of all of these causal demands upon successful communications systems, and the very reality of each can often only be convincingly established by considering different principles in conjunction with one another.

Specifically, *there is often a (partial) conflict between principles.* For example, any pragmatically motivated alternations between object + verb and verb + object order will result in a partial mismatch with the head-final or head-initial orders of other phrasal categories, as fixed by cross-categorial rules of the grammar. A rigid verb-final language (such as Japanese) is unable to relieve centre embedding by postposing the complement into clause-final position. That is, a principle of basic verb position here blocks the grammaticalization of a postposing rule which is frequently grammaticalized in other languages and which is motivated by processing demands. Instead another option has to be found (sentence-initial positioning of the complement). Now, these conflicts actually support the reality of the underlying principles—yet they obscure their effects.

Furthermore, *many causal principles are gradient rather than absolute.* There are different degrees of processing difficulty, of communicative usefulness, even perhaps different extents to which semantic transparency is necessary or desirable (cf. the detailed comparison of English and German in Hawkins 1986 from this point of view). All languages share a common core of grammaticalized categories and structures, e.g. the noun/verb distinction, and the transitive/intransitive distinction. They all obey a lower or least bound on semantic transparency, below which meaning is not readily extractable from form. And there is an upper or highest bound on the tolerated degree of processing difficulty, above which no language is readily processable. But beyond this core and within these bounds languages may exhibit semantic transparency and may respond to processing ease and also functional pressures to varying extents, and these varying extents will result in variation between languages. Some principles are stronger than others to which they are partially opposed and will predominate in more languages. The inherently gradient nature of certain principles may also be reflected in different language quantities. For example, the greater the processing difficulty involved in some structure, the fewer exemplifying languages there will be. Or the more successful the linear order of some numeral system is in providing an early indication of the computational product, the more languages will adopt this serialization. Now, these gradients and varying extents do not diminish the causality of the relevant principles, but they *do* result in counterexamples to any absolute predictions to the effect that, for example, centre embeddings are intolerable and impermissible in languages. Such counterexamples will arise precisely when other principles favour such structures and when the relevant processing principle is not sufficient to guarantee 100 per cent adherence across languages.

How can we contribute to these rather general issues of explanation for language universals? One of the goals of this paper is to reaffirm the value of the typological method in this context. Cross-linguistic variation patterns readily suggest solutions to these problems. With regard to clarifying the precise link between explanans and explanandum, they enable us to eliminate numerous hypotheses and corroborate others, as proposed within current theories of semantics, processing, pragmatics, and syntax. And with regard to the logic of the interaction, variation patterns readily reveal the interaction of contributory principles and enable us to factor these out. From cross-language quantitative data, we can also infer the relative strength of partially opposed principles, and the degree of e.g. processing difficulty when some gradient notion is involved.

These points will be illustrated by considering some examples of left–right asymmetries in syntax and morphology. These asymmetries arise when certain linguistic categories that are predicted by one independently motivated principle to be, for example, leftward-occurring within languages of a given type actually show up on the right whereas the converse fails. When this same principle predicts a rightward occurrence in the languages of the relevant type, there is no leftward skewing and the categories in question do occur to the right. On other occasions the asymmetry may involve a leftward rather than a rightward skewing. It will be argued that these asymmetries are the result of an interaction between competence principles and principles of performance. The former make crucial reference to the grammatical notion 'head of phrase' and to a cross-categorial linearization of heads in relation to non-heads or modifiers. The latter invoke considerations of language processing in real time. Our cross-language data provide suggestive evidence about the precise nature of the underlying competence and performance principles, and about the manner of their interaction.

Three examples of left–right asymmetry will be considered, involving: the positioning of relative clauses; the positioning of sentence complements; and the ordering of morphemes in a word (prefixing versus suffixing).

2. The positioning of relative clauses

2.1. Patterns of cross-language variation

Across languages there is an asymmetry in the distribution of relative-clause orders: the languages that are independently predicted to have the relative clause after the head noun (as in English) do so, the languages that are independently predicted to have the relative clause before the head noun may or may not do so, and in a significant number of cases have postnominal relatives just as in English. The result is a rightward skewing in favour of postnominal relatives overall.

More precise quantitative data are set out in Table 5.2. The ratio of prepositional to postpositional languages, of VO to OV languages, and of NGen to GenN languages is in each case roughly 50–50 in the Expanded Sample of Hawkins (1983). But there is a roughly 70 per cent–30 per cent skewing in favour of postnominal as opposed to prenominal relatives. More significantly the head-before-modifier languages are almost exclusively postnominal, whereas some 40 per cent of otherwise modifier-before-head languages also have the postnominal relative-clause order.

Correlating with the order difference are other linguistic generalizations that will be relevant in this context, involving the expressive power of relative clauses and the marking of subordination. These generalizations have been most thoroughly documented to date in the impressive work of Christian Lehmann (1984).

Lehmann (1984: 168–73, 227–80) observes that prenominal relatives are significantly more restricted in expressive power than postnominal relatives along two dimensions: they exhibit greater 'nominalization' (or non-sentential and nominal-modifier-like status for the relative clause); and much less tolerance of appositive interpretations. He proposes a scale of nominalization, which orders restrictions on the form and expressive power of relative clauses, from the most sentential (and least nominal) clause types at one end, to the least sentential (and most nominal) at the other, roughly as follows: limitations on the illocutionary force of the relative S;

TABLE 5.2. *Relative clause ordering quantities across language types* (*cf.* *Hawkins 1983*)

Head + modifier	Modifier + head
Pr + NP	NP + Po
VO (SVO v. VSO)	OV
NGen	GenN
NRel	RelN v. NRel

Note: 99% of Pr + NP lgs have NRel; 1% have RelN. 61% of NP + Po have RelN; 39% have NRel. 94% of SVO lgs have NRel; 6% have RelN. 56% of OV lgs have RelN; 44% have NRel. 100% of VSO lgs have NRel; 0% have RelN. (The only SVO languages with RelN in the data (total = 4) also have NP + Po.)

The proportions of Pr + NP to NP + Po, VO to OV, and NGen to GenN = roughly 50–50, and the correlations between Pr + NP, VO, and NGen on the one hand, and between NP + Po, OV, and GenN on the other, are very strong indeed.

Abbreviations:

NP + Po	noun phrase precedes postposition	(e.g. *the room in*)
Pr + NP	preposition precedes noun phrase	(e.g. *in the room*)
VO	verb precedes direct object	(e.g. *threw the rock*)
OV	direct object precedes verb	(e.g. *the rock threw*)
NRel	head noun precedes relative clause	(e.g. *the dog that was killed by me*)
RelN	relative clause precedes head noun	(e.g. *the by me killed dog*)
NGen	noun precedes genitive	(e.g. *book of Harry*)
GenN	genitive precedes noun	(e.g. *Harry's book*)

Source: This table is adapted from data in Hawkins (1983, 1984).

restrictions on modal elements; restrictions on tense and aspect; required deletion of verbal complements; required non-finite verb forms; obligatory conversion of the subject to a genitive; restrictions on possible co-occurring arguments of the verb. Prenominal relatives regularly have many more restrictions and occupy positions further down (i.e. to the right of) this scale than their postnominal counterparts. Appositive interpretations are equally restricted for prenominal relatives. If they occur at all, the types of permitted heads are limited. Personal pronouns are regularly excluded as heads of appositive prenominal relatives (cf. Basque, Tamil, Chinese), although pronouns can be perfectly fine heads of relative clauses in postnominal languages. And if an alternative postnominal relative exists in a language which also has a prenominal strategy, the appositive interpretation is most frequently expressed by the former (cf. Basque, Lahu, Turkish).

Subordination indicators in prenominal relatives are of three major types (Lehmann 1984: 49–72). The first type (exemplified by Basque, Lahu, and Chinese) employs a clause-final complementizer, such as *de* in Chinese:

(5) wǒ ba nǐ gěi wǒ de shū diūdiào-le (Chinese)
I Acc (you give me Comp) book lose-Perf
'I have lost the book that you gave me.'

The second type (exemplified by Japanese) has no complementizer at all and relies exclusively on order to indicate relative-clause status. An example is given below. The third type (exemplified by Dravidian and Turkish) employs clause-final participial verb forms:

(6) mīru nāku ic-cin-a pustukamu
(you me give-Pret-Participle) book-Nom
cirigipŏ-yin-adi (Telugu)
tear-Past-3Sg
'The book that you gave me is torn.'

It will be apparent that if a prenominal relative has a subordination indicator at all, that indicator will be in clause-final position. In the case of the participial verbs this regularity follows from the more general fact that all verbs in these head-final languages are normally clause-final. Similarly, the clause-final positioning of the complementizer can also be argued to follow from a higher generalization involving the putative 'head' status of the complementizer: it is strongly characteristic of languages with head-final word orders elsewhere in the syntax, while head-initial languages have initial complementizers (cf. W. P. Lehmann 1978, Zwicky 1985).

2.2. Explanatory hypotheses for relative clause positioning across languages

A number of explanations have been offered for the positioning of relative clauses across languages. Kuno (1974) appeals to the perceptual difficulty of centre embedding to explain why VSO languages invariably have postnominal rather than prenominal relatives. Prenominal relatives would result in centre embeddings when they modify both subjects and objects, whereas postnominal relatives will produce centre embeddings only when they modify the subject of a transitive verb, as shown in Table 5.3. The avoidance of systematic center embeddings is therefore the cause of the relative clause ordering correlations. This same account predicts that SOV languages will only exhibit prenominal relatives, as illustrated also in Table 5.3, while SVO languages should occur roughly equally with both: prenominal relatives will avoid centre embeddings on subjects; postnominal relatives will avoid them on objects.

TABLE 5.3. *Kuno's (1974) centre embedding predictions for relative-clause positioning*

VSO Languages		SOV Languages		SVO Languages	
Prenominal relatives	Postnominal relatives	Prenominal relatives	Postnominal relatives	Prenominal relatives	Postnominal relatives
V (Rel)S[a]	V S(Rel)	(Rel)S V	S(Rel) V[a]	(Rel)S V	S(Rel) V[a]
V (Rel)S O[a]	V S(Rel) O[a]	(Rel)S O V	S(Rel) O V[a]	(Rel)S V O	S(Rel) V O[a]
V S (Rel)O[a]	V S O(Rel)	S (Rel)O V[a]	S O(Rel) V[a]	S V (Rel)O[a]	S V O(Rel)

[a] Centre embedding.

Unfortunately, both predictions are wrong. SOV languages have significant numbers of both relative-clause orders, and SVO languages are almost entirely postnominal (cf. Table 5.2). This account therefore fails to predict the relative-clause distribution, specifically the rightward skewing in favour of postnominal position. Cross-linguistic variation patterns are evidence against Kuno's proposed explanation.

Frazier (1979) proposes a Head Adjacency Constraint for relative-clause positioning and other word orders. The ultimate explanation for this constraint is again a processing one. The constraint stipulates that, in the unmarked case, major phrases follow the head of their mother phrase in prepositional languages, and precede it in postpositional languages. The net result is a set of modifier-head predictions for statistical word-order correlations along the lines of Table 5.1, covering word orders such as those in (7):

(7) modifier + head in Postp lgs: OV; GenN; RelN; etc.
head + modifier in Prep lgs: VO; NGen; NRel; etc.

These line-ups guarantee that heads will always be adjacent when several phrasal categories are combined together to make a larger phrase or sentence. For example, a preposition (as head of PP) when combining with an NP to make a PP will be adjacent to the head of that NP if the ordering of daughter NP constituents is, say, NGen or NRel rather than GenN or RelN, cf. Pr + NGen versus Pr + GenN, Pr + NRel versus Pr + RelN, etc.

More formally, she reasons that on-line semantic interpretation could not take place if X, the head of one phrase, and Y, the head of its modifier (or complement), were separated by the modifier (/complement) of Y. And the ultimate motivation for Head Adjacency is to guarantee that the parser can identify phrasal packages that form coherent semantic units. A violation of Head Adjacency would produce a structure like, for example, (8):

(8) $_{PP}$($_{NP}$(Head Noun + Rel. Clause) Postposition)
Y Complement of Y X

Unfortunately, these and other violations are quite frequent across languages. There are numerous postpositional languages with postnominal relatives in which the relative intervenes between head noun and postposition, as in the following example from Lakhota (cf. Lehmann 1984: 82):

(9) xé wã Tamalpais éciya-pi wã él (Lakhota)
mountain Indef (Tamalpais they-called) Indef on
'On a mountain that they called Tamalpais.'

There are other theories that offer more narrowly grammatical motivations for similar modifier + head versus head + modifier line-ups across languages, e.g. Vennemann (1974), various X-bar theories (Jackendoff 1977, Lightfoot 1979), cf. Hawkins (1983, 1984) for summaries. But none of these predicts the left–right asymmetry of relative-clause positioning.

I suggest instead that the variation data point to an interaction between a (primarily syntactically determined) head-modifier generalization à la Vennemann, etc, and certain processing considerations that are responsible for the rightward skewing. These considerations corroborate the independent predictions for noun-before-relative-clause ordering in head + modifier languages, and are opposed to the relative-clause-before-noun serialization prediction in modifier + head languages, resulting in postnominal relative clauses in some 40 per cent of these cases.

Two processing considerations are supported. First, Antinucci *et al.* (1979) argue that prenominal relatives provide many more opportunities for misanalysing subordinate-clause constituents as main-clause constituents in structures such as (10), exemplified in (11), taken from Japanese:

(10*a*) (NP_S V) NP_S NP_O V NP_S = subject NP; NP_O = object NP
(*b*) NP_S (NP_O V) NP_O V

(11*a*) Inu-ga kande-iru kodoma-ga neko-o nadete-iru
(dog-Nom biting-is) child-Nom cat-Acc patting-is
'The child whom the dog is biting is patting the cat.'
(*b*) Inu-ga ringo-o tabete-iru kodomo-o kande-iru
dog-Nom (apple-Acc eating-is) child-Acc biting-is
'The dog is biting the child who is eating the apple.'

Even though context will disambiguate in many cases, on-line comprehension strategies will regularly misanalyse the initial (NP_S V) in (10*a*) as a main clause, and the initial NP_S (NP_O V) in (10*b*) as a main clause SOV, with subsequent correction of the misanalysis. Recall that subordination indicators in prenominal relatives either do not exist (as in Japanese), or occur in clause-final position in the form of a participial verb or as a complementizer, and that these elements are independently predicted to occur finally in these languages (cf. section 2.1).

The reality of these misanalyses in left-branching languages such as Japanese and Korean has been strikingly confirmed in several experimental studies using Japanese and Korean children. Thus, Harada *et al.* (1976), Asano (1979), and Hakuta (1982) found that virtually no Japanese children up to 8 years in age could correctly interpret sentences like (10*b*). Error analysis indicates that these children almost invariably took the first two noun phrases to be arguments of the embedded verb. There were also significant numbers of errors with the initial subordinate clauses such as (10*a*). Clancy *et al.* (1986) also found that 6-year-old Korean children misinterpret structures like (10*b*) in approximately half the test sentences of Korean, and often misinterpret structures corresponding to (10*a*).

By contrast, the initial position of the head noun in N + Rel languages will regularly avoid misanalysis. There are several reasons for this. In particular, the leftward positioning of the head means that in the left-to-right presentation of a sentence, the head can be recognized first and can be integrated into the sentence structure as a matrix constituent. A subsequent subordinate clause can then be interpreted as a relative-clause modifier. In addition, the majority of postnominal relative clauses have an initial complementizer or relative pronoun (cf. Lehmann 1984), which signals the beginning of the subordinate clause. The position of the head therefore prevents any on-line integration of subordinate-clause constituents with other main-clause constituents to the left (as in the misanalysis of (10*b*)), and the initial subordinator provides a clear structural demarcation between the head and the relative clause. Even in languages without an initial subordinator (such as Lakhota in (9) above, or Dyirbal, cf. Dixon 1972), a syntactic misanalysis of the relative-clause head as a subordinate-clause constituent is a relatively harmless error, since the head is in any case a semantic argument of the relative clause in addition to being a syntactic and a semantic argument of the matrix. Thus, a postnominal version of (10*a*) (*child-Nom* (*dog-Nom biting-is*) *cat-Acc patting-is*) would still assign *child* and *dog* as arguments of *biting*, even if the syntactic head status of *child* was temporarily misanalysed. There is no danger of assigning a matrix argument to some left-branching subordinate clause in which it does not belong semantically. And even the relatively harmless misanalysis of a head NP as a constituent of its relative clause will regularly (though not invariably) be avoided by various language-particular disambiguating strategies such as case marking and word order. For example, compare the relative clauses of (10) with their postnominal counterparts in (10′):

(10′*a*) NP_S (NP_S V) NP_O V
(*b*) NP_S NP_O (NP_O V) V

The first two noun phrases encountered in (10′*a*) are both subject-marked and will normally be interpreted as belonging to different clauses: the first NP_S will be assigned to the matrix; the second NP_S will be selected as subordinate together with its verb; and the remaining NP_O must be a matrix object preceding the main verb and following the subordinate verb. The first two noun phrases in (10′*b*) are matrix subject and object forcing the interpretation of the third NP as a subordinate object, its immediately adjacent verb as subordinate, and the final verb as the matrix verb.

Following the logic of Antinucci *et al.* (1979) we might therefore propose that: if a grammar is to depart from independent syntactic predictions for relative-clause ordering; and if these departures are in response to processing considerations involving clause-boundary recognition; then the departures will guarantee the avoidance of regular on-line misanalyses of relative-clause constituents as matrix-clause constituents.

More generally, let us incorporate Frazier's (1978) parsing principles of Minimal Attachment and Late Closure into the discussion:

> *Minimal Attachment*: attach an incoming item into a constituent structure representation of the sentence using the fewest syntactic nodes permitted by the rules of the language.
>
> *Late Closure*: when possible, incorporate an incoming item into the clause currently being processed.

These principles represent the most general and simple formulations that Frazier could derive from a number of more specific parsing principles proposed by Kimball and others before her. Let us assume, pending evidence to the contrary, that these are universal processing strategies, adopted by all speakers of all languages, and that they predict preferred interpretations and regular misanalyses/garden-path effects, etc. that arise (all things being equal) in all languages. This assumption is not implausible: Frazier is merely claiming that language users make the simplest constituent structure assignment to a sentence that they can, relative to the rules of the language in question. Notice that both principles predict an on-line main-clause SOV analysis for NP_S (NP_O V) . . . in (10*b*), for example, since this will require fewer syntactic nodes (the absence of a subordinate S), and since the inital NPs belongs to the matrix S.

These considerations suggest the hypothesis in (12):

(12) If a grammar is to depart from independent syntactic predictions for word order; and if these departures are in response to considerations of processing; then they will maximize rather then minimize the successful applications of Minimal Attachment and Late Closure.

That is, if a grammar is going to respond to processing needs at all, it will do so by reorganizing its syntactic structures so that the first-pass interpretations in language use are the preferred ones, and misanalyses and garden-path effects are avoided. I have argued, drawing on the insight of Antinucci *et al.* (1979), that postnominal relatives in SOV languages do this—they result in more successful applications of Minimal Attachment and Late Closure than prenominal relatives, and this explains why some 40 per cent of languages that are independently predicted to have the prenominal type exhibit postnominal order, and why the converse fails.

There is a second processing consideration that is supported by cross-language relative-clause data and which is discussed in some detail in Hawkins (1983: 98–102). Here I shall be brief. In the processing of noun phrases, early head recognition is preferred to late head recognition. That is, there are processing advantages to having the head noun occur in a leftward rather than a rightward position in relation to the other daughter constituents of the NP. We can therefore say, parallel to (12), that: if a grammar is to depart from independent syntactic predictions for head ordering within NP; and if these departures are in response to considerations of processing; then the departures will guarantee early rather than late head recognition.

The support for this principle comes from the limitations on expressive power summarized in section 2.1. Notice that a fully sentential relative clause that precedes a head noun will delay the appearance of the head, and that any restrictions on the form and meaning of the relative clause will result in the head being encountered that much sooner (which, it is argued, facilitates the syntactic and semantic processing of the whole noun phrase and its integration into the clause). The reduction of sentence-like properties (and hence the shortening) of relative clauses is much more pronounced in prenominal than in postnominal position; and the capacity for parenthetical and more fully sentential appositive interpretations is correspondingly reduced. Now, some of Lehmann's (1984) nominalization effects do simultaneously reduce the opportunity for clause-boundary misanalysis, thereby implicating (12) as the explanation in this context as well. For example, the genitive marker on the underlying subjects of Turkish prenominal relatives avoids any misanalysis resulting from Minimal Attachment. But other nominalization effects do not necessarily reduce on-line misanalysis (e.g. restrictions on illocutionary force, on modal, tense, and aspectual elements, on verbal complements, etc.), yet they do result in earlier head recognition. Hence, two partially independent processing considerations are implicated.

2.3. Conclusions re relative clauses

We have seen that cross-language variation reveals descriptive patterns. These patterns enable us to dismiss some explanatory hypotheses, to corroborate others, and to propose more general hypotheses for further testing (such as (12)). That is, they clarify and inform the explanatory principles of Universal Grammar. In particular, they reveal the interaction of partially opposed competence and performance principles and contribute to a more precise theory of the interrelations between explanatory principles than we now have. Specifically:

- these patterns enable us to factor out interacting principles (here head-modifier and processing principles);
- by formulating the interaction using if–then statements (if the grammar is going to respond to processing principles, then it will maximize rather than minimize the successful applications of Minimal Attachment and Late Closure) we predict which structures will depart from independent predictions (e.g. relative clauses will create more processing problems than adjectives in this context) and we predict the directionality of these departures (prenominal relatives will postpose, rather than vice versa, thereby maximizing the successful applications of Frazier's parsing principles);
- we avoid the insufficiency problem for explanation discussed in section 1: grammars do not have to respond to processing

pressures, but if they do, we make precise predictions for what they will do (relative clauses will be postposed or reduced);

- we capture the gradient nature of 'processing difficulty', and we can quantify the strength of the underlying processing principles (40 per cent of modifier + head languages postpose their relatives, 60 per cent retain Rel + N; a much higher percentage of languages avoids self-embeddings, presumably for reasons of processing difficulty—hence self-embeddings cause more processing difficulty than prenominal relative-clause positioning).

3. The positioning of sentence complements

3.1. Patterns of cross-language variation

Dryer (1980) has established that the positioning of sentence complements (i.e. sentential NPs) within a clause frequently differs from the positioning of the corresponding non-sentential or simple NPs across languages. For example, it was pointed out in section 1.1 that many SOV languages employ SV*O* order when the direct object is a sentential complement. These different orderings of sentential and simple NPs turn out to be quite systematic. Dryer formulates a frequency hierarchy for sentence-complement positions given here as (13):

(13) clause-final position > clause-initial position > clause-internal position

and a set of implicational universals defining permitted and non-permitted co-occurrences of sentential and simple NP orders in a given language. An example is (14):

(14) If sentential NPs and simple NPs of the same grammatical relation have at least partially different word orders; and if these differences involve *clause-final* and *clause-internal* position; then it will be the sentential NP which exhibits the preference for clause-final position.

Similar universals are formulated for *clause-initial* and *clause-internal*, and for *clause-final* and *clause-initial*, position, with sentential NPs preferring the former member of each pair. The net result of these implicationally sanctioned departures from the basic

TABLE 5.4. *Dryer's (1980) sentence-complement data summarized*

Sentential NP prefers *clause-final* over *clause-internal* position				
Wappo	simple object	only SOV (i.e. clause-internal)	sentential object	normally SVO (i.e. clause-final)
Hopi	simple object	normally SOV	sentential object	often SVO
Persian	simple object	normally SOV	sentential object	only SVO
Yaqui	simple object	only SOV	sentential object	only SVO
Turkish	simple object	normally SOV	sentential object	(finite): only SVO
Wichita	simple object	normally OV	sentential object	normally VO
Latin	simple object	normally SOV	sentential object	normally SVO
Mojave	simple object	normally SOV	sentential object	frequently SVO
Lakhota	simple object	normally SOV	sentential object	frequently SVO
Finnish	simple object	some SOV (some SVO)	sentential object	only SVO
Lithuanian	simple object	some SOV (some SVO)	sentential object	only SVO or OVS (not SOV)
Malagasay	simple object	normally VOS	sentential object	only VSO
Tongan	simple object	many VOS	sentential object	only VSO
Toba Batak	simple object	normally VOS	sentential object	only SVO
Ojibwa	simple object	normally VOS	sentential object	normally VSO
Sentential NP prefers *clause-initial* over *clause-internal* position				
Japanese	simple object	normally SOV (i.e. clause-internal)	sentential object	mostly OSV (the greater the length of O, the greater the preference for OSV)
Hare	simple object	normally SOV	sentential object	frequently OSV
Lithuanian	simple object	normally SOV	sentential object	frequently OVS

Sentential NP prefers *clause-final* over *clause-initial* position				
Persian	simple subject	normally SOV (i.e. clause-initial)	sentential subject	only clause-final (VS, OVS, etc.)
Turkish	simple subject	normally SOV	sentential subject	only clause-final
Woleaian	simple subject	clause-initial and clause-final	sentential subject	only clause-final
Kinyarwanda	simple subject	normally SVO	sentential subject	only clause-final
Thai	simple subject	normally SVO	sentential subject	mostly clause-final
Yaqui	simple subject	only SOV	sentential subject	only clause-final
Tuscarora	simple subject	normally SVO	sentential subject	only clause-final
Wichita	simple subject	clause-initial and clause-final	sentential subject	mostly clause-final
English	simple subject	normally SVO	sentential subject	frequently clause-final (cf. extraposition)
Egyptian Arabic	simple subject	normally SVO	sentential subject	frequently clause-final
Lakhota	simple subject	normally SOV	sentential subject	frequently clause-final
Indonesian	simple subject	normally SV	sentential subject	normally VS
Lithuanian	simple subject	normally SV	sentential subject	both SV and VS
Marathi	simple subject	normally SV	sentential subject	both SV and VS
Blackfoot	simple subject	both SV and VS	sentential subject	only VS
Ojibwa	simple subject	both SV and VS	sentential subject	only VS
Numerous SOV lgs	simple object	optional OSV (i.e. clause-initial)	sentential object	only clause-final

order for simple NPs is the set of preferences for sentence-complement positioning given in (13), which is reflected in the quantities of the relevant structures across languages. The supporting data provided by Dryer are summarized in Table 5.4.

It will be clear that sentential NPs provide another example of a left–right asymmetry across languages. In fact, they exhibit both a leftward and a rightward skewing compared with simple NPs. The rightward skewing is strongest and occurs when sentential NPs that would otherwise be predicted to be in initial or internal position show up in final position. The leftward skewing occurs when sentential NPs that would otherwise be in clause-internal position show up as clause-initial.

3.2. Explanatory hypotheses for sentence complement positioning across languages

This time I would argue that there *is* evidence for Kuno's (1974) centre-embedding-avoidance principle, since clause-internal position for sentence complements is the most infrequent across languages. This immediately raises the question of why relative clauses should differ from complements—the preferred postnominal order for relative clauses produces rampant centre embedding in SOV and SVO languages, and avoids it only in languages with VSO (cf. Table 5.3), and such embeddings are tolerated in large numbers of languages. It also requires us to ask: in what precisely does the processing difficulty of centre embedding consist?

The difficulty posed by centre embedding may be in part attributable to clause-boundary misanalysis of the type predicted by Frazier's (1978) Minimal Attachment and Late Closure. For example, when complementizers are clause-final in an SOV language, a direct-object complement will not be formally marked as such in any left-to-right parsing up until the complementizer is reached, and its daughter constituents can be parsed as belonging to the matrix in a way that parallels the misanalysis of (10) above. However, clause-final complement position is still preferred over clause-internal and clause-initial position in languages in which complementizers are initial and hence structurally disambiguating (cf. Dryer 1980 for discussion). So an additional processing principle is implicated. I suggest that what we are witnessing here is the perceptual difficulty of interrupting main-clause material (cf. Bever

1970). Specifically, the preferred initial over internal order for complements indicates that the delay of a main clause is preferred over its interruption. And clause-final order is preferred overall because it neither delays nor interrupts the main clause.

The difficulties caused by delay and interruption of the main clause can be attributed to an even more fundamental characteristic of the human parser: the need to match arguments with their appropriate predicates quickly and readily while building a semantic interpretation for the whole sentence. Clausal complements are relatively long constituents that must be held in temporary memory before being integrated into the argument-predicate structure of the overall sentence, and their positioning within the matrix will have consequences for the relative ease with which the argument-predicate relations of the matrix can be recognized, and the long subordinate constituent correctly integrated into it. A medial complement is worst because it interrupts the left-to-right processing of the matrix, maximizing the argument-predicate recognition problem, and rendering most acute the temporary memory load caused by the long constituent. An initial complement is better because, although it delays the left-to-right processing of the main clause, it does not necessarily interrupt it, and argument-predicate relations can be more clearly recognized. And a final complement is best of all, because it occurs at a point where the matrix argument-predicate relations have already been established. (Cf. further Grosu and Thompson 1977 for discussion of these points.)

The difference between relative clauses and sentence complements is plausibly related to the fact that relative clauses are semantic and syntactic modifiers of a main-clause argument, and their interpretation is therefore anchored to this main-clause element in a way that is typically not the case with clausal complements, which are simply sentences within sentences. This anchoring presumably facilitates the argument-predicate recognition problem, which we have argued to be at the root of the perceptual difficulty of centre embedding. Since relative clauses pose fewer problems for argument-predicate recognition than sentence complements, they can tolerate more centre embeddings.

Notice finally in this section that the preferred clause-final complements cross-linguistically are right-branching structures. The preferred postnominal relatives of the last section are also right-branching structures. These distributional preferences argue against a recent assertion by Frazier (1985) that left-branching structures are either as frequent or more frequent than right-branching structures across languages. (Note that non-sentential embeddings of e.g. genitive NPs within NPs do not exhibit any left–right asymmetry (cf. Table 5.2), so the claim for preferred left versus right branching rests primarily on sentential embeddings).

3.3. Conclusions re sentence complements

Our conclusions are similar to those for relative clauses. Cross-language variation reveals descriptive patterns. These patterns enable us to dismiss some explanatory hypotheses and to corroborate others. They also reveal the interaction of partially opposed competence and performance principles. Specifically:

- they enable us to factor out the principles responsible for simple NP placement from those responsible for sentential NPs;
- by formulating the interaction using an if–then statement (if the grammar of complementation is going to respond to processing considerations involving centre embedding and argument-predicate recognition, then the departures from simple NP-ordering rules will be in accordance with Dryer's hierarchy (13) and implicational universals such as (14)) we predict which structures will depart from these independent predictions (namely those which create the relevant argument-predicate matching difficulties) and we predict the directionality of these departures (e.g. a sentential NP whose corresponding simplex NP is clause-initial will move to clause-final rather than clause-internal position for processing reasons);
- we avoid the insufficiency problem for explanation discussed in section 1: grammars do not have to respond to processing pressures, but if they do, we make precise predictions for what they will do;
- we quantify the relative strength of the processing difficulties associated with sentence-internal and sentence-initial complements by quantifying the numbers of languages that have avoided these independently predicted orders.

4. The ordering of morphemes in a word: prefixing versus suffixing

4.1. Patterns of cross-language variation

Greenberg (1966) observes that suffixal morphology within the word is much more frequent across languages than prefixing. That is, there is a rightward skewing in favour of stem + affix ordering (as in English *lion* + *s*, *lion* + *ess*), as opposed to affix + stem. More recently, Hawkins and Gary Gilligan have tried to document the cross-linguistic regularities in this area in more detail by examining a 200-language sample (collected by Gary Gilligan, Joan Bybee, and Leon Stassen). From this sample they have extracted certain implicational universals defined on morpheme order within the word and word order within the phrase. These universals are summarized in Cutler, Hawkins, and Gilligan (1985). The major pattern to emerge is that: whenever we can set up such universals, we find that postpositions and/or SOV always imply suffixing, never prefixing; while prefixing implies prepositions and VO, never postpositions or SOV.

The full set of attested and non-attested co-occurrences of affix order and word order in those cases for which implicational universals have been proposed is illustrated in (15):

(15)

	Prefixing	Suffixing
{Pr+NP / VO}	X	X
{NP+Po / OV}	O	X

That is, prepositional and/or VO word orders co-occur with either prefixes or suffixes; postpositions and/or OV co-occur with suffixing only. (Note that implicational universals of this type cannot be set up for all affixes on which we have data. Sometimes all four cells are filled, and hence anything goes.) The result of the pattern in (15) is that there is a skewing in favour of suffixing overall, and hence another example of a left–right asymmetry.

Representative universals taken from Cutler, Hawkins, and Gilligan (1985) are:

(16) If a lg has NP + Po or SOV, gender affixes on N (if any) are

suffixed; conversely, if a lg has prefixed gender affixes, it will have Pr + NP and VO (i.e. neither Po nor SOV);
If a lg has NP + Po or SOV, plural affixes on N (if any) are suffixed with considerably greater than chance frequency (93% of Po, 96% of SOV lgs conform);
If a lg has NP + Po or SOV, nominalizing affixes (if any) are suffixed;
If a lg has NP + Po or SOV, definiteness affixes on N (if any) are suffixed with greater than chance frequency (85% of Po, 92% of SOV lgs conform);
If a lg has NP + Po or SOV, indefiniteness affixes on N (if any) are suffixed;
If a lg has NP + Po or SOV, tense affixes on V (if any) are suffixed with considerably greater than chance frequency (95%+ of SOV lgs conform);
If a lg has NP + Po, mood affixes on V (if any) are suffixed;
If a lg has SOV, mood affixes on V (if any) are suffixed with more than chance frequency (88% of SOV lgs conform);
If a lg has SOV, causative affixes on V (if any) are suffixed with more than chance frequency (86% of SOV lgs conform).

Most of these universals are formulated with NP + Po or SOV as the antecedent of an implication whose consequent is suffixing: e.g. if a language has NP + Po or SOV, GENDER affixes on N (if any) will be suffixed. It follows that if gender affixes are *not* suffixed (and are e.g. prefixed), that language will be neither NP + Po nor SOV, but must be Pr + NP and VO. Cutler, Hawkins, and Gilligan (1985) formulate thirteen separate implicational universals of this type, of which five are exceptionless, while the remainder are statistical in Greenberg's sense, i.e. they hold with more than chance frequency. The number of exceptions is quantified in each case.

4.2. Explanatory hypotheses for morpheme ordering across languages

The distribution of (15) strongly implies the need for two major principles at the explanatory level: one which explains why prefixes occur productively only in conjunction with Pr + NP and VO in these universals, while similar functions in NP + Po and OV languages are performed by suffixes; and another that favours suffixing in both languages types and that is partially opposed to the independent predictions of the first principle for VO and Pr + NP languages. Cutler, Hawkins, and Gilligan argue that the first principle makes crucial reference to the notion 'head of phrase' in both syntax and morphology, and that heads are identically ordered relative to their modifiers at both levels (the Head Ordering Principle). The second principle, responsible for the postposing asymmetry, is argued to be a processing one. Its effects corroborate the Head Ordering Principle's prediction for suffixing in NP + Po and OV languages, and account for why suffixes occur at all in Pr + NP and VO languages.

It has been argued that the notion 'head of a phrase' in syntax generalizes to morphology as well (cf. Aronoff 1976, Williams 1981). Within syntax, heads of phrase preserve category constancy (e.g. N = the head of NP, Adj = the head of AdjP, etc.); within morphology, the categorial status of an immediately dominating lexical category is regularly predictable from an affix, but not necessarily from the stem. Hence, affixes can naturally be regarded as heads. (For a recent and detailed discussion of the definition of 'head' within syntax, and an enumeration of the similarities—and differences—between heads at these two levels, cf. Zwicky 1985). If we accept such a generalization cutting across syntax and morphology, then we have a ready explanation for the implicational universals of (16): head-final order in the syntax (NP + Po and SOV) guarantees head-final order in the word (suffixing); and head-initial ordering in the word (prefixing) guarantees head-initial ordering in the syntax (Pr + NP and VO). That is, these universals define a common ordering for a common (even though abstract) entity at both levels—and in the simplest, unmarked case this is what we should expect. We can accordingly define a common Head Ordering Principle (HOP), as in (17):

(17) *The Head Ordering Principle* (HOP): the affixal head of a word is ordered on the same side of its subcategorized modifier(s) as P is ordered relative to NP within PP, and as V is ordered relative to a direct object NP.

Clearly, the HOP is not the only principle determining the order of affixal morphemes in our implicational universals. If it were, we would expect a perfect line-up between head categories in the syntax and in the word and our universals would be reversible: NP + Po implies suffixing *and* suffixing implies NP + Po; prefixing implies Pr

+ NP *and* Pr + NP implies prefixing. We cannot make this reversal, however, because of the fact that Pr + NP languages are regularly either prefixing or suffixing, as shown in (15). That is, Pr + NP co-occurs with both morpheme types, and suffixing co-occurs with both word-order types, whence the skewing towards suffixing overall.

The processing explanation given for this skewing by Cutler, Hawkins, and Gilligan (1985) will be summarized only briefly in this context. Stems convey primarily lexical-semantic information. The affixes under consideration carry primarily syntactic information (number, gender, case, etc.). Now, all current psychological models of comprehension assume that lexical recognition precedes syntactic and higher-level semantic processing. As a result, the ordering of stem + affix actually mirrors in left-to-right fashion the temporal order of computation for these elements in the compositional process of sentence comprehension (and, it can be argued, production). The stem is processed before the affix. Initial position in a word can also be shown to be more salient than final position in recall and recognition experiments, and this further facilitates the recognition of the lexical stem prior to higher-level processing. Such considerations can be argued to favour suffixing overall. In particular, they corroborate the suffixing prediction of the HOP for NP + Po and SOV languages, and they provide a counterpull to the HOP's predicted prefixing order for Pr + NP and VO languages, causing many of these to be realized as suffixes.

There is a competing explanation for the suffixing preference in the linguistic literature, involving principles of language history and change. This alternative is summarized in Givón (1979) and consists of three steps. Givón observes first that affixes regularly derive historically from independent words, e.g. verbal affixes from auxiliaries. Second, such elements regularly occur to the right of the verb in SOV languages. These languages will therefore go through a progression SOVAux < SOV_{af} which results in verbal suffixes rather than prefixes. Third, all current language families were originally SOV. Today's suffixes are therefore frozen relics of earlier syntactic orders that have meanwhile changed to the VO type in many languages. Hence the suffixing preference.

The crucial step in this argument, the third one, is unfortunately highly questionable. The current distribution of OV to VO is roughly 50–50, i.e. random, as is that of NP + Po and Pr + NP. This distribution provides no foundation for the assumption of a 100 per cent skewing in favour of SOV in the past, and since the erstwhile independent syntactic elements such as auxiliaries typically precede the categories to which they should later attach in VO languages, we lose the explanation for the suffixing preference. Nor are Givón's supporting arguments using syntactic reconstruction convincing. Even for the Indo-European family, whose western branches provide the best attested evidence for the progression from SOV to VO, it has been argued (Hawkins 1982, 1983) that the ultimate syntactic reconstruction for Proto-Indo-European that is most consistent with language universals is VO and Pr + NP rather than the reverse. There are also counterexamples to Givón's claim that today's morphological order reflects yesterday's syntactic order (cf. Comrie 1981: 209–11).

4.3. Conclusions re morpheme ordering

Once again cross-language variation reveals descriptive patterns. These patterns corroborate some hypotheses and eliminate others. And they reveal the interaction of competence and performance principles:

- they enable us to factor out two partially opposed forces (the HOP and the processing principles motivating the suffixing preference);
- by formulating this interaction using an if–then statement (if the morphology is going to respond to a processing preference for stem + affix ordering, then departures from the HOP will be toward suffixing, producing the distribution in (15)) we predict which structures will depart from these independent predictions and we predict the directionality of these departures (prefixes will be realized as suffixes rather than vice versa);
- we avoid the insufficiency problem for explanation discussed in section 1 (the morphology does not have to respond to these processing considerations, but if it does . . .);
- we can also quantify the relative strength of the HOP and processing principles in those language types in which they are in conflict (cf. Cutler, Hawkins, and Gilligan 1985).

Conclusions

I began this paper with a critical look at some competence and performance explanations for language universals that are currently being developed in the linguistic literature. Competence explanations are those that are made in terms of grammatical regularities alone (possibly innately determined ultimately), while performance explanations appeal to various principles of language use (some of which may again be ultimately innately determined, cf. n. 1). I argued that the explanations offered are regularly inadequate as they stand, largely because they take no account of the ways in which different principles interact with one another collectively to define the variation space within which human languages occur. Different principles are often in partial conflict, or they may be gradient rather than absolute, and this complicates the precise predictions that they make. I argued further, using examples of left–right asymmetries, that the typological method can help clarify the logic of this interaction by providing descriptive patterns of variation that enable us to factor out contributory principles, to formulate them more precisely, and to define their mutual interaction. The examples discussed involved interacting principles of different causal types. The same method can readily be extended, however, to clarifying and factoring out causal principles of one and the same type. Different processing principles may often be in partial conflict (e.g. strategies that benefit the speaker versus those that benefit the hearer), as may different semantic principles, etc., and cross-linguistic variation patterns are as potentially revealing in these cases as they are in those we have illustrated involving an interaction of very different causal factors.

6

Semantic Ascent: A Neglected Aspect of Syntactic Typology

John Lyons

1. Introduction

The term 'semantic ascent', which I am using as the title of this article, has been borrowed from Quine (1960: 270–6). How my use of the term relates to, and differs from, Quine's I will explain later (see section 4). For the moment, it suffices to say that under the rubric of 'semantic ascent' I shall be synthesizing and reformulating views that I have expressed in various publications over the years, from 'Towards a "Notional" Theory of the Parts of Speech' (1966a) to *Semantics* (1977).

My general thesis will be that, contrary to what seems to be the majority view among linguists at the present time, much of the semantically relevant syntactic structure of natural languages—and more particularly their categorial structure—is non-universal. At first sight, this thesis might seem to run counter to the principles of notionalism, as these were developed and applied in Lyons (1966a). But the contradiction is only apparent. I will not be denying that a considerable part of what may be referred to loosely as their categorial infrastructure (I do not wish to use here the technical term 'deep structure') is ontologically (and psychologically) determined and common to all natural languages. On the contrary, I will be explicitly reaffirming my commitment to this view, which I first defended (at a time when it was less widely accepted by linguists than it is today) in my 1966 article on the parts of speech. But I will also be arguing, not only (as I did in 1966) that natural languages in their non-universal grammatical and lexical structure determine the ontologically indeterminate differently from one another, but also (and this is the more original part of the present article) that some of them permit higher levels of abstraction (and different degrees of abstraction and objectivity) than others do. It is at this point that I make contact with Quine (1960). But I shall be concerned with other aspects of the ascent from the concrete to the abstract than he was: I will be dealing more particularly with the distinction between what I call first-order and second-order expressions (and entities), on the one hand, and the distinction between extensional and intensional expressions (and entities), on the other. As we shall see, two very different dimensions of abstractness are involved in the drawing of these distinctions. I will begin, however, by making some comments upon my 1966 paper, to which I have referred several times in this Introduction.

2. Notionalism updated and revised

Rather more than twenty years have passed since the publication of Lyons (1966a), the purpose of which was to stimulate discussion, within an overtly generative (and transformational) framework, of issues which seemed to me to have been unsatisfactorily treated in recent mainstream linguistics, both structuralist and generativist. It did not, in fact, succeed in this, its immediate, purpose. Nor did it have any discernible effect upon the development of Chomskyan generative grammar. But it has been quite widely referred to in typological studies, partly for its formulation of a particular methodological principle (which will be restated and reformulated below), but also for its content. Since it is still being cited, either directly or indirectly (via the sections that were absorbed into the relevant chapters of Lyons 1968), and the issues themselves have not lost their topicality, I thought I might usefully make a few comments here on the relevant parts of the original paper, by way of clarification and correction and as a preface to what is said in section 3.

The first point to be made has to do with the term 'notional'. In retrospect, it is clear that I ought to have chosen a different term, because 'notional' has been employed in a variety of different senses, technical and non-technical. However that may be, I took both the term itself and its interpretation from Jespersen (1924) and contrasted it, in two respects, explicitly with 'formal' (another ill-chosen term, perhaps, but one that was commonly used in this way at the time: cf. Lyons 1968: 135–7). Notional grammar, in contrast with formal grammar, was held to be (i) semantically determined and (ii) universal. As for (i), I would now prefer to use 'ontological', which captures more precisely than does 'semantically determined' the particular aspect of the traditional theory of the parts of speech that I was anxious to defend: the assumption that the meaning and distribution of the major grammatical categories were basically, or prototypically, dependent upon and determined by the structure of the external world. (Actually, the term used in Lyons (1966a) was 'semantically based', which the advent of so-called generative semantics in the late 1960s made potentially ambiguous.)

As far as the question of universality is concerned, it is perhaps worth noting that the context in which the paper was written was one in which theoretical linguistics had not yet been influenced by Chomsky's then but recent introduction of the principles of universal grammar into the theory and methodology of transformational-generative grammar. There were, and are, in any case considerable differences between Chomsky's conception of universal grammar and the one which I put forward in Lyons (1966a)—and which, with certain qualifications, I still hold. But there is no need to go into that question here. What should be emphasized is that the substitution of the term 'ontologically determined' for 'semantically determined' is not without implications for the question of universality. Semantically determined grammar might well be non-universal (and many structural linguists have, of course, held that the semantic structure of each language is unique). Ontologically determined grammar, on the other hand, must indeed be universal—at any rate, in the sense and to the degree that universality was attributed to ontologically determined grammar in Lyons (1966a) and is being attributed to it here.

There are other more or less important terminological and notational changes that I would make if I were writing Lyons (1966a) today. Most of them are such that the failure to make them in the original article does not affect the substance of the argument. Some of them, however, are worth mentioning here, if only briefly.

(i) The term 'part of speech' is used ambiguously throughout the article, as it was in traditional grammar, to denote, on the one hand, classes of lexemes and, on the other, classes of (word) forms of various kinds. There are many reasons why it is important to use the term 'part of speech' with greater care and perhaps to restrict its applicability, distinguishing it, as I have done elsewhere, from 'form-class' (cf. Lyons 1977: 423 ff.). But one good reason for doing so in the present context is that it makes it possible to say, for example, that different forms of the same lexeme, which would all be described traditionally as nouns, verbs, etc., belong to different syntactic classes. At least one contemporary theory of generative grammar to which reference was made in the article did take this line (cf. Shaumjan 1965).

(ii) I would now distinguish forms from expressions, reference from denotation, sentences from utterances, and acceptability from grammaticality (as in Lyons 1977). And having drawn the relevant distinctions, I would be careful to point out that sameness and difference of distribution, to which a considerable appeal is made in the course of argument, can only be sensibly discussed relative to more or less well-acknowledged ontological assumptions. Apart from anything else, some of the asterisks assigned to certain of the sample hypothetical utterances (or sentences?) in Lyons (1966a) would need to be removed. Linguists are more careful with asterisks nowadays than they used to be and more sophisticated about the difference between grammaticality, meaningfulness, and various kinds of acceptability (cf. Householder 1973). In the present article I will tacitly draw the necessary distinctions, notationally and terminologically, when it is important to do so. But I will not labour them unnecessarily.

(iii) I have already referred to the fact that Lyons (1966a) was written within the framework of contemporary transformational-generative grammar. It was, however, in certain respects avowedly non-Chromskyan. Rightly or wrongly, I argued that current theories of transformational grammar needed to be radically revised in various ways. In particular, I suggested that the rules of the base component should operate upon two different kinds of elements, (i) categories (or constituents) and (ii) features, the former being classified as nouns, verbs, adjectives, etc. (i.e. as major lexical or phrasal categories) and the latter as what I referred to as secondary grammatical categories (tense, mood, aspect, etc.). I also noted that the view of the nature of 'deep' structure that I was arguing for appeared 'to lie somewhere between that adopted by Chomsky (1965) and his followers, on the one hand, and that of Lamb (1964) and Halliday (1966), on the other, as well as having something in common with Shaumjan's (1965) approach' (Lyons 1966a: 209–10). Towards the end of the article, I further suggested, somewhat tentatively, that the base component of a transformational grammar should be formalized in terms of categorial grammar rather than phrase-structure grammar. I do not wish to go into these various details here. Syntactic theory, both Chomskyan and non-Chomskyan, has moved on since 1966; and it would be tedious, and rather pointless, to relate some of these more specific points to present-day theories of syntax. It may however be worth mentioning that several scholars have been working with categorial grammar in recent years. It is no accident that categorial grammar should have been attractive to logicians and formal semanticists like Montague (1974), Lewis (1972), etc., since it formalizes in a particularly elegant way the combinatorial properties of the major syntactic categories; and these inherent combinatorial properties may be held to be ontologically determined, as they were assumed to be in Lyons (1966a) and indeed by Husserl, Leśniewski, and Ajdukiewicz, the originators of categorial grammar. In short, categorial grammar formalized that part of what is pre-theoretically identifiable as acceptability which I have more recently called (using a traditional term in a partly traditional way) categorial congruity (cf. Lyons 1981: 154). As for featurization, this has of course been carried much further recently both by Chomsky himself and, more extensively perhaps, in such non-Chomskyan theories of generative grammar as Generalized Phrase Structure Grammar (cf. Horrocks 1987: 65–8, 169–73; van Riemsdijk and Williams 1986: 42 ff.; Radford 1981: 109–12). A general point that I would want to make here is that, when Chomsky (1965) appeared (between the writing of the first version and the final draft of Lyons 1966a), I was pleased to note the renewed interest in universal grammar that it betokened, but disappointed that no attempt was made to discuss the soundness of the traditional theory of the parts of speech (cf. Lyons 1966b).

(iv) One of the most serious defects of Lyons (1966a) was the failure to draw a distinction between nouns and what I later called nominals—between Ns and NPs in the most widely used Chomskyan notation (between N and N-(double-)bar, in X-bar notation). Failure to draw this distinction does not invalidate entirely the main points in the argument. But it does obscure the fact that the universality of such lexical categories as N, V, A, etc. is a quite different question from that of the universality of such phrasal categories as NP, VP, AP, etc.

This defect is remedied in Lyons (1977: 423 ff.). In the later work it is argued, I think convincingly, that phrasal distinctions are more universal than lexical distinctions; or, at least, that nominals (NPs) are more universal than nouns (Ns). It was always clear, for example, that Nootka (and related languages) had a category of NPs, even if they lacked a distinct lexical category of Ns (cf. Lyons 1977: 433). It is the category of NPs (nominals) that is of primary concern in the present paper. It is worth noting, however, that, although the weight of modern descriptive evidence seems to suggest, contrary to what I had assumed on the basis of earlier statements by Sapir, Swadesh, and others, that Nootka does have a distinction between nouns and verbs (or non-nouns) at the level of lexical categories (cf. Schachter 1985: 11–13; Anderson 1985: 155–7), it is still in principle possible for a language to have nominals (NPs) and predicates (VPs) without having lexically distinct categories of nouns and verbs. I might also mention, at this point, the fact that (again contrary to what I took to be the case in Lyons 1966a), Japanese is nowadays usually said to have a distinction between verbs and adjectives. Granted that this is the correct view of the matter, granted even that the distinction between adjectives and verbs is descriptively more soundly based in the languages of the world than I (and many other linguists) assumed at the time (cf. Dixon 1977), it does not follow that it is as important as the distinction between nouns and non-nouns. In any event, it is important to emphasize that the question is not simply one of the presence or absence of a particular categorial distinction in a particular language, but also one of the relative importance of the distinction in question (measured by the number of criteria that are satisfied or the linguist's ease or difficulty in applying them). The distinction between verbs and adjectives (and more generally between any two categories) is drawn in terms of several criteria which may or may not apply independently and which may even be in conflict. There is little doubt that the distinction between verbs and adjectives is less important in the structure of Japanese than it is in, say, Latin or even English. But independently of such considerations, the very fact that the question whether a language has or has not such and such a category can be raised, discussed, and answered in the way it has been in recent typological work is proof of the applicability of the methodological principle that I was defending in Lyons (1966a). In fact, I would claim that the principle that I made explicit was one that many traditional grammarians have tacitly applied in the past, so that the descriptions of particular languages that they produced were by no means as badly vitiated as the definitions that they (officially, as it were) used would suggest.

(v) Another serious defect of Lyons (1966a) was the failure to draw a distinction between entity-referring and place-referring expressions. (There is some mention of locative expressions in the original paper, but the point made there is of limited import: cf. Lyons 1966a: 229.) It is obvious that there is an ontological distinction to be drawn between entities and places. It is also arguable that places (as distinct from spaces) are ontologically secondary, being identifiable as such by virtue of the entities that are located in or near them. Be that as it may, there is no question but that locative expressions in many languages are to be distinguished syntactically from nominal expressions. It is worth noting, in this connection, that, looked at from an ontological point of view, locative expressions are demonstrably the prototypical or nuclear members of Chomsky's fourth major lexical category: what he currently calls adpositions, and defines in terms of the features [−N] and [−V], the absence of both nominality and verbality (1988: 68). But this is too big a question to tackle here. For present purposes it suffices to observe that adpositional phrases are a subclass of what are traditionally classified as either adverbs or adverbial phrases (with some adverbial phrases, in certain languages, being subclassified as prepositional phrases, by virtue of the typologically restricted criterion of having a preposition as their head) or as case-marked nominals. Now, it is a fact of considerable typological significance that in some languages place-referring expressions overlap more or less with entity-referring expressions. This is the situation, to a limited extent, in English. Conversely, in other languages case-marked entity-referring expressions are morphologically or lexically identical with place-referring expressions. This is of course the whole basis of localism, which is not mentioned in the 1966 article, though it is in subsequent publications, including Lyons (1977). Localism was not part of my thinking in 1966 (though I had some familiarity with it): it became so to some degree, as it became part of the thinking of other scholars in Edinburgh in the late 1960s and early 1970s, largely under the influence of Anderson (1971a, 1977, etc.) and Miller (1985, etc.). The degree to which languages encourage the hypostatization of places by assimilating the expressions that denote or refer to them to entity-denoting or entity-referring expressions is as interesting a typological question as the one that we are pursuing here. The only point to be made in the present context, however, is that there can be no language-independent ontological justification for grouping places with persons, animals, and things as the prototypical denotata of nouns. Traditional definitions of the noun which do this (if they are intended as definitions of universal grammar, rather than as definitions valid for some languages but not others) are therefore to be rejected.

(vi) There is yet another distinction which I failed to draw clearly in the 1966 article: this is the distinction between entities and substances. (I am here using 'substance' in the non-Aristotelian sense. In Aristotelian, and scholastic, terminology 'substance' and 'entity' are more or less synonymous. And it is this by now almost obsolete sense of 'substance' which gave rise to the term 'substantives' for what, in modern grammatical terminology, are normally called nouns: see below, section 3.) As we shall see later, Quine is one of the very few major logicians and philosophers of languages, until recently, to have paid sufficient attention to the implications of the fact that attested natural languages distinguish entity-referring and substance-referring expressions to different degrees and in different ways (by means of 'a provincial apparatus of articles, copulas and plurals' (1960: 60)). Meanwhile let me simply note that, although this is not made fully explicit in Lyons (1966a), the whole tenor of the argument there is that, although a syntactic distinction between count nouns and mass nouns is by no means universal, in any language that has this distinction, it is the former, rather than the latter, which constitute the nuclear, or prototypical, members of the class of nouns. Here, I part company with Quine (1960), who (though he does not express himself in quite this way) takes the denotata (or, as he would say, referents) of mass nouns to be ontologically more basic than those of count nouns and to function, logically, as proper names.

We come now to the restatement of the methodological principle, the justification of which was the main point of Lyons (1966a) and which has been widely accepted in recent typological studies. My original formulation of the principle in question was couched in the metalanguage of purely descriptive, not to say taxonomic, linguistics of the time. This being so, it may appear to have been made to depend for its success upon the validity of the rigid separation of what were presented as two quite different, and chronologically distinct, operations, the first being carried out independently of, and before, the second: (i) that of establishing the membership of the major grammatical categories within each language, and independently for that language, on purely (so-called formal) distributional grounds; (ii) that of naming, or labelling, the categories across languages (as N, V, A, etc.) on notional grounds. It is, of course, doubtful whether it is possible, even in principle, to operate with distributional discovery procedures. But the principle can be formulated in wholly non-procedural terms and without regard to the comparison of one language with another. The crucial question, from a methodological point of view, is simply that of avoiding circularity in the completed description of the language, in which morphology (if relevant), syntax, and semantics are all integrated. Circularity is easily avoided (and was no doubt often avoided in practice) if the following crucial theoretical point is understood: that, because the grammatical categories of natural languages are partly, but only partly, determined by the language-independent structure of the world (i.e. ontologically), the ontological definitions of these categories are applicable only to their nuclear, or prototypical, members. As far as nouns are concerned, the prototypical denotata are persons, animals, and other discrete physical entities (but not places): i.e. what will be referred to in section 3 as first-order extensional entities. Nouns which denote first-order entities are what are traditionally referred to as concrete nouns; and it is the distinction between concrete and abstract nouns—or, rather, the distinction between concrete and abstract nouns (Ns, whether lexically simple or composite) and nominals (NPs)—that is of primary concern in this paper. Abstract nouns (and nominals), as a subclass of nouns (and nominals), are by definition non-prototypical, or non-nuclear, nouns. Languages may or may not grammaticalize the ontological distinction between concrete and abstract, the distinction between entities and places, the distinction between entities and substances, etc., but if they do, the various subclasses of nouns whose prototypical members denote something other than physical entities will be various kinds of non-prototypical, or non-nuclear, nouns. It follows that a particular noun, in a particular language, may be non-nuclear in at least two distinguishable ways: (i) it may be a non-nuclear member of the nuclear class of (concrete) nouns, such as 'cloud' in English; (ii) it may be a nuclear member of a non-nuclear subclass (i.e. satisfying the ontological definition for nuclear members of that subclass), such as 'water' or 'idea' in English.

Granted this distinction between nuclearity and the two kinds of non-nuclearity, let me now make explicit a principle which has probably guided the practice of grammarians throughout the ages without having been formulated in these terms. This is that, with respect to any ontologically defined grammatical category, X, no language can have only non-nuclear members. For example (to take first the case of non-nuclear members of the nuclear subclass of nouns): no language could have a class of concrete nouns all of which were like 'cloud' or 'river' in English: 'cloud' and 'river' are, of course, rightly classified as concrete nouns in English, because they are assimilated grammatically to the class of nouns which includes 'boy', 'tiger', and 'table'. Similarly (to take the second kind of non-nuclearity), no language could have a class of nouns all of whose members denoted places, rather than entities. A language might very well have a grammatically distinct class of place-denoting expressions, but if they were not assimilated grammatically to a class of entity-denoting expressions, they simply would not be called nouns. The import of this general principle will be made clear, as far as the distinction between abstract and concrete nouns (and nominals) is concerned, in the following section, where it will be argued that abstract expressions presuppose, and are parasitic upon, concrete expressions, but not conversely.

3. Concrete and abstract nominals

Our principal concern in this article is with a particular aspect of the traditional distinction between concrete and abstract expressions: more especially, with the ontological basis for this distinction. Much of what follows is simply a reformulation of what is said, or a making explicit of what is implicit, in Lyons (1977: 442–50). It does, however, incorporate a very important terminological and conceptual revision involving the reclassification of what I previously called third-order nominals as second-order intensional nominals and the introduction of an intensional correlate for first-order (extensional) nominals. Let me begin, however, by making some general comments on the traditional distinction between concrete and abstract expressions.

It is difficult to say just how long the distinction between concrete and abstract expressions has been part of traditional grammar (and logic). The *Oxford English Dictionary* (*OED*), in its entry for 'concrete', notes that the term 'was applied by the early logicians and grammarians to a quality viewed (as it is actually found) *concreted* or adherent to a substance, and so to the word expressing a quality so considered, viz. the adjective, in contradistinction to the quality as mentally abstracted or withdrawn from substance and expressed by an *abstract* noun'. Thus, the adjective 'white' is said to denote 'the concrete quality or quality in the concrete', whereas the noun 'whiteness' is held to denote 'the abstract quality or quality in the abstract'. We are told, however, in a note appended to the entry itself, that subsequently the term 'concrete' was 'extended also to substantives involving attributes' (e.g. 'fool', 'sage', 'hero') and that it 'has finally been applied by some grammarians to all substantives not abstract, i.e. all those denoting "things" as distinguished from qualities, states, and actions', and that 'the logical and grammatical uses have thus tended to fall asunder and even to become contradictory'. The situation has been further confused, it may be added, by the usage of some modern logicians, including Quine (1960: 118–24), who call both the adjective 'white' and the noun 'whiteness' abstract terms, the former being distinguished from the latter as a general rather than a singular term.

For a modern definition which self-evidently has its roots in the scholastic tradition, we may turn to Springhetti (1962), where abstract nouns are said to be those 'quae actionem seu notionem aliquam, non aliquid per se exsistens, indicant' ('which denote some action or concept without independent existence'). A concrete noun, in contrast, is defined as one 'quod rem vel animans exsistens, vel ut tale consideratum, designat, non vero qualitates vel habitus (seu modos essendi)' ('which denotes an existent thing or animate being, or one that is considered to be such, but not qualities or attitudes (or modes of being)'). Examples given for the class of abstract nouns are 'pietas' ("piety"), 'pulchritudo' ("beauty"); and for concrete nouns 'hortus' ("garden"), 'homo' ("human being"), 'Deus' ("God"), 'equus' ("horse"), 'multitudo' ("multitude"). Two of the examples given here, it will be noted, are somewhat puzzling, in view of the way concrete nouns are defined (unless they are held to be covered by 'considered to be such'): 'hortus' and 'multitudo'. (It may also be worth remarking that, in contrast with other familiar definitions, on the one hand, animate beings, rather than persons, are here opposed to things, and, on the other, there is no mention of places.) But it is by no means uncommon to find that the examples given in grammars and dictionaries fail to satisfy the criteria set forth in the definitions themselves. This is, of course, at the heart of the general criticism that is commonly, and rightly, made of the traditional definitions of the parts of speech (and of their subclasses) and of the use that was made of them. What is of particular interest to us here is to note, on the one hand, the evident source of the distinction between concrete and abstract nouns in scholastic speculative grammar (NB the term 'modi essendi') and, on the other, the persistence of the distinction and of the terms in which it is drawn right down to the present day, in works which, unlike Springhetti (1962), would not see themselves, one assumes, as being rooted in the scholastic tradition.

I have already quoted from the *OED* (which, as we have seen, draws our attention to some of the inconsistencies and problems attaching to the traditional distinction between abstract and concrete nouns). Let me now give some definitions from two other recent dictionaries of linguistics. (Not all the glossaries and dictionaries of linguistics available to me have entries for 'abstract' and 'concrete'.) In Hartmann and Stork (1972: 2) an abstract noun is defined as one 'referring to a non-material concept, e.g. *happiness* or *courage*'; (and, we are told, it 'rarely takes a determiner such as *a* or *the*, and if used in the plural the meaning may be changed. *Kindness*: *kindnesses*'), whereas a concrete noun is defined as one 'referring to a material object, e.g. *table* or *animal*' (and a material noun 'may take any determiner and usually forms a plural'). Interestingly different, though equally traditional, is the definition found in Richards *et al.* (1985: 56), where a concrete noun is defined as one that 'refers to a physical thing rather than a quality, state or action', 'book', 'house', and 'machine' being given as examples of concrete nouns, in contrast with 'happiness', 'idea', and punishment'. What is different, from an ontological point of view (if we equate 'physical' and 'material'), is that the one definition talks of (non-material) concepts and the other of qualities, states, or actions as the denotata (or, in their terminology, the referents) of abstract nouns. I would not wish to press this difference unduly. But the ontological status of the denotata of (different classes of) abstract nouns is the subject of this paper. I have drawn attention to this otherwise unimportant difference between the two definitions that I have just quoted in order to prepare the ground for a distinction that I wish to draw, and exploit typologically, below: the distinction between extensional and intensional abstract expressions. And this distinction, which has been obscured by the confusions and equivocations associated with the definition and application of the term 'abstract' in traditional grammar, is, in my opinion, not only of the most profound philosophical significance, but also of considerable importance for theoretical linguistics. One further point may be made with reference to the dictionary entries that have just been quoted. This has to do with the examples of abstract nouns. None of them denotes what would normally be regarded as a physical property, such as whiteness or hardness (as an attribute of some physical object or other). And yet, on the assumption that 'abstract' and 'concrete' are complementary classificatory terms, nouns like 'whiteness' and 'hardness' must presumably count as abstract (and they would seem to satisfy at least one of the two definitions of abstract nouns just given).

The general points I am making here are simply that, if I may so express it, there are intuitively different kinds or degrees of abstractness and that the traditional two-way distinction of abstract and concrete runs into problems, however it is drawn. To illustrate these two points further, let us look rapidly, first, at two reference grammars of English, and then at Chomsky's treatment of the distinction between concrete and abstract nouns in *Aspects*.

In a once very popular and eminently traditional school grammar of English, originally published in the late nineteenth century, we find that nouns are subclassified as proper, common, collective, material, and abstract; that the first four subclasses 'are all concrete; *i.e.* they denote *objects of sense*'; and that 'an abstract noun relates to *qualities*, *states*, etc. . . . which are thought of *apart from* any object of sense. *For example*: We know that a stone is *hard*. We also know that iron is *hard*. We also know that a brick is *hard*. We can therefore speak of *hardness* apart from stone, or iron, or brick. "Abstract" means "drawn off" (abstracted in thought from the object. Hence *hardness* is an abstract noun; while *stone* or *brick* or *iron* is a concrete noun' (Nesfield 1939: 17–18). Here, it will be noted, we have as the sole example of the subclass of abstract nouns one which denotes a physical property (but a property that has been 'abstracted in thought' from physical objects in which it is instantiated). Worth mentioning, too, is the assumption, surely ill founded, but not uncommon, that all the other subclasses of nouns are necessarily non-abstract. I do not propose to deal with this issue here. As we shall see immediately, some grammars recognize the existence of abstract count nouns. And there is no reason why collectives or proper nouns should not be divisible into both concrete and abstract subclasses (in certain senses of abstract, anyway).

In Quirk *et al.* (1972), a more comprehensive, more recent, and linguistically more sophisticated reference grammar, we find two interestingly different formulations of the distinction—different from one another and different from Nesfield's: (i) 'broadly speaking, nouns can be characterized naturally as "stative" in that they refer to entities that are regarded as stable, whether these are concrete (physical) like *house*, *table*, *paper*, or abstract (of the mind) like *hope*, *botany*, *length*' (1972: 48); (ii) 'Cutting across the grammatical count/mass distinction we have then a semantic distinction into concrete (material) and abstract (immaterial) nouns . . . though concrete nouns are mainly count and abstract mainly mass', with, as examples of concrete count nouns, *difficulty*, *worry* (in contrast with *bun*, *toy*), and, of mass abstract nouns, *music*, *homework* (in contrast with *iron*, *butter*) (1972: 129). Here 'of the mind' in (i) seems to mean something very different from "abstracted in thought". Setting that point aside, however, I particularly want to emphasize the fact that, whereas the count/mass distinction (and the proper/common distinction) is taken, apparently, to be purely grammatical, the concrete/abstract distinction is described as semantic. In my view, all three distinctions, in any language in which they are relevant, are rooted in ontological distinctions which may or may not be grammaticalized in the structure of particular natural languages.

We now come to Chomsky's (1965: 75 ff.) treatment, where the concrete/abstract distinction figures in the discussion of two unrelated theoretical issues: (i) the cross-classification problem; (ii) the status of so-called selection restrictions. One of these, (i), is not, of itself, particularly relevant to our present topic. It is perhaps worth noting, however, in passing that Chomsky restricts the concrete/abstract distinction, in English at least, to mass nouns: more precisely, in his feature analysis, to non-count nouns. (Incidentally, Chomsky handles the concrete/abstract distinction in terms of the two-valued feature [$\pm$Abstract], whereas Dubois *et al.*

1972 operate with [±Concrete]. In neither case are the implications of the choice of one notation, rather than the other, investigated. But the formalism does, of course, carry certain implications.) As for (ii), it would now be generally agreed, perhaps, that sentences such as 'Sincerity admires John' are perfectly well formed in terms of the grammatical structure of English. Chomsky's whole discussion proceeds on the assumption, common enough at the time, that sentences such as these are either syntactically or semantically ill formed and must be defined as such by a generative grammar of the language. As I said earlier, linguists are now much more sophisticated than they were twenty years ago in their discussion of this particular question. The point that I want to emphasize here is that in *Aspects* there is no discussion at all of the ontological basis of the distinction between concrete and abstract nouns, as there is no discussion of the ontological basis for the differences among the major lexical categories: noun, verb, adjective, etc. In fact, here, as generally, Chomsky was (and, apparently, still is) content to operate, uncritically, with the categories and subcategories of traditional grammar. But I will not pursue any further the details of Chomsky's treatment. I have taken it as one further example of the persistence of the traditional concrete/abstract distinction, of the confusion that surrounds it, and of the uncritical way in which it has been maintained not only in everyday dictionaries and reference grammars, but even in more specialized theoretical works, from the earliest times to the present day.

One final point that might be made on the basis of the definitions, traditional and modern, that we have looked at is the following: they are all either wholly or primarily ontological (as far as lexical nouns are concerned) and, in those cases where syntactic criteria are invoked (such as combining with a determiner or taking plural suffixes), these criteria are obviously applicable to typologically restricted subclasses of natural languages.

We may now embark upon the more constructive part of our task. But we cannot get started without making certain assumptions. (What follows at this point is a revised, updated, and abbreviated version of Lyons 1977: 438 ff.) The assumptions that I am making are not philosophically uncontroversial, but they are certainly defensible. They are often referred to as the assumptions of naïve realism, because they correspond more closely with the metaphysics of unsophisticated everyday usage than certain traditional versions of philosophical realism, Platonic, Aristotelian, etc. In doing so, I am, like Quine, 'beginning with ordinary things'. As he points out:

> if we improve our understanding of ordinary talk of physical things, it will not be by reducing that talk to a more familiar idiom; there is none. It will be by clarifying the connections, causal or otherwise, between ordinary talk of physical things and various further matters which in turn we grasp with the help of ordinary talk of physical things. . . . The familiar material objects may not be all that is real, but they are admirable examples. (Quine 1960: 3.)

One may follow Quine thus far without accepting his full-blooded empiricism.

The first ontological assumption that I will make, then, is that the external world contains a number of individual persons, animals, and other more or less discrete physical objects. That it is difficult to draw the line precisely between what counts as a discrete physical object and what does not, does not invalidate the assumption itself. Naïve realism is compatible with the view that the ontological structure of the physical world is to a considerable degree indeterminate. What is important, from our point of view, is that it is possible to identify a sufficient number of what are indisputably individual physical objects. We can then accept, as appears to be the case, that it is the lexical and grammatical structure of particular languages that draws the line for us in unclear cases (e.g. with respect to the ontological status of mountains, rivers, etc.); and different languages draw the line in different places. There is at least this degree of truth in the so-called Sapir–Whorf hypothesis (which is of course no longer as fashionable as it used to be): that we perceive and describe the world in terms of the categories imposed upon it by the languages we use. To this degree at the level of first-order entities, properties, and relations, as also at the higher levels created by conscious or unconscious semantic ascent, we can say that ontology recapitulates philology (see section 4).

Physical objects are what I call first-order entities. They are such that they may be referred to, and properties may be ascribed to them, within the framework of what logicians call first-order formal languages (of which the lower predicate calculus is the best known). The properties of first-order entities are, by virtue of this fact, first-order properties. Similarly, the relations that hold among first-order entities are first-order relations; and they too can of course be satisfactorily formalized within the framework of first-order formal languages with many-place, relational, predicates.

In the class of first-order entities, persons occupy a privileged position; and the distinction between persons and non-personal entities is lexicalized or grammaticalized, in various ways, in many, and perhaps all, natural human languages. There is also operative in many languages, if not in all, a hierarchy within the classificatory scheme that is employed to describe or refer to first-order entities such that persons are more strongly individualized than animals, and animals more strongly individualized than inanimate things. For example, the distinction of singular and plural in the grammatical category of number may apply only, or predominantly, in respect of expressions referring to persons; the pronoun system, gender system, or classifier system may reflect the privileged position of persons; and so on. Ontologically different subclasses of first-order entities, such as human beings or other biological species, are traditionally referred to as natural kinds: i.e. classes of entities that exist in nature and have something in common. (Semanticists have been paying considerable attention recently to words that denote natural kinds, but for reasons rather different from those that concern us here.) For our purposes, let us simply note that it is characteristic of these different classes of first-order entities that, under normal conditions, they are relatively constant as to their perceptual properties; that they are located, at any point in time, in what is, psychologically at least, a three-dimensional space; and that they are publicly observable.

The ontological assumption that I have just spelled out is, of course, the one that underpins the traditional definition of nouns (and nominals), and more particularly of the subclass of nouns (and nominal expressions) that is distinguished as concrete rather than abstract and as count rather than mass—a class of expressions which denote (or refer to) persons and things. (It will be noted that I have deliberately omitted places, for reasons given earlier in this section. It will also be noted that I have systematically correlated nouns with denotation and, parenthetically, nominals with reference.) Applying the methodological principle that was put forward in the preceding section, we shall say of any language that has a distributionally distinct class of expressions that denote (or refer to), prototypically, persons, animals, and things that the language in question has a class of concrete nouns (or nominal expressions). Whether the language also has one or more classes of abstract nouns (or nominal expressions) is another matter. But before we move on to a discussion of that question let me repeat a point that was made at the end of section 2. This is that, although a language might in principle have concrete, but not abstract, nouns (or nominal expressions), no language could have abstract nouns (or nominal expressions) without having concrete nouns (or nominal expressions). In other words, the existence of abstract nouns (and nominal expressions) presupposes, and is parasitic upon, the existence of concrete nouns (and nominal expressions). This principle was not made as explicit as it might have been in Lyons (1966a), but it was taken for granted in the argument that was presented there and in subsequent work (cf. Lyons 1977: 428 ff.).

First-order nominals, as we have seen, are by definition members of the expression-class whose nuclear (or proto-typical) members are used characteristically to refer to first-order entities. Second-order nominals may be defined, in similar fashion, as expressions that are used characteristically to refer to second-order entities. The ontological status of what I am calling second-order entities is, however, more controversial. Whereas first-order entities, according to the assumptions of naïve realism, exist independently of language, the individuation (and therefore the existence as entities) of second-order entities depends crucially, it may be argued, upon the structure of the languages that we use to talk about them. For a second-order entity is either a hypostatized first-order property or a hypostatized relation, event, process, or state of affairs involving first-order entities. It is the fact that they are hypostatized (i.e. treated as entities) which makes them, in the eyes of certain philosophers, metaphysically suspect. One such philosopher, of course, is Quine.

Second-order extensional entities differ from first-order (extensional) entities in several ways; and they fall into various subclasses. But we need not go into these finer ontological differences (cf. Lyons 1977: 443–5). There are just two points to be made here. The first is that, although propositions containing expressions referring to second-order entities cannot be represented in the lower (first-order) predicate calculate, they can be represented, more or less satisfactorily, in its higher (second-order) extension, in which it is permissible to quantify over predicates. (It is arguable that neither the lower nor the higher predicate calculus is satisfactory for the formalization of the semantic structure of natural languages, in that they cannot properly represent the difference between static properties and relations, on the one hand, and dynamic situations, such as events and processes, on the other. But that is another matter.) The second point of importance in the present connection is the fact that in many familiar and well-studied natural languages, including English, most second-order extensional nominals are created by a synchronically productive process of syntactic nominalization, traditionally referred to as gerundival. For example, corresponding to the sentence 'John sings in his bath' (or rather to a class of sentences whose members differ from one another in tense and/or aspect: *sings*, *is singing*, *sang*, *was singing*, etc.) we have the nominal (NP) 'John (**or** John's) singing in his bath', which is used, characteristically, to refer to the situation of John's singing in his bath.

We may now move on to what I have referred to elsewhere as third-order entities: 'such abstract entities as propositions, which are outside space and time' (Lyons 1977: 443). The term 'third-order' was justifiable in that it correctly indicated that such entities are more abstract than second-order entities. My usage has been rightly criticized, however, on the grounds that it is in conflict with standard logical terminology. Intensional objects such as propositions do not stand in the same relation to second-order (extensional) entities as the latter do to first-order (extensional) entities. There is the further point that, as I shall explain presently, within the class of intensional entities one can, and should, draw a distinction between propositions and so-called individual concepts (to use the traditional term) which exactly parallels the distinction between second-order and first-order extensional entities.

Both second-order extensional entities and propositions are traditionally described as abstract, as are the expressions used to refer to them. There is, however, a crucial difference. Second-order extensional entities, though they are more abstract, in one sense, than first-order extensional entities, are not abstract in the sense of being non-physical. They are publicly observable and, unless they are instantaneous events, have a temporal duration (i.e. some kind of physical existence). Propositions, in contrast, are unobservable and cannot be said to exist, occur, or be located in either space or time. Propositions are such that 'true', rather than 'real', is more naturally predicated of them; they can be asserted or denied; they can be reasons, but not causes (except in so far as their psychological correlates are the objects of thought and exercise a causal influence on human mental processes and subsequent activity). As we saw in the earlier part of this section, this crucial ontological distinction between the two kinds of abstract entities, extensional and intensional, is thoroughly confused in traditional grammar.

We have noted that reference to second-order entities is made most commonly, in English and other languages, by means of phrases formed by the syntactic (and, in some cases, morphological or lexical) process of nominalization. But there is a fairly clear difference, in some languages at least, including English, between the set of nominalizations that is appropriate for the one purpose and the set of nominalizations that is appropriate for the other. (For some discussion of the range of possibilities that are actualized in the languages of the world, see Comrie and Thompson 1985; Noonan 1985.) Generally speaking (this generalization will, however, be heavily qualified presently), gerundival constructions are used to refer to second-order entities and *that*-clauses to propositions. For example, 'John's singing in his bath' could refer to the situation of John singing in his bath (*I heard John singing in his bath*), whereas 'that John be singing in his bath' might refer to the corresponding proposition (*I know that John is singing in his bath*). 'John's arrival', on the other hand, may be used to refer either to the event of John's arriving or to the proposition that corresponds to it (*I witnessed John's arrival* in contrast with *John's arrival has been confirmed*).

Logicians who draw a distinction between sentences and propositions frequently identify propositions with the meanings of sentences. To my mind, there are at least two reasons for not doing this. First, strictly speaking it is not propositions that are expressed by sentences, but propositional functions, or propositional content; propositions, in which the reference of the constituent nominal expressions is fixed in context, are expressed by utterances. Second, there is more to the meaning of sentences than propositional content (cf. Lyons 1981: 119–42): the propositional content of a sentence is therefore comparable with an open formula of formal logic (i.e., a formula containing one or more free variables).

I have described propositions as intensional entities. But what does this mean? The term 'intension' (to be distinguished from 'intentional', with which it is however etymologically connected) here, as elsewhere, stands in contrast with 'extensional'. In traditional logic the extension of an expression is the class of entities to which it is correctly applied and its intension is the set of essential properties which determined its applicability. The sense in which 'intensional' is opposed to 'extensional' in the present context is ultimately related to this traditional distinction between a class and its defining properties. But the use that is being made of the distinction in the present connection is one that has come to the fore in modern formal logic.

Let us begin by drawing a distinction between two kinds of worlds: an extensional world and intensional world. An extensional world is simply a set of individuals which have certain properties, are related to one another in various ways, engage in various situations, and are located each in a certain place. An extensional world can be identified, initially at least, with what is commonly referred to as the external world: more precisely, since the external world is changing continuously from one state to another through time, with a state of the external world at some point in time. An intensional world, in contrast, is a model, or description, of some actual or potential extensional world—of the extensional world that it purports to represent.

We can now relate the notions of truth and reality in the following way. If true, a proposition will be true in some intensional world, W_I; and it will be true of some (actual or potential) extensional world, W_E. To say that a proposition is true in W_I implies that it exists in W_I; to say that it is true of W_E implies that the situation which it represents exists in W_E. (Both W_I and W_E will be sets of world, rather than single worlds, since a proposition may be true in many members of W_I and true of many members of W_E. This opens up the possibility of identifying a proposition, formally, with the intensional world (or set of intensional worlds) in which it is true. I have exploited this possibility elsewhere, though rather informally, and will say no more about it here: cf. Lyons 1977: 809–23.) This way of talking about the truth of propositions brings out the connection between truth and existence that is implicit in the correspondence theory of truth. As reality (being in an extensional world) is the mode of existence appropriate to first-order and second-order extensional entities, so truth (being in an intensional world) is the mode of existence appropriate to intensional entities.

From what has been said it will be clear that propositions are the intensional correlates of second-order extensional entities. Following some, but not all, logicians, I will assume that first-order extensional entities also have their intensional correlates in W_I. These are what many logicians, following Carnap (1956: 41; etc.), call individual concepts. It is important to realize, however, that they are not necessarily concepts in any traditional sense of the term. Nothing has been said here which would imply that intensional entities, propositions, propositional functions, individual concepts, have any kind of transcendental, immanent, or even psychological reality. What has just been said is compatible with nominalism, realism, or conceptualism; it is equally compatible with the rejection of any or all of these traditional approaches to the so-called problem of universals. Nowadays logicians and philosophical semanticists seem to be less concerned about the once hotly debated issue of ontological or ontic commitment. Even the neo-nominalists, like Quine (1960), seem to be prepared to accept the point of view expressed by Carnap (1956), that the decisive issue for the semanticist is not the alleged ontological or ontic question of the reality of abstract entities such as intensions, but their practical usefulness and explanatory power for the job that they have to do in the description of natural (and non-natural) languages.

There is no space here to justify, or to develop further, the two dimensions of the ontological basis for the traditional distinction between concrete and abstract expressions that has just been outlined; and, for the limited purposes of this paper, there is no need to do so. (As mentioned above, what has been presented in the immediately preceding paragraphs is, in essence, a revised and abbreviated version of Lyons 1977: 438 ff.) As far as first-order entities and expressions are concerned, the distinction between extensional and intensional reference has long been familiar to semanticists and has been exploited to good effect in the clarification and formalization of what, since Quine (1960: 141 ff.), we have been accustomed to call referential opacity. But there are many other logico-linguistic problems in addition to 'those coping e.g. with perplexities of lion-hunting or believing', which cry out for a controlled use of the technique of 'semantic ascent as a means of generalizing beyond examples' (Quine 1960: 274). To mention just one: it now seems to me to be impossible to make sense of (i.e. to describe systematically and without contradiction or incoherence) various kinds of existential constructions (including negative existentials and existential causatives) otherwise than by invoking the distinction between intensional and extensional reference (cf. Lyons 1977: 723). But that must be the subject for another paper.

It is the distinction between extensional and intensional second-order expressions that I have in mind in calling attention—and I am hardly doing more than that—to a neglected aspect of syntactic typology. Generative grammarians and semanticists working within the framework of generative grammar no longer operate, explicitly or implicitly, with the assumptions (i) that all phrasal and clausal complements are transformationally derived from S; and (ii) that, since the process of (so-called) complementization is without semantic effect ('transformations do not change meaning'), grammatically distinct complements are semantically equivalent. It is now generally accepted that these assumptions are indefensible in the light of such obviously non-equivalent pairs of sentences as (cf. Noonan 1985: 103):

(1) I remembered that I closed the door.

(2) I remembered to close the door.

But, as I have noted elsewhere, there are less obvious, but none the less clearly demonstrable, cases of semantic—and indeed, more narrowly, truth-conditional—non-equivalence, such as

(3) I remembered closing the door.

(4) I remembered myself closing the door,

which to the best of my knowledge had not been so widely recognized.

The difference between (1), on the one hand, and (3) and (4), on the other, can be accounted for, in terms of the ontological distinctions outlined above, as follows (on the assumption that they are being used, under normal conditions, to make descriptive statements). In uttering (1) the illocutionary agent is using the *that*-clause to refer to a proposition (i.e. an intensional entity), but in uttering (3) or (4) he or she is using the grammatically distinct gerundival complement to refer to an act (i.e. to a second-order extensional entity)—an act in which he or she was involved as the agent. Admittedly, the current perceptual or experiential awareness of his or her involvement in the act of closing the door is, if I may so express it, memorial and, in that sense, purely mental, rather than perceptual. But that fact does not of itself bring it within the scope of the philosopher's catch-all category of so-called propositional attitudes. (cf. Lyons 1987: 175). In this case, the generalization that I made earlier about the semantic difference between *that*-clauses and gerundival clauses in English is clearly valid: the reference in (3) and

(4) is to an entity presented as extensional, and not to some intensional, or psychological, correlate. As to the difference between (3) and (4), this is explained, intuitively at least, by saying that what is being reported in (3) is the illocutionary agent's reliving in memory—his or her memorial re-experiencing as the agent—of the act of closing the door; and in (4) the quite different mental act or state of perceiving or witnessing this act, as he or she might perceive (i.e. see, hear, etc.), from outside as it were, a situation in which he or she was not, or had not been, involved as the agent. The fact that one is more commonly in the position of being able, or wanting, to assert the propositional content of (3) than that of (4) is simply a fact of life and does not make (4) in any way semantically or grammatically anomalous or less normal, or even stylistically more highly marked in any interesting sense, than (3). English happens to provide us, in this respect, with an exploitable syntactic difference between two constructions—a difference, incidentally, which casts doubt on any simplistic application of the transformational notion of equi-deletion—which we can, and do, readily exploit to describe two different classes of situations. (All we have to do, as competent users of English, to see that (3) and (4) are truth-conditionally non-equivalent, is to imagine that the utterer of (4) is truly reporting his or her memory of seeing a filmed record of himself or herself closing the door—and act of which he or she may have no experiential memory, so that (3) would be false. The semantic difference between (1) and each of the others is evident enough, I take it, to require no commentary.)

It is, in fact, the difference between a class of complement-constructions including (1), on the one hand, and a class of constructions including (3) and (4), on the other, that I wish to focus upon as I bring this section to its conclusion. But before doing so, I must qualify the generalization made above about the semantic difference between *that*-clauses and gerundival complements in English, and in three respects.

First, I must make it clear that I am not unaware of the existence of a whole range of particularly interesting examples of *that*-constructions in English operating as complements of verbs like *perceive*, *hear*, etc., which seem to make reference simultaneously both to propositions and to the situations that they describe (or, more generally, that are directly or indirectly correlated with them in terms of their descriptive content). One such example might be

(5) John saw that it was raining.

There is, of course, one straightforward interpretation—with *see* being understood as a verb of mental activity (comparable with *realize*)—in which the *that*-clause refers solely to a particular proposition. But there is also a more complex interpretation, 'which describes the experiential situation in which John's acquisition of the propositional knowledge that it is raining derives from his perceptual knowledge of conditions in the external world' (Lyons 1987: 175). Such sentences, which have been discussed in considerable detail by Barwise and Perry (1983: 171 ff.), do not invalidate the distinction drawn above between the two classes of constructions and the two ontologically distinct classes of potential referents. On the contrary, they support the distinction itself, by showing that there are complex transitional cases involving, or appearing to involve, both extensional and intensional referents simultaneously (as there are complex cases of simultaneous, or conjoined, first-order extensional and intensional reference).

Second, there are, unquestionably, many exceptions to the generalization that *that*-clauses refer to propositions and gerundival constructions to situations. And there are many semantically and syntactically different subtypes of complements and, more generally, of nominal expressions in English that would need to be considered in order to set proper limits to the generalization itself and to put it in a broader typological context. Some of these have been discussed from a typological point of view and compared with semantically and syntactically similar constructions in a fairly wide range of languages by Noonan (1985) and by Comrie and Thompson (1985), but within a somewhat different classificatory framework from the one that I would use and without drawing the ontological distinctions in the way that I have done.

Third, it might be objected that the interpretation of particular utterances in the everyday contexts in which they occur is often both indeterminate and indeterminable in terms of the ontological distinctions that I have been drawing; that the distinctions themselves are theory-laden; that ordinary, unreflecting, users of the language (and non-ordinary users of the language, like philosophers and linguists, in much of their otherwise ordinary life, when, as Wittgenstein would have said, their minds are not idling) are unaware of applying them, and for the purpose in hand do not need to do so, in the daily round of business, recreation, and social intercourse; and that, when the semanticist seeks to impose a fixed and determinate interpretation upon this or that uncontextualized or decontextualized sentence, he is guilty of distorting the facts in the light of his preconceived theoretical ideas. There is a good deal of force in this objection. And it is, of course, of much more general import than the context in which it has just been raised might suggest. It is an objection which, if pressed, might seem to undermine the very foundations of descriptive semantics (and pragmatics), as currently practised. But I do not think that it can, or need, be pressed to this point, either in general or in the present instance. There is a sufficient degree of theory-neutral determinacy in the lexical, grammatical, or semantic structure of languages for us to be able to say with confidence, often, if not always, that this or that distinction is indeed grammaticalized or lexicalized in such-and-such a language, even though the distinction in question is not always clear-cut and, when it is, is not always exploited in everyday, unreflecting, usage. And I believe this to be the case in respect of the distinction that I have drawn between second-order extensional and intensional expressions. That some such distinction as I have been explicating, in my own terms, holds for the constructions in question, in English and in some other languages, has long been recognized by grammarians of different theoretical persuasions.

Granted the validity of the generalization that has just been made (and duly qualified) about the meaning of *that*-clauses and gerundival complements in English, the question that now arises is whether all languages provide their users with grammatically distinct expressions for referring to second-order extensional and intensional entities. It is a question that cannot be answered, I believe, on the basis of current work on language typology.

Certain closely related questions are raised and, up to a point, answered in the recently published three-volume compendium edited by Shopen (1985*a*, *b*, *c*). For example, we are there told that some languages have no morphological processes for creating lexical nouns from verbs in so-called action nominals, but that 'clauses can be nominalized and used in various nominal contexts' (Comrie and Thompson 1985: 391). This is consistent with the more general point made in section 2, that a language might have syntactically formed nominals (NPs) without necessarily having lexical nouns (Ns). And it prompts two further questions: (i) whether any language that has second-order nouns, extensional or intensional, will necessarily have second-order nominals formed by productive grammatical processes; (ii) whether any language that has lexically simple second-order nouns (like 'event', 'act', 'state', on the one hand, and 'fact', on the other, in English) will necessarily also have lexically complex or compound second-order nouns (formed by a more or less productive process of lexical nominalization). These two implicational universals would seem to follow from the principles set forth in section 2. Whether they are in fact valid is, of course, a matter for empirical investigation.

Again, it is claimed that 'in apparently all languages with action nominalizations, it is possible to leave the subject unexpressed, the nominalization then referring to an abstract type of activity' (Comrie and Thompson 1985: 384). Presumably what is at issue here, from a semantic point of view, is (in my terms) the distinction between second-order extensional singular and general expressions. The question whether all languages provide their users with various kinds of singular and general abstract expressions is of considerable importance for anyone who is interested in the notion of semantic ascent (as Quine 1960 has demonstrated). And it is one that could be profitably discussed in respect of the two kinds of second-order expressions, intensional as well as extensional, with which we have been principally concerned in this paper.

Finally it should be noted that, as was mentioned earlier, in his discussion of several kinds of complementation in a variety of languages, Noonan (1985: 90ff., 133) does indeed recognize a syntactic difference between two classes of constructions which is comparable with the one that has engaged our attention (and makes a number of interesting and relevant semantic generalizations), but from a different point of view from the one adopted here.

The distinction itself has not, then, been completely neglected by typologists, but its connection with what, following Quine (1960), I am calling semantic ascent does not appear to have been investigated in relation to a wide and representative sample of the world's languages. Hence the title of this paper. Before we turn, in the next section, to the notion of semantic ascent itself and to my interpretation of it, I may perhaps make one additional comment. Although we may not be able to answer the question whether all languages have syntactically distinct classes of second-order extensional and intensional expressions on the basis of current work in typology, we can hazard the guess that they do not. There are plenty of other examples of semantically relevant syntactic distinctions being present in some languages but not in others (e.g. the distinction between relativization and nominalization, cf. Comrie and Thompson 1985: 394) to suggest that this might well be the case. The fact that we cannot answer the specific question that I have raised (and many similar questions) is of course in part due to the fact that we still lack a more theory-neutral, standardized, framework for the typological description of languages than is at present available.

4. 'Ontology recapitulates philology': a philologist's view

As I explained in section 1, the term 'semantic ascent' comes from Quine (1960): one of the most stimulating and controversial works in the philosophy of language, and one of the most significant to have appeared this century, but one which has not had the influence in linguistic semantics that it ought to have had. As I have already noted, it is to Quine that we are indebted, not just for the term 'referential opacity', but also for much subtle discussion of the phenomenon itself and much of the seminal work on its formalization. Quine, too, must be given the credit for laying the foundations of the modern study, by formal semanticists, of mass nouns and nominals. To the best of my knowledge, his notion of semantic ascent has not, however, been taken up by either philosophers or linguists and developed in the way in which I wish to develop it here.

The quotation that I have used as the heading for this section—a witty adaptation of Haeckel's famous slogan, 'ontogeny recapitulates phylogeny'—is also taken from Quine (1960: vii), who attributes it to James Grier Miller. As for Quine's interpretation of the amended slogan (I will give my own interpretation of it presently), it is to be noted, first of all, that he couples it with Otto Neurath's famous analogy about progress in science: 'Wie Schiffer sind wir, die ihr Schiff auf offener See umbauen müssen, ohne es jemals in einem Dock zerlegen und aus besten Bestandteilen neu errichten zu können' ('We are like mariners who have to rebuild their ship on the high seas, without ever being able to strip it down in dock and construct it afresh from the best available components'). Quine explicitly invokes Neurath's analogy on several occasions in the course of the work, pointing out, in the very first section of

Chapter 1 (entitled 'Beginning with ordinary things'), that it is not only the scientist, but also the philosopher, who has to rebuild at sea 'plank by plank while staying afloat' (1960: 3). And he makes it clear that what he calls 'semantic ascent' is just such a process of rebuilding at sea. ('Our boat stays afloat because at each alteration we keep the bulk of it intact as a going concern.') When Quine asserts that philosophers and scientists 'are in the same boat', he implies that there is no difference in the last resort between philosophy and science. He is thinking primarily, no doubt, about the physical sciences. On the more general, and perhaps also more contentious, point that he is making I have no view. But I do believe that the difference between theoretical linguistics and such branches of philosophy as metaphysics, epistemology, and the philosophy of language, in certain areas including semantics, is far from being clear-cut. The whole of the present paper and of other work from which it derives rests on that belief. It also rests on the belief, which again I share with Quine, that both linguistic and philosophical semantics (in so far as they can be profitably distinguished) have to be grounded in common-sense ontology: that they have to start with ordinary things.

So much then for the use that Quine makes of the Neurath analogy. Before I come to the slogan that I have taken as the heading for this section, let me make a comment or two about the subheading, and more particularly about my use of the term 'philologist' in this context. This stands in implicit contrast with 'philosopher'; and I have used 'philologist', rather than 'linguist', principally of course because 'philology' is employed in the slogan. Actually I do not draw a very sharp distinction between 'linguist' and 'philologist'. But I would maintain that, in so far as there is a distinction to be drawn, 'philology' is indeed appropriate in the present context. The notions that we have been operating with, and more particularly the notions that support the distinction between concrete and abstract nouns and nominals, originated in traditional grammar and, as we have seen, have been taken over, often uncritically, in modern theoretical linguistics. My own discussion of them is very much in the spirit of the philological tradition, but reinterprets this in the light of more recent linguistic theory.

I have said that Quine (1960) is one of the most significant works in the philosophy of language to have appeared this century. It is also one of the most linguistically sophisticated. It is certainly more sophisticated in its appeal to linguistic theory of its own day and to the accumulated findings of descriptive linguistics than most other philosophical works on language of that period. It is also more sophisticated, it may be added, than many that have appeared since, although some of these give the impression of being more radical—less traditional, not to say less old-fashioned—than, in fact, they are, because of their use of a certain amount of modern terminology and their concern with formalization.

To be contrasted with Quine's approach (and the one that I am following here) is that of an author like Cresswell:

> What is a thing? Obviously, anything at all is a thing. I do not mean only physical objects but anything our language can talk about: numbers, sets, properties, events, attitudes of mind and the like. Of course, there are all sorts of interesting questions about what these things may be, but they are not my questions. (1985: 70.)

In the note referring to this passage, he explains:

> in saying that everything is a thing, I am being unabashedly Platonistic. It seems to me that, in dealing with the semantics of natural language, this is right. For I think we do speak as if all these things existed, and I follow Emmon Bach (1983) in assuming that the illuminating way to study natural language is to ask what sorts of entities it presupposes. (1985: 164.)

It is not only in respect of its ontological exuberance, or so-called Platonism, that Cresswell's attitude is to be contrasted with Quine's. Also to be noted is his use of the expressions 'our language' and 'natural language', in the singular, and his apparent assumption that all natural languages have the same semantic, if not the same, grammatical structure. Quine, of course, explicitly rejects this assumption; and so do I.

To judge from recently published works in both philosophical and linguistic semantics, Cresswell is by no means alone in holding the views that he expresses in the passage that I have just quoted. I have quoted his formulation of them, partly because they are expressed in a particularly clear and forthright fashion and partly because Cresswell is, of course, one of the most influential of modern formal semanticists. Currently fashionable though they may be, the attitudes and assumptions in question are eminently challengeable.

First of all, it is, to say the least, misleading to say that a language presupposes the existence of anything. Some natural languages, but not all, provide their users with the means of asserting or denying the existence of entities (of various kinds). Others, and presumably all, permit their users to refer to entities (of various kinds) and in so doing to commit themselves to the existential presuppositions that are associated with the act of reference. It does not follow from these facts, however, that all languages permit, still less oblige, their users to commit themselves to the view that the referents of all kinds of referring expressions, concrete or abstract, are ontologically on a par. Quine, as we shall see, in his explication of the notion of semantic ascent, expressly dissociates himself from this view of what used to be called ontological, or ontic, commitment. I too, in the somewhat different interpretation of 'semantic ascent' that I am presenting in this paper and in the account that I gave of the ontological basis for the distinction between concrete expressions and (different kinds of) abstract expressions in section 3, have deliberately avoided commitment to an undifferentiated notion of existence.

As for the assumption that the semantic structure of all natural languages is identical—or, to be more specific, in the context of the present discussion, that whatever can be referred to in one natural language can be referred to in any natural language—this assumption too can, and must, be challenged. There is an enormous amount of careful and detailed empirical work to be done on the structure of a genuinely representative sample of the languages of the world before anyone can be at all confident about the degree to which different natural languages permit or facilitate the drawing of ontological differences of the kind that we have been concerned with in this paper. But there is strong prima-facie evidence to suggest that not all the distinctions drawn in one language can be drawn, or at least can be readily drawn, in all. In section 3 I have concentrated upon only one particular distinction, which can be associated with the syntactic difference in English, and in certain other languages, between two kinds of nominalization, and I referred in passing to other distinctions or subdistinctions of a similar nature. But there are many other dimensions of the distinction between concrete and abstract expressions that I have not even mentioned. It is interesting to note, for example, that Cresswell's illustrative list of abstract entities ('numbers, sets, properties, events, attitudes of mind and the like') overlaps only partly with Quine's ('points, miles, numbers, attributes, propositions, facts, or classes', 1960: 270–1). I have said nothing at all about the ontological status of most members of both of these sets of examples.

When it comes to the interpretation of the slogan 'ontology recapitulates philology', I am closer to Quine in spirit than in detail. As I have made clear already, I do not share his empiricism. I am prepared to grant that the external world has far more structure independently of its linguistic categorization by human beings than he would countenance, and I thus do not give the same ontological primacy to the denotata (and referents) of mass nouns (and nominals) as he does. And there are many other respects in which my view differs from his. In fact, it is not absolutely clear, to me at least, how Quine himself interprets the slogan. But I do not propose to speculate upon the finer points of Quine's interpretation. Instead, I will simply give my own interpretation, and that only in outline in so far as this is relevant to the principle topic of this paper: the two dimensions of the distinction between concrete and abstract expressions which were explained in section 3.

In order to interpret the slogan in the way in which it can be most profitably interpreted, we may begin by drawing a distinction between implicit and explicit, or systematic, ontology and a similar distinction between implicit and explicit philology. (The terms 'implicit' and 'explicit' may not be ideal for this purpose, but they will serve.) The general thesis of this paper has rested on a number of assumptions associated with what I called notionalism in section 2, including the following: (i) the world is, up to a point, structured independently of the grammatical and lexical structure of languages and, up to that point, determines the grammatical and lexical structure of natural languages to be as it is, rather than otherwise; (ii) particular languages may extend the scope of their grammatical categories and will develop their vocabularies, differently in the case of different languages, and in so doing will, in their turn, determine (i.e. give structure to) what is, a priori and independently of language, ontologically indeterminate. Now, to the degree that (i) and (ii) hold true and ordinary users of a particular language are even tacitly aware of the correspondence that exists between the structure of their language and the structure of the world, we can say that such-and-such an ontology is implicit in that language, as we can also say that ordinary users' knowledge or awareness of the grammatical and lexical structure of their language is implicitly philological. So, if both ontology and philology are understood to be implicit, in the interpretation of the slogan, we can take 'Ontology recapitulates philology' to be no more than a witty formulation of a moderate version of Whorfianism.

It is not however Whorfianism, as this is usually understood, that concerns us here: i.e. we are not concerned with the influence that the average native speaker's tacit knowledge of the structure of his or her language (allegedly) exerts upon the creation or reinforcement of his or her everyday ontological assumptions. What is of interest, in the present context, is the explicitation and explication by linguists (or, as the slogan would have it, philologists) of the ontologically relevant structural distinctions encoded in particular natural languages and the systematic and controlled exploitation of these distinctions in the service of science (including linguistics) and philosophy. If what we are exploiting in this way is one or other of the many distinctions between concrete and abstract expressions (or more or less abstract expressions) that can be drawn, we are involved in the process that Quine (1960) has called semantic ascent.

There is, of course, potentially at least, a negative, as well as a positive, side to the process of semantic ascent. There is the danger, not only of multiplying entities beyond necessity, but also of attributing to abstract entities the same kind of existence as one attributes to concrete (first-order extensional) entitles—or even a different kind of ideal or transcendent existence which would make them, as it were, more real than real. But this danger is avoidable, in the formalization of the language of science (including the metalanguage of linguistics) either in the way that Quine suggests (by invoking the distinction between the formal and the material modes of discourse, cf. Quine 1960: 271) or otherwise. The important point is to be aware of the danger and to arm oneself with the necessary technical distinctions, precisely formulated and systematically applied. In my exploitation of the two distinguishable dimensions of the distinction between concrete and abstract expressions in English (a very modest attempt at ship-building on the high seas), I have not been guilty, I trust, of the creation of 'entia non grata' or of imputing to them the wrong kind of existence (Quine 1960: 243 ff.).

As for the positive value of semantic ascent, this has to do with the notion of expressive power. For example, any (natural or non-natural) language that can refer to and quantify over classes (as can the higher predicate calculus, in contrast with the lower predicate calculus as standardly interpreted) is, by virtue of this fact and in this respect, a higher-order language and is more powerful, or richer, than a lower-order language that cannot: there are generalizations that can be made in the higher-order language that cannot be made at all, or cannot be made as economically, elegantly, and revealingly, in the lower-order language. This same point holds true, I would submit, in respect of the two rather different dimensions of the distinction between concrete and abstract expressions that I have been discussing in this paper.

Coupled with my explication of a particular aspect of the distinction between concrete and abstract expressions and my exploitation of these two dimensions of the distinction for typological purposes (in the metalanguage of linguistics) in section 3, there has also been made explicit the hypothesis that (as it may now be formulated) natural languages may differ in expressive power because one encodes and makes exploitable, and the other does not, this or that kind of distinction between concrete and abstract expressions. There is, of course, a familiar and disreputable version of this hypothesis: 'the more advanced a language is, the more developed is its power of expression of abstract or general ideas' (Jespersen 1924: 429). But the fact that one version of the hypothesis, resting upon anecdotal and by now thoroughly discredited 'accounts of the languages of barbarous races', has quite rightly fallen into disrepute does not mean that there is no substance to the hypothesis itself, as I have presented it. It is a hypothesis which, as I said at the end of section 3, is worthy of dispassionate empirical investigation.

Whether I have carried my readers with me or not in my explication of the distinction between what I call first-order and second-order extensional and intensional nouns and nominals and in my association of this composite, two-dimensional, distinction with the notion of semantic ascent, I hope at the very least to have shown that linguists, in their descriptions of particular languages and in their theorizing about the structure of language in general, should no longer expect to get away with the kind of uncritical acceptance of the traditional distinction between abstract and concrete expressions which, as we saw at the beginning of section 3, is still common and which has by now, to put it mildly, outlived its usefulness.

7

Participant Roles, Synonymy, and Truth Conditions

Jim Miller

Almost all current work on semantics pays at least lip-service to truth conditions. While it seems obvious that truth conditions have a part to play in semantic analysis (but cf. the interesting critique and history of truth-conditions in Baker and Hacker (1984)), their application always involves the assumption that an objective reality can be discovered and that objective semantic structures can be established. Anyone who has tackled, let us say, the category of aspect in a foreign language is well aware that neither the latter assumption nor the notion of truth conditions applies straightforwardly, since they ignore the latitude allowed speakers by a given language. King (1983) and Smith (1983) have drawn attention to the problems of aspect. This paper looks at the problem of participant roles.[1]

The fundamental problem was discussed by Quine in a well-known paper entitled 'The Problem of Meaning in Linguistics'. Thirty-five years after Quine gave the lecture on which his paper is based, the problem remains no less severe and no less crucial. In this paper I discuss the problem with respect to participant roles—any area of language would suffice but participant roles present peculiarly interesting features in relation to cognition. In his paper, Quine (1963: 61) considers the task of studying speakers of English and speakers of Pike's mythical language Kalaba.

If we could assume that our Kalaba speaker and our English speaker, when observed in like external situations, differed only in how they say things and

[1] The preparation of this paper has been greatly helped by E. K. Brown's discussion of participant roles in E. K. Brown and J. E. Miller, *Syntax: A Linguistic Introduction to Sentence Structure* (London, 1980).

not in *what* they say, so to speak, then the methodology of synonymy determinations would be pretty smooth . . . But of course the trouble is that not only the narrowly linguistic habits of vocabulary and syntax are imported by each speaker from his unknown past . . . It is not even clear that it makes sense to think of words and syntax as varying from language to language while the content stays fixed; yet precisely this fiction is involved in speaking of synonymy, at least as between expressions of radically different languages.'

At stake are the cognitive representations that speakers of different languages construct on the basis of external stimuli. While the phrase 'cognitive representations' is exciting, investigations of cognitive representations can too easily slide into conjecture and hot air. This paper is not directly concerned with cognitive representation, but it is concerned with the criteria on which semantic analyses are established. This concern relates to cognitive representations via the principle that a good semantics is based on thorough analyses of morphology and syntax and via the assumption that the morphology and syntax, the code, of a particular language is not accidental but does offer clues to cognitive representation. Let us look first at the principle and then briefly at the assumption.

The principle has been widely applied in European linguistics, the most skilled exponent being perhaps Benveniste, whose example is followed by many contemporary French linguists. It was applied in much transformational work of the sixties. (Though some of the work led to the rightly criticized Generative Semantics, it is useful to recall that it was the model that was hopeless: many of the analyses that were styled 'generative semantic' are still of intrinsic interest—allowing for the excesses and errors in individual pieces of work.) The principle is lacking in much recent work in generative grammar, logic, and cognitive science, which it is why it is worth while illustrating its application to participant roles.

The assumption that the syntax and morphology of a given language offer clues to cognitive structure is far from new and unknown. It informs much historical linguistics of the last century and a half and a growing body of work in current synchronic linguistics. (Generative grammar is excluded from that comment: the term 'cognitive' in that domain relates to concerns rather different from those under examination here.) It is essential to proceed circumspectly, but the following references indicate that the cause is promising.

Slobin (1973) points out that children learning their native language acquire semantically consistent grammatical rules early and without significant error, and attempt to use grammatical markers with semantic consistency. Historical change in syntax and morphology indicates that adult speakers of languages operate on the same principle. Jackendoff (1983) and Langacker (1982) have demonstrated that, synchronically, grammatical patterns can be put in correspondence with semantic patterns, and Lakoff and Johnson (1980) have demonstrated the pervasiveness of metaphor in English—by metaphor is meant that semantic analysis must deal, not with some 'objective' reality, but with the construction put upon external stimuli by the speakers of a given language.

It is important to note that acceptance of the view that grammar offers clues to cognitive structures does not necessarily lead to the Sapir–Whorf hypothesis. In the first place, recent work—cf. for instance Miller (1985) and Stassen (1985)—suggests that languages do not differ fundamentally with respect to e.g. tense, aspect, case relations, though differences do arise in the details of language systems and in the interaction of lexical items with grammatical categories. In the second place, the proposed relation between grammar and cognition is neutral with respect to the question of whether cognition moulds grammar or vice versa.

Syntax and morphology, then, are the necessary basis for semantics. As will become clear from the discussion of participant roles, various phenomena are relevant: word order, agreement and government, the signalling of grammatical categories (the occurrence of case affixes is particularly important for participant roles), the occurrence of prepositions, the occurrence of different verbs in related constructions, and transformational relationships (as found in the work of Z. S. Harris). Note that the syntactic and morphological facts to which appeal is made are all on the surface. None depends on principles peculiar to a particular formal model.

An aside is required here to emphasize that the previous statement should not obscure the fact that the phenomena do result from the analysis of various languages and are not immune to the vagaries of individual interpretation. For instance, in the sentence *Sue lent her essay to Arthur*, *to* does not contrast with any other prepositions: it is what Matthews (1981: 59–68) calls a marker. That is, it is regarded not as a full word but as an automatic marker occurring with a given verb in a given construction. In *Sue carried the parcel to London*, *to* is a full word. For Matthews it is a determiner, which means that it contrasts with a limited number of other prepositions, such as *through*, *round*, *towards*, and *about*. The difficulty is then to decide whether markers can be assigned a meaning. In terms of the amount of information carried, the *to* in *Sue lent her essay to Arthur* is clearly redundant: it adds no new bits of information to those expressed by the other words in the sentence. In contrast, in the example with *carried*, *to* does contribute information.

To say that an item in a particular example contributes no new information may be quite justified, but to say that the item has no meaning (distinguishing between *meaning* and *information*) is a different move. Some analysts make the move, other analysts, taking a different perspective, maintain that e.g. *to* has the same directional meaning in both the *lent* and *carried* examples. The latter view is adopted here.

Exactly parallel arguments are applied by some analysts to case-affixes. For instance, Babby (1986: 171), distinguishing between semantic and syntactic case marking, asserts that if the case of a noun phrase is uniquely determined by the other categories in a given sentence then it is entirely predictable and cannot therefore make a direct contribution to the overall semantic interpretation. This assertion rests on the confusion of information and meaning—not to mention neglect of the fact that a particular utterance related to a given Russian sentence may be so distorted that the addressee makes sense of it only by latching on to the case affixes. The approach adopted here disagrees with Babby's, though the argument is not presented in detail. The interested reader is referred to Miller 1985 and the references therein, and to Jackendoff 1983 and Langacker 1982.

What, then, of participant roles? They have been in and out of favour with theoretical linguists, receiving attention between 1967 and 1972, retreating to the background for a while, and now becoming popular once more. In particular, they provide an alternative to the traditional grammatical relations, which now look suspect as candidates for a general theory of syntax; they appear in the Government and Binding model as Theta roles; they are relevant to various areas of syntax—cf. Wasow 1981, Foley and Van Valin 1984, Bresnan 1982, and many others; they are a central component of situation semantics.

Participant roles are usually treated as self-evident and universal: neither Bresnan nor Wasow, for example, shows concern for the validity of the roles they employ. In discussions of cross-language data it is usually assumed that the roles assigned to a particular construction in one language will be assigned to the corresponding construction in other languages. Practically no attention is given to the problem of how roles are established in linguistic analysis and how the number of roles can be constrained. (The consistent exception is Starosta's work—cf. Starosta 1982—with other one-off exceptions being Cruse 1973 and Schlesinger 1979).

This paper discusses certain constructions in English and other languages in order to focus on the problem of meaning equivalence between constructions in one and the same language and between constructions in different languages. The principle is applied that semantic analysis must take grammar into account, and this application has certain consequences.

(i) Sentences within one and the same language that are equivalent in meaning may require different participant roles.
(ii) Sentences in different languages that are equivalent in meaning may require different participant roles.

The opposite approach, implemented most recently in Foley and Van Valin (1984) is what Starosta (1982) calls the 'silent movie' approach. (It is this approach that Quine attacks in the passage cited earlier.) According to this approach, the analyst considers examples of different but equivalent constructions and asks whether they can be applied to an imaginary silent film in which an event unfolds without commentary or captions. The idea is that, although a given event might be described in different ways, there is one invariant event involving the same action/state/process and the same individuals in the same roles. This approach unfortunately ignores the fact that events are not interpreted directly, but via language, and languages possess different constructions which encode different images. That is, linguistically there are different constructions encoding different events and implications hold between the constructions. The appropriate treatment is to handle the constructions separately and to state the relationships by means of implicational rules, rather than postulating an invariant semantic structure with which the various syntactic structures correlate.[2]

[2] The following discussion assumes a prototype theory of participant roles. For example, in *I gave the puppy to Sue*, *the puppy* refers to an animate creature to which something happens: *the puppy* is a central example of a patient. In *I gave John a punch*, quite apart from the fact that *a punch* is a second object, *a punch* relates to peripheral example of a patient. I would argue nonetheless that the syntax presents it as a patient.

It will be helpful to work towards the more complex examples by first considering some relatively simple ones. (1) is borrowed from Foley and Van Valin (1984: 30).

(1) The sun emits radiation.

This English sentence presents *the sun* as the agent, the entity that performs the emission of radiation. At the same time *the sun* is also a source, the place from which the radiation comes. All this information can be captured in a semantic analysis [SUN CAUSE [RADIATION COME FROM SUN]]. Consider now (2).

(2) The mugger took the money from Fred.

(2) presents *the thief* as agent, doing something to a patient, *the money*. The thief removes it from a 'place', namely *Fred*, who plays the role of source. So far the analysis is apparently straightforward, but difficulties are caused by (3), which is related in meaning to (2).

(3) The mugger robbed Fred of the money.

Foley and Van Valin (1984: 30) assign *Fred* in (3) the role of source as well as that of undergoer—equivalent to patient as used here. On the basis of the above and other examples, they propose a set of 'objective' roles such as source, agent, patient, instrument, experiencer, which are specific to particular predicates. In addition, they propose the 'generalized semantic relations', or macroroles, of actor and undergoer, which are not to be equated with the case roles of Fillmore or the thematic relations of Gruber. Various participant roles can function as actor or undergoer, and a number of grammatical processes are stated in terms of the latter, especially actor.

Actor and undergoer are further described by Foley and Van Valin (1984: 32) as constituting an interface between syntactic relations such as subject and semantic relations such as case roles, but they are also described as universal semantic relations. It is not clear how elements can be both semantic relations and an interface between semantic and syntactic relations, but it is clear from the discussion, and especially from the diagram on p. 186 of their book, that they need the interface because they are caught between the demands of logic for an objective logical structure and the inescapable linguistic fact that natural languages regularly fail to provide a syntactic structure running parallel to the desired logical structure.

Thus, for the 'grammatical semantics' school the syntax of (3) presents *Fred* as a direct object and therefore as a patient, which is the only role assigned to *Fred.* For Foley and Van Valin, *Fred* is logically a source, which means that the source in the logical structure is mapped on to undergoer in the interface, which in turn is mapped on to the direct object in the syntactic construction.

But why should *Fred* in (3) be regarded as logically a source? (3) certainly implies (2), and vice versa, but the fact is that (3) can be seen as presenting the mugger as operating directly on Fred, as separating him from his money. Fred, so to speak, moves, but the money stays still. In support of this account, note that (2) and (3) contain different verbs. The occurrence of different lexical items in different sentences is usually considered an obstacle to a transformational relationship between those sentences—cf. (4) below—and it is important that *steal* denotes an action applied to possessions, whereas *rob* denotes an action applied to possessors. If the analysis is accepted whereby (2) and (3) are treated as separate syntactic constructions related by implication, the relationship between them is captured but the syntax is respected and the need for an interface of general semantic roles as in Foley and Van Valin is removed.

In the light of the preceding discussion, further examples can be brought into consideration. Most of them have three place verbs, with the exception of (4).

(4*a*) The library is to the right of the museum.
(*b*) The museum is to the left of the library.

(4*a*, *b*) describe the same situation. There is no action; merely the location of entities. Utterances related to (4*a*, *b*) could be produced with respect to one and the same photograph, but no analyst has yet suggested that (4*a*, *b*) should be assigned the same logical structure. Presumably one obstacle is the presence of the different lexical items *right* and *left*, and another is that although the sentences apparently share the same truth conditions, they certainly do not share the same pragmatic conditions. (4*a*) takes the museum as the point of orientation and is appropriate when the addressee knows the museum but not the library, and vice versa for (4*b*). (4*a*) implies (4*b*), and (4*b*) implies (4*a*), but they cannot be assigned the same logical structure.

The examples in (5) are very familiar but no less interesting for that.

(5*a*) The men loaded the lorry with bricks.
(*b*) The men loaded bricks on to the lorry.

Although (5*a*, *b*) contain the same verb *loaded*, it is well known that they differ in truth conditions: (5*a*) relates to a model situation in which the lorry is completely loaded with bricks, whereas (5*b*) relates to two model situations, one in which the lorry is completely loaded, and one in which it is not. The difference in truth conditions matches the syntax. In (5*a*) *the lorry* is the direct object and has the role of patient. The action is applied directly to the lorry and the patient is completely affected by the action unless there are signals to the contrary: e.g. the phrase *partly loaded* instead of *loaded*. In (5*b*), *bricks* is the direct object and patient, the action applies directly to the bricks and affects them completely, but it is left open what might be the exact effect on the lorry.

What are the participant roles in (5*a*, *b*)? From their analysis of similar examples on pp. 86–7 of their book, Foley and Van Valin would assign them the same logical structure, in which *bricks* are theme (entities whose location or movement is described are themes) and *lorry* is locative. If the grammar of the examples is heeded, the assignment of roles is different: in (5*a*) *lorry* is patient and *bricks* is a locative (or perhaps comitative), whereas in (5*b*) *bricks* is patient and *lorry* is locative (or perhaps goal). On this analysis, the differences in syntax—word order, occurrence of preposition, and choice of preposition—are accompanied by a difference in truth conditions and a difference in participant roles.

The importance of the examples in (4) is that they differ in syntax, seem to share the same truth conditions, but are assigned different semantic structures. The importance of the examples in (5) is that they differ in syntax and truth conditions, and the argument advanced here, based on the assumption that grammatical differences are accompanied by semantic differences, is that they also differ in participant roles.

Other pairs of examples do not differ in truth conditions but do have different syntax and therefore different semantic analyses, in particular, differences in participant roles and in the assignment of roles to lexical items. Examples that work like *load* are exemplified in (6)–(8).

(6*a*) We sprayed the wall with slogans.
(*b*) We sprayed slogans on the wall.

(7*a*) They hung pictures on the walls.
(*b*) They hung the walls with pictures.

(8*a*) She planted the garden with spring flowers.
(*b*) She planted spring flowers in the garden.

The difference in truth conditions between the members of each pair parallels the difference between (5*a*) and (5*b*), and similarly for the grammatical differences and the participant roles. *With* signals a comitative, *in* and *on* a locative. The crucial difference in participant roles has to do with which participant is presented as patient and therefore, *ceteris paribus*, as directly and completely affected by the action. Other three-place verbs occur in two constructions but without a change in truth conditions, as illustrated in (9)–(13).

(9*a*) He engraved an epitaph on the stone.
(*b*) He engraved the stone with an epitaph.

(10*a*) She inscribed their names on the page.
(*b*) She inscribed the page with their names.

(11*a*) The stonemason marked a sign on the stone.
(*b*) The stonemason marked the stone with a sign.

(12*a*) They issued rifles to the policemen.
(*b*) They issued the policemen with rifles.

(13*a*) Italians supply ice-cream to the Scots.
(*b*) Italians supply the Scots with ice-cream.

These constructions are not particularly exciting, but they illustrated the possibility of having differences in participant role not accompanied by differences in truth conditions. The fact that one can occur without the other is not alarming, provided we accept the central role of verbs in clauses and the fact that verbs can have idiosyncratic properties. In the above examples it may be that the idiosyncracy belongs to groups of verbs rather than to individual lexical items: *engrave*, *inscribe*, and *mark* seem alike, as do *issue* and *supply*.

With respect to *supply* and *issue*, and also *give*, *show*, *tell*, *teach*, *bring*, and *send*, Givón (1984b: 158) comments that in unsolicited English discourse the bulk of dative/benefactive participants appear as direct objects, especially when expressed by a pronoun. The direct object denotes the most affected entity, which registers the change of state caused by the action. Among the participants in the actions denoted by the above verbs, human entities are more likely to be seen as central than inanimate entities. Givón talks of the recipient (goal) appearing as the direct object. The preceding discussion favours an analysis in which the direct object denotes the patient. That is, consistency is achieved: all direct objects denote patients, the grammar is respected, and the semantic facts noted by Givón are taken into account. Quite simply, patients are more central, and more directly affected by an action, than goals (Givón's recipients).

Some verbs are restricted to a particular construction. For example, *fill* and *cover* are restricted to the *with* construction, *place* and *pour* to the *on/into* construction. Cf. (14)–(15).

(14*a*) She placed the books on the table.
(*b*) She covered the table with books.
(*c*) *She placed the table with books.
(*d*) *She covered books on the table.

(15*a*) She poured water into the bath.
(*b*) She filled the bath with water.
(*c*) *She filled water into the bath.
(*d*) *She poured the bath with water.

The reason for the asterisk is not far to seek. The action denoted by *cover* applies to surfaces but not to entities that are moved onto surfaces, and vice versa for *place*. The action denoted by *pour* applies to liquids but not to containers for liquids. (These remarks relate to protypical situations and ignore the possible but not prototypical situation described by *The tip-up truck tipped up and poured the old baths into the pit*.)

The essential point of examples (14), (15) is this. (14*a*) is an *on* construction, (14*b*) a *with* construction. They differ in meaning in the same way as *loaded the lorry with bricks* and *loaded bricks on the lorry*. The difference in truth conditions and the differences in word order and preposition are reinforced by a difference in verb.

For many of the examples above a solid case has been made for the view that the sentences in each pair represent different syntactic constructions and different semantic constructions. For the *supply* examples the case might seem weaker, but it must be borne in mind that the original analysis by Fillmore, with a single deep structure from which one or other NP was chosen to be the surface subject, will not do either. The difficulty is that talk of one or other NP being chosen as surface subject gives the impression that the difference between the constructions is minor. Closer examination reveals rather large syntactic differences. The choice of surface subject and object is reflected in a range of other constructions: e.g. clefts, pseudo-clefts, adjective + infinitive constructions. Cf. (16)–(18).

(16*a*) It is ice-cream that Italians supply to the Scots.
(*b*) It is the Scots that Italians supply with ice-cream.

(17*a*) What Italians supply to the Scots is ice-cream.
(*b*) ?Who the Italians supply with ice-cream are the Scots.

(18*a*) The Scots are certain to be supplied with ice-cream by Italians.
(*b*) Ice-cream is certain to be supplied to the Scots by Italians.

The argument based on data such as (16)–(18) was that subjectivization in a transformational framework is a deep rule that precedes many other major transformations, such as cleft-formation and subject-raising. The conclusion was that subject-assignment could not be accommodated in a transformational framework. The analysis advocated here does not presuppose a transformational framework but the data is none the less relevant. It shows that the distinction between e.g. (13*a*) and (13*b*) is not isolated but is part of a network of syntactic distinctions that point to (13*a*) and (13*b*) being indeed different and independent constructions, not merely variants of a single construction.

Important points in the preceding discussion are that the placing of a noun phrase in direct-object position is not semantically vacuous and that differences of verb (*inter alia*) oblige the analyst to postulate different syntactic and semantic structures. These points become even more important when data from languages other than English are examined. For example, Fillmore (1963: 47–8) talks of the purely formal character of the direct object and equates the English *furnish someone with something* to the French *fournir quelque chose à quelqu'un*. Extending the principles of analysis from English alone to inter-language data, we must regard the French construction as presenting the goods as patient, whereas the English construction presents the acquirer of goods as patient.

The corresponding Russian constructions are of interest with respect to choice of verb. The English verb *furnish* occurs only with the acquirer of goods as direct object. The French *fournir* typically has the goods acquired as direct object. Russian possesses two verbs: *snabžat'* ('supply, furnish') takes as direct object the noun denoting the acquirer of goods, as in (19), whereas *postavljat'* ('supply, deliver') takes as direct object the noun denoting the goods, as in (20).

(19) Knigami nas snabžaet rajonnaja biblioteka
with books us supplies district library
'The district library supplies us with books.'

(20) Knigi nam postavljaet rajonnaja biblioteka
Books to us supplies district library
'The district library supplies books to us.'

It was proposed above that the English constructions with *supply* be assigned different semantic structures. Russian, by virtue of the different verbs, forces the different semantic structures on the analyst: one (=(20)) corresponding to the French *fournir*, the other (=(19)) corresponding to the English *furnish*. Note that the Russian examples have the same word order, but the nouns are in different cases, equivalent to the different prepositions in English. In (19) *knigami* is an instrumental case form and *nas* is an accusative case form. In (20), *knigi* is an accusative case form and *nam* is a dative case form.

There are instances where Russian has one construction corresponding to two English ones. An example is provided by the English verb *present*, which occurs in both the constructions illustrated in (13*a*) and (13*b*). The corresponding Russian verb is *podarit'*, which occurs in only one construction, corresponding to that in (13*a*). Cf. (21).

(21) Zavedujuščij podaril inženeru zolotye časy.
(The) manager presented to (the) engineer (a) gold watch

The crucial fact is that *podaril*, a three-place verb, is accompanied by three nouns, one of which is *inženeru*, a noun in the dative case. *podarit'* denotes an action that applies directly to gifts, and *inženeru* denotes the goal to which the gift moves.

At this stage in the discussion Givón's remarks on *supply*, *give*, *show*, etc. are pertinent. The Russian examples show that with *podarit'* and *postavljat'* the noun denoting the recipient is in the dative case and the recipient is presented as a goal, whereas with *snabžat'* the noun denoting the recipient is in the accusative and the recipient is presented as a patient. In both constructions the human recipient is presented as central: in (19) because the appropriate noun is the direct object, and in (20) and (21) because the noun denoting the recipient is adjacent to the verb in spite of being in the dative case.

In other languages the centrality of the human non-agent participant is increased by a downgrading of the gift. Blansitt (1984) cites the Latin example (22).

(22) Rubrium corona donasti.
Rubrius-Acc crown-Abl you presented
'You presented Rubrius with a crown.'

The important feature of (22) is that *corona* is in the ablative case, and that the ablative case, especially with inanimate nouns, has instrumental meaning. That is, an action was performed on Rubrius, using the crown. (A similar comment applies to (16).)

A word of caution is required concerning Russian. (19) and (20) are convenient in that they have completely different verbs, *snabžat'* and *postavljat'*, but the contrast between Russian and English is often more subtle. Consider (8*a*, *b*) and (23*a*, *b*).

(23*a*) Maša sowed the field with wheat.
(*b*) Maša sowed wheat in the field.

Corresponding to *planted* and *sowed* in the (*a*) examples, Russian has *zasadila* and *zasejala*, as in (24).

(24*a*) Maša zasadila sad cvetami.
Maša planted garden with flowers
(*b*) Maša zasejala pole pšenicej.
Maša sowed field with wheat

Corresponding to *planted* and *-sowed* in the (*b*) examples, Russian has *posadila* and *posejala*, as in (25).

(25*a*) Maša posadila cvety v sadu.
Maša planted flowers in garden
(*b*) Maša posejala pšenicu v pole.
Maša sowed wheat in field

The verb denoting the basic action of planting as applied to plants is *sažat'*. Forms such as *sažaem* ('we sow') denote the action in progress. Another set of forms, such as *posadila* in (25*a*), present the action as completed. Historically both sets of forms derive from the root *sad*, but it is a moot point whether Modern Russian has a single lexical item, say *sad*, realized by two sets of forms, or whether two lexical items should be recognized, *sažat'* and *posadit'*.

The verb in (24*a*) denotes a 'derived' action of planting as applied to areas of ground—gardens, fields, etc. The action is presented as completed, and the form is *zasadila*, which is parallel to *posadila* but has a different prefix, *za*. The forms that denote the action in progress are based on *sad* historically but have undergone palatalization: e.g. *zasaživaet* ('is planting').

The imperfective form consists of the prefix *za-* and the root *sad*, together with the suffix *-iv*, the linking vowel *a*, and the third-person singular non-past affix *-et*.

Corresponding to *sow*, Russian has forms such as *seet* ('is sowing') and *poseet* ('will sow') for the basic action applied to seed, and forms such *zaseet* ('will sow') and *zaseivaet* ('is sowing') for the derived action applied to areas of ground.

The essential points are these. Russian does not have two completely different verbs corresponding to *plant* or *sow*, but it does possess verb forms with different morphology. The differences in derivational morphology reinforce the syntactic differences mentioned above. In a formal grammar in which all morphology is handled in the lexicon there would be no temptation to derive the surface constructions from a single deep one: all the constructions would be independently generated in order to receive the correct verb from the lexicon. Finally, note that many analysts of languages such as Russian assume that more complex morphology reflects more complex (or less basic) meanings. If this assumption is correct, the morphology of the Russian verbs in the above examples supports the intuition that *planted* in (8*b*) is more basic than *planted* in (8*a*).

One last comment on morphology. (15) illustrates the completely different English verbs *pour* and *fill*. Russian does have a separate verb corresponding to *fill*, namely *dopolnit'*, but it also has verb forms which translate into English as *filled*, *fill*, etc., but which are based on the root corresponding to *pour*. These verb forms denote only the filling of containers with liquid. Cf. (26):

(26*a*) Ivan lil pivo v kružku
Ivan poured beer into mug
(*b*) Ivan nalil kružku pivom.
Ivan filled mug with beer
(*c*) Ivan dolil kružku.
Ivan topped up mug

Examples (19)–(26) are drawn from a language where two different constructions are available, either with the same verb or with different verbs: i.e. either different roots or the same root but different derivational morphology. (Lemaire (1983) discusses in detail the Latin examples of the sort in (22) and related constructions.) In some languages only the construction in (19) is available for verbs of telling, giving, and showing. That is, the noun denoting the recipient of goods is the direct object of the verb and thereby patient. Givón (1984b: 159) cites examples from the Uto-Aztecan language Ute. Talking of the obligatory promotion of benefactives (recipients/goals) to direct object, he continues the usual unsatisfactory analysis. In the light of the above discussion, Ute must be regarded as presenting the recipient of goods as patient, as operated on directly by the agent. This is recognized by Blansitt (1984: 146), who comments that in languages like Ute the bitransitive recipient or beneficiary may be the cognitive equivalent of unitransitive patient. This is precisely in accord with the above analyses.

The final part of this paper looks at data demonstrating that the participant-role analysis of a construction in one language may be disconcertingly different from the analysis of the equivalent construction in another language. The data is from Nichols (1984: 188–90). She discusses example (27), from Chechen-Ingush.

(27) da:s woʕa: urs tiexar
father-Erg son-Dat knife-Nom hit
'The father stabbed his son.'

According to Nichols, 'the subject is ergative, the person or object struck (henceforth I use the term "target") is in the dative, and the weapon or instrument in the nominative'. *Urs* ('knife') is the direct object, and the combination of nominative object and verb can undergo semantic specialization: e.g. *tuop tuoxan* ('rifle-hit') is equivalent to *shoot* and not *beat with a rifle*. This semantic specialization is not to be interpreted as a sign of noun incorporation. Rather, 'the verbs of hitting have abstract and very general meanings which are not well captured in their English glosses'.

These comments by Nichols are very much in the spirit of this paper. A suitable gloss of (27) is 'The father hit the knife to his son'. That is, the father is presented by the language as operating directly on the knife, causing the knife to move to the son. In terms of roles, the knife is patient and the son, as Nichols says, is the target—in my terms, the goal. (1) is the typical construction for three-place verbs in Chechen-Ingush—e.g. verbs of giving, putting, spreading, etc.—which Nichols interprets as verbs of movement, the nominative noun denoting the thing moved.

Languages such as Chechen-Ingush offer striking examples of cross-language divergence affecting languages belonging to unrelated language families. It was precisely such striking examples from Hopi that set Whorf investigating the idea of linguistic relativity. It is worth while reminding ourselves at this point that the Sapir–Whorf hypothesis is not argued for in this paper. The notion of Standard Average European is out, since the bulk of the data, from European languages of the Indo-European family, indicates that SAE may be elusive. (In any case, many of the features regarded by Whorf as peculiar to e.g. the Hopi verb are found in Indo-European languages too.) Moreover, there is no assumption that speakers of Chechen-Ingush view the world in a fundamentally different fashion from speakers of Russian or English. Rather, Chechen-Ingush possesses only one construction for describing situations involving a weapon, someone using the weapon and someone on whom the weapon is used. The available construction presents the weapon as one of the central participants, as patient, and the person attacked as less central, as the goal: cf. the English *The father threw the knife at his son*.

The typical English or Russian construction presents the person attacked as the patient. Speakers of Chechen-Ingush may well be able to appreciate the view conveyed by the English sentence: the essential mistake to avoid is imposing the role structure of the English example on to the Chechen-Ingush example. Truth conditions have a part to play in semantic analysis but used uncritically and unsubtly they distort our understanding of language system and language use. Too much emphasis has been laid on interpretation of sentences both by the analyst and by the native speakers of a given language. It is time to reintroduce the notion that speakers construct reality and that human languages reflect their constructions.

8

Prepositional Relatives and Syntactic Marginality*

S. G. Pulman

1. Introduction

This paper investigates the properties of sentences like these:

(1*a*) He gave her a cake with pink icing on (it).
(*b*) There was a cupboard without much room inside (it).
(*c*) The house was surrounded by a garden with blue flowers in (it).

The phrases of particular interest are the NPs with what appears to be a PP modifier beginning with 'with' or 'without'. What is interesting about them is the gap, or understood NP position, they appear to contain, making them structurally and semantically somewhat like relative clauses, hence the name. As indicated, an overt pronominal NP can also appear in this position, resulting in an exactly synonymous sentence. If it were not for this fact it would be tempting to try to analyse the 'gap' as merely an intransitive use of a usually transitive preposition. However, while there is some support for this approach in that some clearly transitive prepositions do not happily occur in this construction without a pronoun:

(2*a*) . . . a station with several lines from it (*θ)
(*b*) . . . . the bus stop with the people at it (*θ)

I have not been able to find any examples of strictly transitive

* This paper was written in 1984, and thus takes no account of developments in syntactic theory since that time. I am grateful to two anonymous referees, and to the following people for their comments and suggestions (the usual absolutions apply to them): Bob Borsley, Ted Briscoe, Keith Brown, Gerald Gazdar, Steve Harlow, David Kilby, Ken Safir, and Anthony Warner.

prepositions which absolutely cannot appear with a gap in some context or another: On a good day I am happy with things like:

(3*a*) ?Probably the station with the fewest lines from is Liverpool Street.
(*b*) ?The table with the least room at is that one by the window.

Since the allegedly intransitive uses are in fact interpreted as if they were transitive, the line of least resistance leads to the tentative conclusion that all occurrences are transitive, and that if there is no overt NP complement to the preposition, there is an understood NP of some sort.

To my knowledge, the Prepositional Relative construction (henceforth PR) has not appeared in the literature before, although a closely related form is mentioned in Quirk *et al.* (1972: 6.46, 327–8), as is a semantically similar form without the final preposition or gap (14.34, 963). Siegel (1983) also discusses a similar usage of PPs headed by *with*. The related form is perhaps just a special case of PR, but it has slightly different properties, involving NPs which refer, roughly speaking, to 'things which can be worn' and is restricted to the prepositions *on* and *off*.

(4*a*) She came out without any make-up on.
(*b*) I saw a man with a hat on.
(*c*) There was a man with his shoes off in the armchair.

Alone, these restrictions would not necessarily distinguish the form from the examples in (1), but whereas those in (1) and their like can all have the possibly resumptive, certainly anaphoric, pronoun instead of the gap, those in (4) cannot:

(5*a*) He gave her a cake with pink icing on it.
(*b*) *I saw a man with a hat on him.

This restriction apart, this quasi-idiomatic form seems to have pretty much the same properties as the other examples of PRs.

The properties of PRs can be catalogued as follows:

(i) When there is a gap, it is interpreted as identical in reference to the head NP modified by the *with*(*out*) PP.

(ii) If a pronoun appears in that position it too is interpreted as identical in reference to that NP, as in (5*a*). However, a full definite NP can also appear in that position: under these circumstances, the

NP must be understood as identical, or intersecting in reference, or at least as inalienably linked in some way to the head NP.

(6*a*) . . . a cake with pink icing on the top.
(*b*) . . . a house with a window in the roof.
(*c*) . . . a cottage with flowers in the garden.

The quasi-idiomatic form also behaves similarly in this respect:

(7) . . . a man with a hat on his head.

If the link is not easy to make, the results can be more than a little strange:

(8*a*) . . . a cake with icing on the fruit loaf.
(*b*) . . . a man with a hat on my head.

The properties of the NPs involved here seem to be very similar to those often referred to as 'pronominal epithets', as in:

(9) As for John, I can't stand the fool.

(iii) Just as with sentential relatives, PRs can have a restrictive or a non-restrictive reading, although the inherent meanings of *with* and *without* mean that ambiguities are not common:

(10*a*) There was only one cake (,) without icing on.
(*b*) We have two new buckets (,) with no holes in.

(iv) Although the prepositions preceding the gap are usually classed as locatives, not all locatives are equally felicitous (?*at*, ?*into*), and not all of those that do appear are uncontroversially locative semantically speaking (for example, *in* in (10*b*) expresses a property of the bucket rather than the whereabouts of a non-existent hole).

(v) The phrase beginning *with*(*out*) is arguably what it appears to be, a PP: it can appear in the usual preposed positions:

(11*a*) With all those holes in, the bucket is useless.
(*b*) Without any icing on, the cake will look unfinished.

And, somewhat less easily, clefted:

(12*a*) It was without any icing on at all that the cake was eventually delivered.
(*b*) It was with the marigolds in that the garden looked most attractive.

However, in these examples, we do not have the PR interpretation: the PP seems to be behaving as an optional VP modifier, just like any other PP. Perhaps the appropriate semantic analogy here is with the type of relative clause illustrated in:

(13) We went to the Tate yesterday, which John has never enjoyed.

Here there is a range of possible antecedents for the relative which are not determined syntactically.

As the canonical forms of (11) and (12) indicate, PRs can also apparently be generated in the VP:

(14*a*) The bucket is useless with all those holes in.
(*b*) The cake will look unfinished without any icing on.
(*c*) The cake was eventually delivered without any icing on at all.
(*d*) The garden looked most attractive with the marigolds in.

This is presumably exactly what would be expected if they are like ordinary PPs. That they are indeed modifying the VP in (10) is suggested by the semantic contrast with (15):

(15*a*) The bucket with all those holes in is useless.
(*b*) The cake without any icing on will look unfinished,

in which only a restrictive reading is present. It is possible that all those in (14) should be regarded as instances of the non-restrictive form, or analogous to the presumably closely connected use of *with*(*out*) introducing 'small clauses' like:

(16) The room looked peaceful with the cat sitting next to the dog.

Note that the restrictive forms can in fact be extraposed:

(17*a*) I saw a cake yesterday with green icing on.
(*b*) I'll get the bucket for you with all those holes in.

(vi) The stranded preposition heads a full PP: the usual PP specifiers can appear there:

(18) . . . a wood with a path right/straight through

(vii) PRs can be paraphrased by ordinary relative clauses whose main verb is 'have', and there are also ordinary full sentences corresponding to these:

(19*a*) . . . a cake which had pink icing on (it)
(*b*) . . . a bucket which didn't have any holes in (it)

(*c*) The cake had pink icing on (it).
(*d*) The bucket didn't have any holes in (it).

As indicated, both of these forms can have either a gap or a resumptive pronoun.

(viii) The dependency between the head NP and the 'gap' is interpreted as for wh-movement type unbounded dependencies. However, syntactically speaking, if it is a dependency, it is a relatively 'bounded' one:

(20) *We bought a house with green slates on the roof of it./θ.

2. Marginality

The PR construction might be described as a marginal one in several senses. The most obvious one is that, in some everyday sense, one's powers of expression would not be radically affected if PRs were not present in the language, unlike, for example, true relative clauses, or other semantically equivalent types of nominal modification. Secondly, there is some speaker variation over the status of examples of the construction. All speakers accept the forms in (4); all accept the version of (1) in which the resumptive pronoun is present, but some speakers do not accept the examples with gaps in. (If you found the last sentence unacceptable, then you are one of those speakers.) For those speakers who are not troubled by gaps, all the judgements are fairly clear for the cases given so far, and analogous examples can be freely constructed, indicating that the construction is live and productive. Some speakers, while rejecting examples like (20), do accept examples like:

(21*a*) . . . a door with a wedge jammed in
(*b*) . . . a jar with the lid firmly screwed on

where the gap is not quite so bounded, appearing inside some type of reduced relative clause, but some report a preference for the version with the pronoun in when the gap is so far away from the head NP. This type of variation means that the construction counts as 'marginal' in the sense of Chomsky (1982: 39).

To call a construction 'marginal' invites two contrasting attitudes to it. On the one hand, it can be argued that not too much weight should be placed on theoretical conclusions drawn from the analysis of such constructions, for their marginal status should be taken as the reflection of the fact that they are not central or core grammatical phenomena. In this sense, 'marginal' means 'marked' or 'unexpected'. Markedness needs to be correlated with some other factor if this is to be a categorization with any objective content: relative rarity in the languages of the world, processing problems, difficulty or lateness of acquisition, etc. An example of a construction which might count as marginal in this sense is 'tough movement', which, though found in several different languages, resists satisfactory analysis within the current theory of transformational grammar, and which that theory might therefore expect to provide difficulties for the language learner, which it apparently does, not being satisfactorily mastered until the age of 9 or 10 by some children. (See Chomsky 1981 for some recent attempts at analysis, Jones 1983 for a history and critique, and C. Chomsky 1969 for the evidence on learning difficulties). The fact that tough movement has been an exception to central grammatical principles in successive analyses (to the Minimal Distance Principle in Standard Theory, to the Tensed S and Specified Subject Conditions in the theory of Chomsky 1973 (analysed as NP movement, that is), and to the Theta Criterion in Government and Binding theory), is therefore not a good reason to abandon those principles, for the fact that tough movement is then in a well-defined sense an 'unnatural' construction provides a way of explaining its marginality.

On the other hand, it can also be argued (Chomsky 1982: 39) that a marginal construction should reveal core grammatical structures and processes, since if it is a marginal construction it might be assumed that the language learner is presented with very little evidence as to its properties, whatever they may be. On the general principle that where knowledge is attained without evidence, that knowledge must be partly the result of innate structure, the properties of marginal constructions should be expected to reflect deep principles of Universal Grammar, and should at the very least not contradict these principles. It would therefore be very satisfying under these assumptions, if an analysis developed for more central constructions proved to extend without alteration to marginal phenomena. Such a situation could also be taken as providing further evidence in favour of that analysis, both on the general principle that a good scientific theory ought to extend to new instances of phenomena in its domain, and by the more specific line of reasoning just sketched. This is the pattern of argument put forward by Chomsky (1982), where he attempts to show that the marginal 'parasitic gap' construction follows directly from the basic principles of independently needed mechanisms of the theory of Government and Binding.

Clearly, one cannot maintain both views of marginality simultaneously, for together they provide insulation against every possible counterexample: if a construction cannot be handled by the theory, it must be marginal in the first sense, and if it can be, then it is marginal in the second sense. And there are problems about both views taken independently: if a construction is marginal in the sense that it contradicts principles of core grammar, as tough movement appears to do, then it presumably has the same logical status with respect to the theory as do ungrammatical structures, structures which violate other syntactic constraints, say. But that makes it puzzling that one type of structure violating principles of Universal Grammar can be learned, whereas another type of structure cannot: the obvious response that no positive evidence is forthcoming for one type of violation is not as easy to substantiate as one might think: see, for example, Brame 1983, who presents examples from real life of violations of many constraints. Such violations are encountered surprisingly often, often enough, at least, to make this response something which needs some arguing for.

Under the second view of marginality there is a different source of paradox: if a marginal construction actually falls under core grammar, what makes it marginal? Examples which simply obey grammatical principles straightforwardly surely ought not to display the speaker variation and uncertainty of judgement which singled out the construction as marginal in the first place. Under this latter conception of marginality, the marginality itself has to be explained by supplementary principles, like those which might be postulated to explain difficulty of processing, and so on: but these principles in turn need independent justification. Notice also that if such principles are available, they might also be involved in the first type of marginality: for example, tough-movement judgements for adults are on the whole fairly clear, once interference from superficially similar constructions has been factored out, and this might be taken as evidence that the construction should be part of core grammar. The difficulty for learners then might be explainable in terms of their possible use of heuristic strategies which work well for the most part, but which break down on 'tough' constructions. At a stage where a learner has only these strategies to go on, or where she/he places excessive reliance on them, things would look as if tough movement had not been mastered at all, whereas, grammatically speaking the competence might have been acquired, but is not fully being exploited. What happens when tough movement is finally 'acquired' is that the child simply drops or changes the unsatisfactory heuristic. If this type of analysis could be generally sustained, then both the marginality and the (eventual) learnability could be explained.

3. Prepositional relatives in GB theory

The analysis of the PR construction appears to present some difficulties for the framework of GB theory. Within that theory, the properties and interpretation of gaps or missing elements are determined by principles which also apply to overt elements: roughly speaking, missing or empty categories are treated just as if they were actually present, thus explaining their properties in a completely unmysterious way. The relevant notions of the theory of Government and Binding, as expounded in Chomsky (1981, 1982), are as follows:

(i) major lexical categories are governors; in particular, a preposition governs its object;
(ii) the governing category of an item is the 'smallest' NP or S in which it is governed;
(iii) the Theta Criterion: roughly, given ($XP_i \ldots t_t$), XP and t must have the same thematic role (agent, etc.) if they are coindexed.
(A) An anaphor (overt, like reflexives, or empty, like NP-traces) must be bound by an element in an argument position within its governing category.
(B) A pronominal (overt or empty) must not be so bound.
(C) An R-expression (a full lexical NP, or a WH-trace) must not be so bound.

The distributional facts argue for a structure like (22) for PRs. The empty category NP*d* is governed by the preposition *in*. This makes NP*c* its governing category. However, if (22) is an appropriate structure for these constructions, then the principles of the binding

(22)

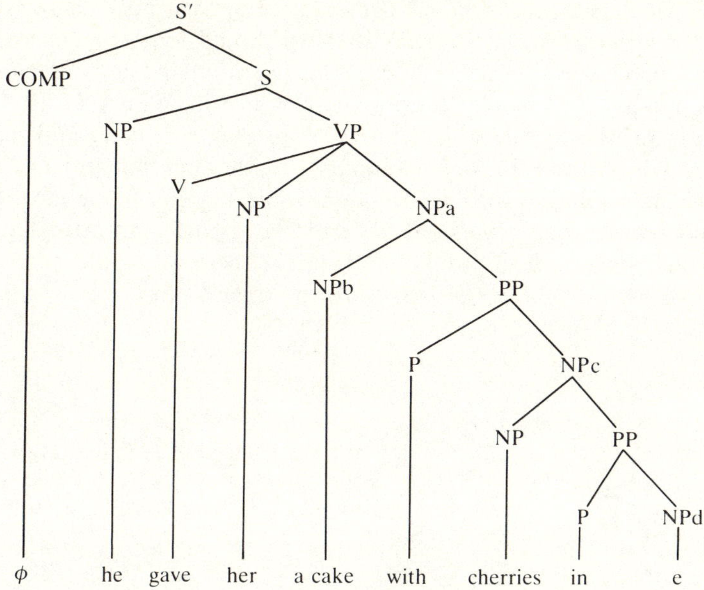

theory appear to rule out NP*d* as any of the realistically possible types of empty NP. PRO, which is both an anaphor and a pronoun, can logically speaking only be consistent with both of principles A and B simultaneously if they are not able to apply to it at all, i.e. if it has no governing category. PRO is thus limited to positions where it is not governed, like the subject position of an infinitival sentence. But NP*d* in (22) is clearly a governed position, so it cannot be PRO. An alternative analysis of NP*d* as an NP-trace, a non-pronominal empty anaphor, is not possible without violation of principle A, for NP*d* is free in NP*c*, its governing category. If NP*a* is somehow taken to be the governing category, then NP*d* is bound correctly, by NP*b*, but now we have a violation of the Theta Criterion: the NP movement it would be necessary to postulate has taken place to a position that presumably already has an independent theta role, since it is subcategorized for by the verb. The empty NP*d* cannot be regarded as a parasitic gap, for in these sentences there is no licensing trace for it to be parasitic upon, and in the case of sentences like (15), where there is a trace, this potential host is in the wrong configuration: characteristically, and crucially, for Chomsky's analysis of them, parasitic gaps must not be *c*-commanded by their host. The analogy with relative clauses suggests that we should look for an analysis involving wh-movement from NP*d* position, the only remaining possibility that would be consistent with principles A–C. But wh-movement only takes place into Comp, and there is no evidence of any wh-phrase in the only Comp in (22), nor does that sentence have the interpretation such a derivation would suggest. In the case of the full relative-clause versions, where there is a Comp available, we would have a second difficulty too, for there we would appear to have two wh-phrases moving into the same Comp.

(23)

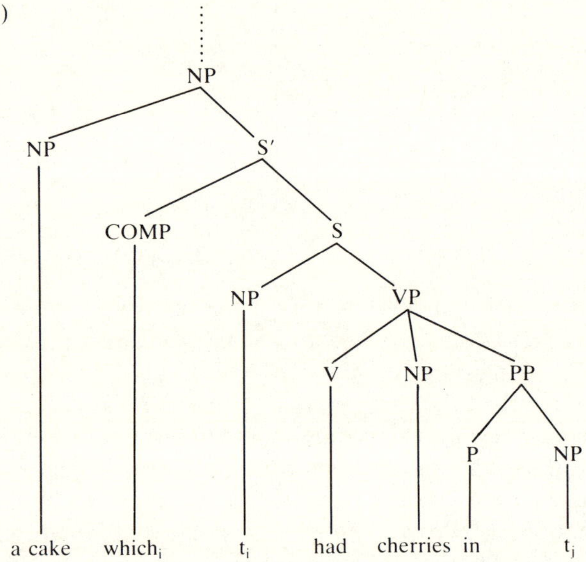

The obvious way out of these difficulties (unless it is simply maintained that the PR construction is marginal in the first of the two senses discussed earlier) is to pursue the possibility of a hidden Comp position in PP. Then an analysis involving wh-movement, or possibly movement of an 'empty operator', as in Chomsky (1982: 30-1) can be made, consistent with the principles of the Binding theory, and providing, apparently, an appropriate semantic or logical form. Notice that there are at least two possible ways of approaching an analysis which would give the necessary structure. An analysis could be attempted on which prepositions can govern an S′, in which wh-movement can take place, with the wh-phrase subsequently deleted. This type of analysis has in fact been offered by Jayaseelan (1983) for certain temporal PPs which are taken to contain a gap. Whatever the merits of the analysis for that range of phenomena, it is not one which is particularly plausible here, for it would involve ascribing S′ status to the complement of *with*(*out*) for which there is absolutely no distributional evidence.

(24)

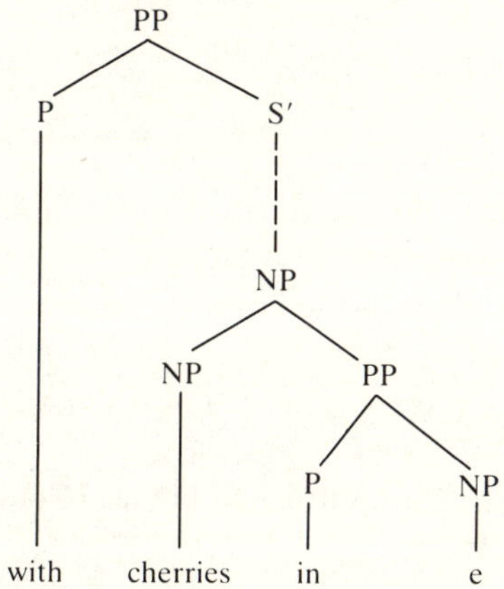

The mechanisms needed to enable the . . . *cherries in* sequence to be regarded as some form of S′ would have to be so powerful as to allow virtually anything to be analysed as S′. This is not a consequence which anybody's theory would regard as desirable, presumably, since the empirical content of such analyses would evaporate.

A second type of analysis would locate the Comp as a sister to PP under PP′, giving a structure like (25).

Such a proposal has been advanced for English and other languages by van Riemsdijk (1978). He argues that all PPs (PP′s, that is) contain a Comp to which wh-movement can take place, as shown in (25), and that wh-movement from inside PP always takes place through this Comp. Against the obvious objection that there is never either an overt Comp or an overt wh-phrase in this position, van Riemsdijk has two replies. He appeals to the principles in Chomsky (1973) for the interpretation of wh-constructions (i.e. for translation into 'logical form'), which he says rule out automatically any overt

(25)

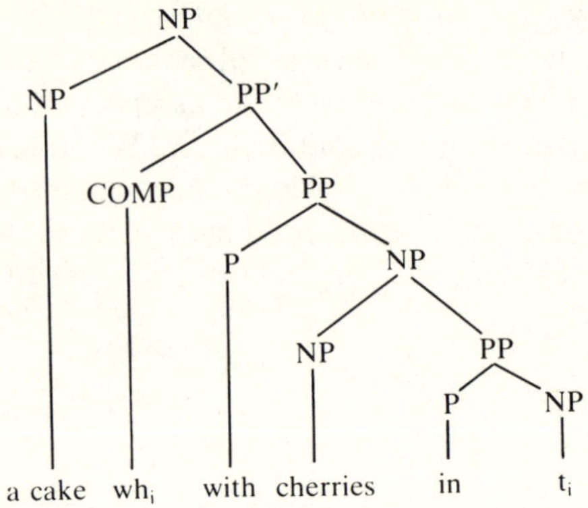

wh-phrases in this position. He claims that 'no new machinery is needed to account for the fact that wh-phrases may not occur in the P‴ Comp in surface structure' (1978: 230). These principles are, in outline:

(26*a*) in [Comp [wh-phrase] +WH] . . . t . . . bind t with wh-phrase.

(*b*) assign a wh-phrase not in Comp to some higher [Comp . . . +WH] and interpret as in (*a*).

(*b*) is there to account for multiple wh-cases, some of which must be left in place. Any structure containing a wh-phrase which does not get interpreted via (*a*) and (*b*) will be filtered out. However, while these principles, along with other conventions, will account satisfactorily for the cases van Riemsdijk discusses, and all cases of wh-phrases stranded in intermediate Comps, there are other cases which he does not discuss which are not handled correctly by the principles. On his theory, for example, a sentence like (27*a*) would have a D-structure as in (27*b*):

(27*a*) Who did you talk to?

(*b*) [S′ [Comp . . . +WH] you did talk [PP′ [Comp . . . +WH] to who]].

The correct derivation involves the application of wh-movement successively into both Comps. If only one wh-movement takes place, being optional, the result is correctly filtered out, since the wh-phrase is in an intermediate Comp. However, this Comp is only 'intermediate' if the topmost Comp is also +WH: if it is not—and nothing in the theory guarantees this—the principles will accept a structure like:

(28) *you talked who to

and assign it, by (26*a*), a logical form like:

(29) you talked [for which *x* to *x*].

There is nothing in van Riemsdijk's framework to rule out a surface structure like (28), or a logical form like (29): indeed, his own analysis of 'sluicing' below requires that both should, with different verbs, be legitimate. Thus it is not true that the non-existence of wh-phrases in Comps in PPs follows from the theory with 'no new machinery'.

The second reply concerns 'sluicing', originally discussed by Ross (1969). Van Riemsdijk argues that this construction, though outside the domain of sentence grammar proper, provides convincing direct evidence of overt wh-movement in PPs. Sluicing is illustrated by the following examples:

(30*a*) John bought a book, but I don't know which one.
(*b*) (i) John bought a book. (ii) Which one?

What appears to be an ordinary wh-phrase can either appear as a sentence fragment in a response to an appropriate preceding sentence, or as a complement to some indirect question taking a verb. Ross analyses sluicing as due to a syntactic deletion rule operating on a full sentence form, but van Riemsdijk argues that in both cases the wh-phrases are base-generated as such, either independently, or as complements. On his analysis, the fragments are not fragments or reduced sentences of any sort, but ordinary phrasal categories with a +WH feature on them, or in the case of PP', on their Comp. The indirect question verbs, he says, are simply subcategorized to take any +WH complement and so the presence of NP, AdjP, AdvP, AdvP, and PP′ complements when they are +WH, but not otherwise, is provided for automatically:

(31*a*) John bought a book, but I'm not sure [NP which one].
(*b*) John bought a book, but I'm not sure [PP′ where from].
(*c*) John bought a book, but I'm not sure [PP′ from where].
(*d*) John finished the race, but I'm not sure [AdvP how quickly].
(*e*) John ran a long way, but I don't know [AdjP how far].

Sentences like (31*b*) demonstrate the existence of overt wh-movement into PP′ Comp and have the structure shown in (32).

(32)

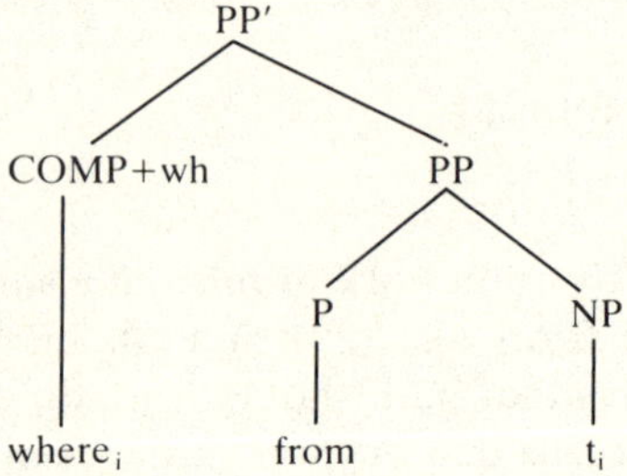

In the case of sentences like (31*c*) the +WH feature is on the PP′ directly, not in Comp, and so no wh-movement takes place.

While this analysis would provide some supporting evidence for a Comp and for wh-movement in PP if it could be sustained, unfortunately it cannot be. Van Riemsdijk's assumption that the sluiced items in (31) are base-generated as ordinary wh-phrases is fairly directly contradicted by their behaviour under conjunction, where any two types of phrase can be conjoined:

(33*a*) John bought a book, but I don't know [NP which one] or [PP what for].

(*b*) Bill raced this morning, but I don't know [AdvP how quickly], [AdjP how far], or [PP where to].

(*c*) He bought a stereo and insists on telling everybody [PP how much for], [NP which make], and [S′ where he got it from].

As the last example indicates, ordinary indirect-question constituents will also happily conjoin with them.

Secondly, there are some examples involving *why*, where the sluiced elements do not seem to form a phrasal constituent, but where these elements will still conjoin with the more normal sort:

(34*a*) I know he wants to leave quickly, but I don't understand for what reason or why tomorrow.

(*b*) He wanted to study something abstruse, but what for, why linguistics, and why at MIT I just don't know.

A more plausible analysis, which would preserve the merits of van Riemsdijk's but overcome these two difficulties, would be to treat the sluiced elements as indeed a reduced S′ indirect-question constituent, whose internal construction is not subject to sentence grammar, involving as it does substantial interpretation of empty elements under discourse control. (See, for example, Levin 1982, who takes an approach partly along these lines, within the framework of Lexical Functional Grammar). On this treatment it would be expected that, like other indirect questions, they can involve wh-movement to an S′ Comp position. This explains their appearance inside sentences as complements of *know* etc., accounts straightforwardly for their otherwise mysterious behaviour under conjunction, since they are now all instances of S′, and treats examples like (31*b*) and (*c*) as differing only in that in (*c*) the entire PP has been fronted rather than just the wh-phrase: an option which of course it would be impossible to prevent, given that it is now just a standard case of wh-movement. Some aspect of the pragmatic analysis must explain why some elements not in Comp cannot be empty (e.g. *from* in (*31b*)), but this will be needed on anybody's analysis for examples like (34). As far as sentence grammar is concerned, then, nothing else needs to be said about the purely syntactic properties of the sluicing construction, and the non-syntactic properties of examples like (30*a*) will be explained by whatever proves to be necessary (again, necessary on anyone's analysis) to explain exchanges like (30*b*).

This analysis of sluicing solves the problems raised by van Riemsdijk's, but unfortunately it also removes any motivation for a Comp or wh-movement in PP. Any wh-movement now takes place to S′ Comp, and there is no evidence left for Comps elsewhere. We must conclude, if this possibility is no longer available to us, that there is no well-motivated analysis within GB theory which does not conflict with at least some of the basic principles of that theory, in its current incarnation. As a marginal construction, then, the PR construction must be treated as analogous to tough movement rather than to parasitic gaps, with the resulting problems over learnability left to be faced. For the case of PRs, these problems might even be worse: there is no evidence that the construction is difficult to learn, but that is perhaps just because nobody has looked yet.

4. Prepositional relatives and GPSG

Within the framework of GPSG the PR construction can be described easily enough. While it would be stretching a point to say that all the properties of the PR construction followed directly from other things in the GPSG theory (as Chomsky claims for the GB analysis of parasitic gaps), they are at least not grossly inconsistent with any of its basic principles.

Let us assume that the instances of the construction that are purely prepositional are, though not sentential, nevertheless similar to relative clauses in that they are specified as being + R. The default value for R is −, and all other PPs will have this value. *With* and *without* will be the only prepositions which are + R. The full relative *have* version of the construction, however, is dominated by a sentential category which also is + R. Let us capture the properties of this constructions via a subcategorization feature which I will write as + with (rather than the usual unmemorable rule identifying number); hinting at the semantic identity between these senses of *have* and *with*. The feature + with will be associated with main verb *have* as it appears in the full relative or sentential versions. We need in the grammar the following Immediate Domination rules:

(35*a*) NP → NP, X2[+R, −N]
(*b*) PP[+R] → H, NP/NP
(*c*) VP → H[+with], NP, PP/NP

Rule (*a*) generalizes over PR and other relative postnominal modifiers. Subject to the problem mentioned below, they will get treated like any other such modifier, thus accounting for the extraposition facts. (If the clefted versions arise via a metarule operating on a PR introduced directly into VP, such a VP rule or metarule will also be necessary.) Rule (*b*) regards a PR as not itself a slashed category, but one which introduces a slashed category. Notice that the dependency here is potentially unbounded: it is not clear how to ensure that we can rule out examples like (20) while allowing still examples like (21). Here we err on the side of generosity. Notice that the Head Feature Convention will ensure that the only prepositions that can occur in the trees licensed by (35*b*) will be *with* and *without*. Rule (*c*) accounts for the full relative and sentential versions with *have*. Examples of the structures assigned by these rules are given in (36) (note that I am assuming the Slash Termination Metarule of Gazdar and Pullum (1982) but display traces for clarity).

I assume that the resumptive pronoun versions are treated as suggested in Gazdar (1981: 162) and that this type of treatment can

(36a)

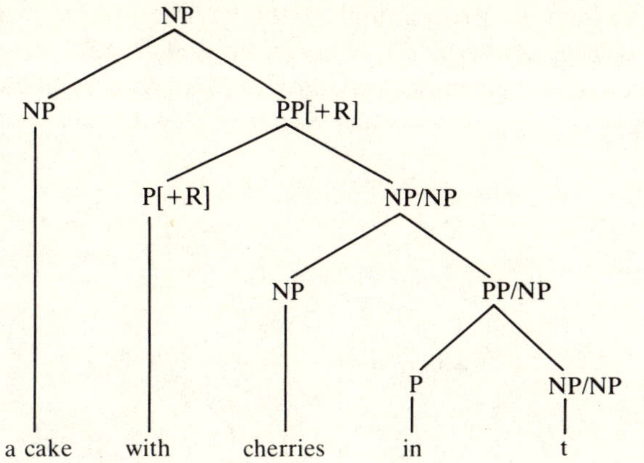
NP
NP
PP[+R]
P[+R]
NP/NP
NP
PP/NP
P
NP/NP
a cake
with
cherries
in
t

(36b)

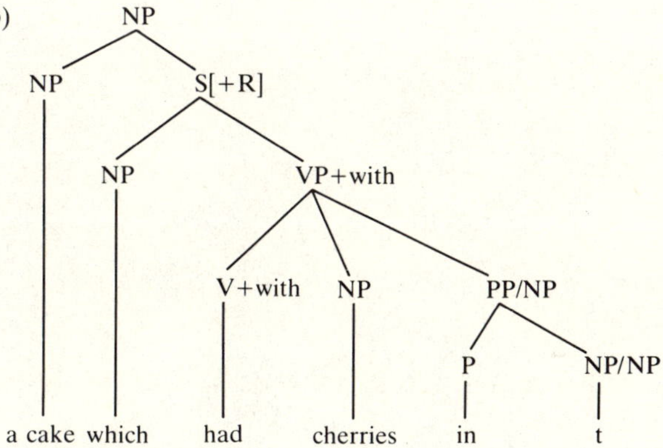
NP
NP
S[+R]
NP
VP+with
V+with
NP
PP/NP
P
NP/NP
a cake
which
had
cherries
in
t

(36c)

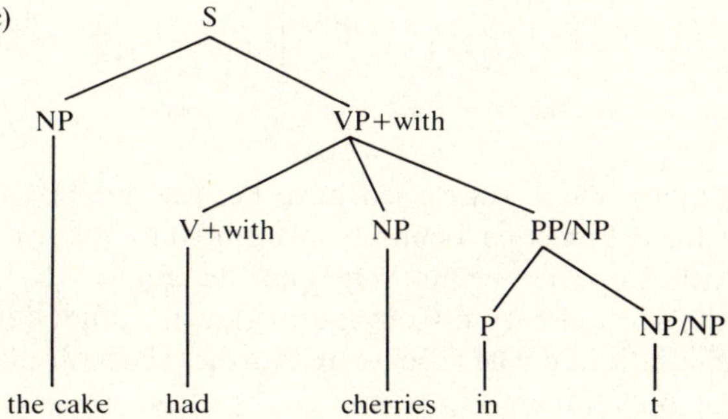
S
NP
VP+with
V+with
NP
PP/NP
P
NP/NP
the cake
had
cherries
in
t

be extended to include 'pronominal epithets'. These rules interact fairly straightforwardly with the other rules and feature instantiation principles of the grammar, giving rise to structures like (37).

(37a)

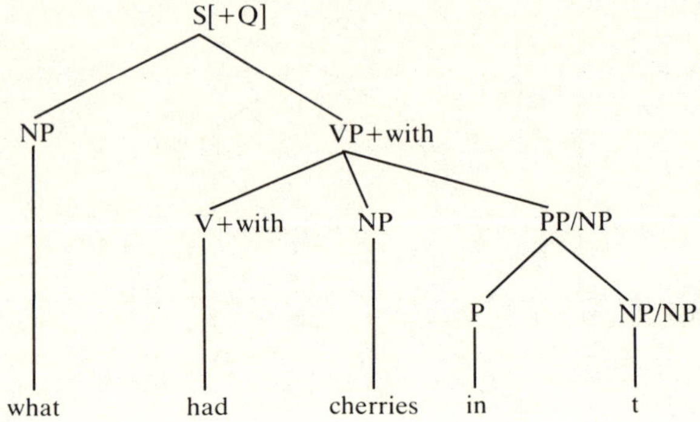

(37b)

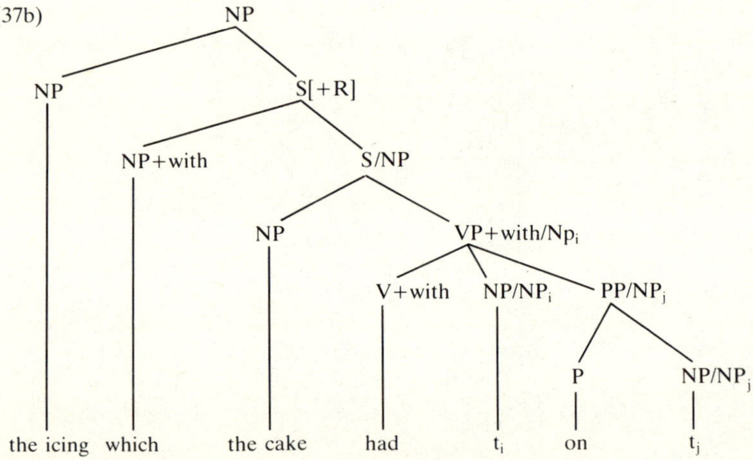

Although two of the three rules used have been stipulated, their general form is for the most part entirely unsurprising. The features +R and +with appear on mothers and daughters in strict obedience to the Head Feature Convention (Gazdar and Pullum 1982). The instantiation of rule (35*c*) with a further slash, displayed in (37*b*), is the only other one permitted by the Foot Feature

Principle (Gazdar and Pullum 1982). Although I have not given the semantic translation parts of the rules in (35), there would appear to be no obvious difficulties in formulating them. From the point of view of a language learner equipped with an innate set of GPSG prejudices about the possible forms of grammar, learning the PR construction is a matter of associating with a particular small set of lexical items an idiosyncratic feature to the effect that they can introduce a version of a regular complement which has a /NP instead of a full constituent. All the other properties of the construction seem to follow automatically.

5. Conclusion

Marginality, as we might expect, turns out to be a highly theory-dependent notion. While the prepositional relative construction is clearly a marginal one in the man-in-the-street sense, it is marginal in different ways when considered from the point of view of a particular syntactic theory. From the standpoint of GB theory (at least of the version considered here), PRs seem to be more akin to problematic constructions like tough movement, being apparently a straightforward counterexample to central principles of the theory. If so, they might be predicted to present similar difficulties of acquisition. From the point of view of GPSG, however, PRs are a minor, lexically conditioned variation on an already existing mechanism, and should present very little difficulty to the learner once the appropriate lexical items have been singled out. In this respect, PRs have more the status of parasitic gaps for GB.

9

The Status of Exclamative Particles in Modern Spoken French

Andrew Radford

1. Introduction

Ever since the pioneering work of Rosenbaum (1967) and Bresnan (1970, 1972), linguists have been fascinated by the syntax of the special kind of particles typically used to introduce complement clauses such as those bracketed below:

(1*a*) I think [*that* you are wrong].
 (*b*) We're anxious [*for* you to win].
 (*c*) I wonder [*whether* he'll manage it].
 (*d*) I doubt [*if* he really understands her].

In more recent work, particles such as those italicized in (1) have become known as *complementizers* (because they generally serve to introduce complement clauses). A second class of words whose syntax has been the focus of a great deal of attention in recent work (cf. e.g. Chomsky 1973, Bresnan 1976, Chomsky 1980, Koopman 1984, and Chomsky 1986) are *wh-words*, so called because in English most of them begin with *wh-*; some of these are illustrated in (2) below:

(2*a*) I don't know [*who* he is after].
 (*b*) I wonder [*what* she is doing].
 (*c*) I don't know [*which* she will choose].

A similar distinction between complementizers and wh-words has played a central role in discussions of French syntax—for example, in Kayne's (1976) analysis of relative clauses, and Obenauer's (1976) analysis of interrogative clauses. For those not familiar with these works, we can illustrate the distinction in relation to the following pair of sentences:

(3*a*) Je ne savais pas *que/si* tu allais partir.
'I didn't know that/if you were going to leave.'

(*b*) Je ne savais pas *où/quand/pourquoi/comment* tu allais partir.
'I didn't know where/when/why/how you were going to leave.'

In (3*a*) we might argue that *que* and *si* are simply invariable 'grammatical particles' which play no syntactic or thematic role within the proposition they introduce (e.g. they never function as an adjunct, or an Agent), but simply serve to mark a complement clause as interrogative or non-interrogative; not surprisingly, therefore, they are omitted in the corresponding main-clause declarative or interrogative sentence: cf.

(4*a*) Tu vas partir (declarative).
'You are going to leave.'

(*b*) Tu vas partir?/Vas-tu partir? (interrogative)
'Are you going to leave?'

By contrast, wh-words like *qui* 'who', *quoi* 'what', *quand* 'when', *comment* 'how', *où* 'where', and *pourquoi* 'why' do indeed play an obvious syntactic or thematic role within the sentences they introduce: for example, *où* 'where' in (3*b*) functions as a Goal complement of *partir* 'leave'—i.e. it indicates ignorance about the destination of the addressee. Given that wh-words play an essential syntactic/thematic role within propositions, they (unlike complementizers) *must* appear in the corresponding main-clause structures: cf. the contrast between (4) above and (5) below:

(5) *Où/quand/pourquoi/comment* vas-tu partir?
'Where/when/why/how are you going to leave?'

Although there has been extensive discussion about whether particular relative or interrogative words (especially relative and interrogative *que* 'that/what?') are best analysed as complementizers or wh-words, comparatively little attention had been focused on the status of exclamative particles in French until the publication of Milner 1978 and Gérard 1980. Both of these authors agree that the distinction between *complementizer* and *wh-word* is fundamental to an understanding of the syntax of exclamatives in French, and that both types of exclamative particle are found in Modern French. For example, both studies agree that exclamative *si* 'if' found in sentences such as:

(6*a*) *Si* elle est belle!
'Is she pretty!'
(*b*) Regarde *si* c'est pas mignon.
'Look how cute it is.'

is a complementizer. Likewise, both studies agree that the italicized expressions in literary examples such as (7) below are wh-words:

(7*a*) *Que* de trésors on perd dans sa jeunesse! (Musset)
'How many treasures one loses in one's youth.'
(*b*) *Combien* souvent j'eus à l'entendre répéter! (Gide)
'How often I heard it repeated!'
(*c*) De *quel* prestige s'auréolait pour moi le nom de Gauthier! (Gide)
'What prestige the name of Gauthier was gilded with for me!'

and both authors support their analyses with a substantial array of empirical arguments.

Where there is disagreement between Milner and Gérard, however, is over the question of how to analyse the italicized expressions in 'standard' exclamatives such as:

(8*a*) *Qu*'elle est bavarde!
'How talkative she is!'
(*b*) *Comme* il s'habille mal!
'How badly he dresses!'

and how to analyse their counterparts in colloquial exclamatives such as:

(9*a*) *Ce qu*'elle a fait peu de bruit!
'How little noise she made!'
(*b*) *Qu'est-ce qu*'on a rigolé, toi et moi!
'What a good giggle we had, you and me!'
(*c*) *Comment qu*'elle roule bien, cette voiture!
'How well it runs, that car!'

Milner maintains that exclamative *que* 'that/what', *comme* 'how', and *ce que* 'it that' are all wh-expressions; and he implies a similar status for *qu'est-ce que* 'what-is-it that' by commenting (1978: 266 n. 1) that it 'fait couple avec *que*' (i.e. it behaves like *que*). He does not, however, comment on the status of exclamative *comment que* 'how that'. Gérard, on the other hand, proposes a diametrically opposed analysis—namely that, in Modern French, exclamative *que/comme/ce que/qu'est-ce que/comment que* have all come to function as complementizer expressions. She further maintains that an interesting historical change has been taking place in twentieth-century French whereby complementizer-exclamatives have been gaining ground at the expense of wh-exclamatives, to the extent that the former have now completely ousted the latter in colloquial speech. More precisely, Gérard argues that whereas Classical (seventeenth-century) French had only three simple exclamative complementizers (*si* 'if', *comme* 'how', and *que* 'that'), Modern French has seen the creation of three new *compound* complementizers, namely *ce que* 'it that', *qu'est-ce que* 'what-is-it that', and *comment que* 'how that'. Moreover, she maintains, the three exclamative wh-words of Classical French (*combien* 'how much', *quel* 'what', and *que* 'what' in its so-called partitive use in sentences such as (7) above) have now fallen out of use in popular French (surviving only in the literary language), and instead have been replaced by the newly created compound complementizers *ce que/qu'est-ce que/comment que*. Thus, in place of the Classical French wh-exclamatives illustrated in the (*a*) examples below, we find the newer complementizer-exclamatives illustrated in the corresponding (*b*) examples (we use the abbreviation *wh* for 'wh-exclamative', and *comp* for 'complementizer exclamative'):

(10*a*) *Combien* mignon c'est! (wh)
'How cute it is!'
(*b*) *Comment que* c'est mignon! (comp)
'How cute it is!'

(11*a*) *Quelle* jolie voiture il a achetée! (wh)
'What a nice car he (has) bought!'
(*b*) *Qu'est-ce qu*'il a acheté une jolie voiture! (comp)
'What a nice car he (has) bought!'

(12*a*) *Que* d'argent il dépense pour les filles! (wh)
'What a lot of money he spends on girls!'
(*b*) *Ce qu*'il dépense comme fric pour les nanas! (Comp)
'What a lot of bread he spends on chicks!'

If this claim is substantiated, then it would amount to a major historical restructuring of the syntax of exclamative sentences in

French. Indeed, we might perhaps see a parallel with the tendency in popular French to replace wh-relatives by complementizer relatives, so that in place of the standard genitive wh-pronoun *dont* 'whose' in relative clauses like (13*a*) below, we find a popular construction involving the use of the complementizer *que* 'that', as in (13*b*):

(13*a*) la maison *dont* j'habite le premier étage
'the house which I live on the first floor of'
(*b*) la maison *que* j'en habite le premier étage
'the house that I live on the first floor of'

If so, then the restructuring of exclamatives could be seen as part of a wider historical change affecting a range of wh-constructions.

Fascinating though Gérard's hypothesis is, it does of course depend crucially on the assumption that the italicized expressions in examples like (8) and (9) above are in fact complementizers. But, as we have already seen, this is by no means an uncontroversial assumption—it is, for example, explicitly rejected by Milner for *que* 'that/what', *comme* 'how', and *ce que* 'it that', and implicitly for *qu'est-ce que* 'what-is-it that'. The obvious question that arises therefore is: 'In Modern French exclamatives, are *que/comme/ce que/qu'est-ce que/comment que* wh-expressions or complementizers—and how can we tell?' This is the central question which I shall address myself to in this paper. It seems to me that a sensible way to go about answering the question is to draw up a list of criteria which characterize the differences between complementizers on the one hand and wh-expressions on the other in relatively clear cases independent of exclamative structures, and then subsequently to attempt to apply these criteria to exclamative sentences like (8) and (9) to determine the status of the italicized expressions in the light of these criteria. In the next section, we propose just such a set of criteria; our discussion is somewhat simplified for the sake of clarity of exposition. I should perhaps emphasize that the criteria given there are formulated specifically in relation to French; some of them generalize to other languages, while others are more language-specific.

2. Criteria differentiating complementizers from wh-expressions

The first criterion I shall propose is morphological in nature: that is, complementizers tend to be invariable monomorphemic particles which do not inflect for number, person, gender, or case; whereas wh-expressions tend to share the morphemic properties of categories they belong to (for example, a wh-NP has typical nominal properties), and thus *may* be polymorphemic in nature, and may be variable in form. Given this criterion, it seems clear that interrogative *lequel* 'which one?' in French cannot be a complementizer but must be a wh-pronoun, since it has the pronominal property of inflecting for number and gender, as we see from (14) below:

(14) *Lequel/Laquelle/Lesquels/Lesquelles* va-t-il acheter?
'Which-one(s) Masc. Sg/Fem Sg/Masc Pl/Fem Pl will he buy?'

But by contrast, interrogative *si* 'if' in sentences such as:

(15) Je me demande *si* elle va réussir.
'I wonder if she will succeed.'

is an invariable monomorphemic particle, and hence (by this criterion at least) a plausible candidate for complementizer status.[1]

Now let us turn to a number of *syntactic* criteria. Firstly, wh-phrases play a grammatical function (e.g. subject, complement, adjunct, etc.) and/or thematic role (e.g. Agent, Patient, Goal, etc.) internally within the proposition they introduce, whereas complementizers do not: thus, in:

(16) Je me demande [*qui* Jean va sortir].
'I wonder who John's going to take out.'

the wh-pronoun *qui* 'who' has the grammatical function of direct object of the verb *sortir* 'take out', and the thematic function of a

[1] This criterion is not without posing problems, either for French, or more generally. For example, complementizers may exhibit some degree of morphophonemic variation: thus, the declarative complementizer *que* in French has the allomorph (i.e. variant form) *qui* in structures like:

(i) Laquelle crois-tu *qui* est partie?
'Which one do you think has left?'

Potentially even more problematic is the fact that Irish has complementizers which appear to inflect for tense and negativity, according to McCloskey 1979. And the complementizer *dat* in Flemish seems to inflect for number, person, and gender, according to Haegeman 1983. However, it would be unwise to jump to hasty conclusions about data from other languages, since there are numerous other possibilities which might be explored—e.g. the question of whether such complementizers are in fact contracted sequences of a complementizer plus a clitic pronoun.

Patient argument of the same verb. By contrast, the interrogative complementizer *si* 'if' in:

(17) Je me demande [*si* Jean va sortir Marie].
'I wonder if John's going to take Mary out.'

has no such internal grammatical or thematic function within the *sortir* proposition: e.g. it is not a subject, complement, or adjunct of *sortir*, nor an Agent, Patient, or Goal argument of *sortir*. On the contrary, *si* 'if' is a particle which stands outside the proposition itself, and serves to mark the embedded proposition as being interrogative. It has no grammatical or thematic function *internally within* the proposition itself.

Two further criteria follow from the fact that wh-phrases have a grammatical role to play within the clauses they introduce, but complementizers do not. Firstly, clauses introduced by wh-phrases typically exhibit a 'gap' (in the sense of Chomsky 1977) internally within the clause, whereas those introduced by complementizers do not. We can illustrate this 'gap' phenomenon in relation to our earlier examples (16) and (17) above. In (16), precisely because the wh-pronoun *qui* 'who' functions as the direct object of *sortir* 'take out', it is not possible to put some other nominal expression like *Marie* in the normal postverbal position associated with direct objects—hence the ungrammaticality of (18) below (where the prefixed asterisk serves to indicate that the sentence is ungrammatical):

(18) *Je ne sais pas *qui* Jean va sortir *Marie*.
'*I don't know who John's going to take Mary out.'

One way of describing this phenomenon is to say that there is a 'gap' in the postverbal object position in (16), so that this position must obligatorily be left empty (how to make the term 'gap' technically more precise is not a question which need concern us here). By contrast, clauses introduced by complementizers contain no such 'gaps', so that although the presence of the wh-pronoun *qui* 'who' in (18) excludes the presence of a direct object such as *Marie*, the presence of the complementizer *si* 'if' in (17) does not.

A second consequence of the fact that wh-phrases play a grammatical or thematic role within the clauses they introduce is the fact that we find *co-occurrence restrictions* (in the sense of sub-categorization or selection restrictions) holding between wh-expressions and elements in the clauses they introduce, but not between complementizers and constituents in the clauses they introduce. So, for example, a clause such as:

(19) Il allait se passer quelque chose d'étrange.
'There was going to happen something strange.'

can freely co-occur with (i.e. be introduced by) either of the finite clause complementizers *que* 'that' and *si* 'if': cf.

(20) Je ne savais pas *qu*'il/*s*'il allait se passer quelque chose d'étrange.
'I didn't know that/if there was going to happen something strange.'

But by contrast, the clause in (19) can only be introduced by some wh-words, not others: cf.

(21) Je ne savais pas *quand*/**combien* il allait se passer quelque chose d'étrange.
'I didn't know when/*how much there was going to happen something strange.'

Hence, we find co-occurrence restrictions holding between wh-expressions and the clauses they introduce, but not between complementizers and the clauses they introduce.

A further characteristic which wh-phrases possess is that the syntactic relations which they bear to elements within the clauses containing them are subject to *island constraints* (in the sense of Ross 1967). One such condition in French is what we might call the Prepositional Island Constraint: informally, this can be regarded as specifying that:

(22) No constituent outside a prepositional phrase can be syntactically related to a constituent inside a prepositional phrase.

A constraint such as (22) would provide a principled account of the ungrammaticality of relative-clause structures such as (23) below:

(23) *le type *dont* j'ai parlé [*à la copine*]
'*the guy whose I spoke to girlfriend'

What's wrong with (23) is that the wh-pronoun *dont* 'of-whom' is a syntactic dependent of the noun *copine* 'girlfriend'; but *copine* forms part of the bracketed prepositional phrase, and *dont* is clearly positioned outside that prepositional phrase, so resulting in violation of the Prepositional Island Constraint (22). By contrast, since complementizers never function as syntactic dependents of any element within the proposition they introduce, they are not in principle subject to island constraints. Thus, in (non-standard) popular French, the wh-relative structure in (23) above would be replaced by the complementizer-relative in (24) below:

(24) le type *que* j'ai parlé [*à sa copine*]
'the guy that I spoke to his girlfriend'

In (24) there is no syntactic link between the complementizer *que* and the noun *copine*, and hence no violation of the Prepositional Island Constraint (22).

There are a number of other no less important syntactic differences between complementizers and wh-phrases. Thus, as Kayne (1972) notes, initial wh-phrases trigger Stylistic Inversion (i.e. postposing of a non-clitic subject), whereas complementizers do not: cf.

(25*a*) Je ne savais pas *combien de temps* allait rester **ton copain**.
'I didn't know how long your friend was going to stay.'
(*b*) *Je ne savais pas *si*/*qu'*allait rester **ton copain**.
'I didn't know if/that your friend was going to stay.'

Thus, the bold-printed subject **ton copain** 'your friend' can be postposed in (25*a*) but not (25*b*) because the subordinate clause in (25*a*) is introduced by the wh-phrase *combien de temps* 'how much time' in (25*a*), but by the complementizers *si* 'if' and *qu*(*e*) 'that' in (25*b*).

A parallel difference between complementizers and wh-words can be seen in respect of Subject Clitic Inversion. As Kayne (1972) has argued in detail, this is an entirely different phenomenon from Stylistic Inversion: for example, whereas Stylistic Inversion is found in main and subordinate clauses alike—cf.

(26) (Je me demande) quand est parti *ton père*(?)
'(I wonder) when did your father leave?'

Subject Clitic Inversion by contrast is found only in main clauses: cf.

(27*a*) Quand *est-il* parti?
'When did he leave?'

(*b*) *Je me demande quand *est-il* parti.
'I wonder when he left.'

What is of more direct concern to us here is the fact that the presence of a complementizer (but not a wh-expression) at the beginning of a clause blocks the application of Subject Clitic Inversion. One piece of evidence in support of this claim comes from popular French wh-question paradigms like:

(28*a*) Où il est allé?
'Where has he gone?'
(*b*) Où est-il allé?
'Where has he gone?'

(29*a*) Où qu'il est allé?
'Where has he gone?'
(*b*) *Où qu'est-il allé?
Where that has-he gone?

Here we see that Subject Clitic Inversion can optionally take place in (28) where the clause is introduced by the wh-word *où* 'where', but contains no complementizer. But inversion is blocked in (29), apparently by the presence of the complementizer *que* 'that'. The obvious conclusion to draw is thus that complementizers block Subject Clitic Inversion. A second piece of evidence which supports this conclusion comes from the fact that yes–no echo questions permit inversion if they are not introduced by a complementizer: cf.

(30) SPEAKER A: Est-elle partie?
'Has she left?'
SPEAKER B: *Est-elle* partie? Pourquoi tu veux savoir?
'Has she left? Why do you want to know?'

However, clitic inversion is blocked if the echo question is introduced by the interrogative complementizer *si* 'if': cf.

(31) SPEAKER A: Est-elle partie?
'Has she left?'
SPEAKER B: Si elle est/**est-elle* partie? Pourquoi tu veux savoir?
'Has she left? Why do you want to know?'

It thus seems clear that complementizers block Subject Clitic Inversion, whereas wh-expressions do not.

Another difference between wh-expressions and complementizers is that (as Gérard 1980 notes) wh-expressions can occur as independent phrases in elliptical constructions, whereas complementizers cannot (perhaps because their intrinsic function is to introduce clauses)—hence the contrast in:

(32*a*) Je me demande quand il va arriver, et *avec qui.*
'I wonder when he will arrive, and with whom.'
(*b*) *Je me demande quand il va arriver et même *si.*
'I wonder when he will arrive and even if.'

Moreover, a wh-phrase can occur clause-initially with a complementizer in popular French as in (33*a*) below, but not one complementizer with another as in (33*b*), or one wh-phrase with another as in (33*c*):

(33*a*) Je me demande *comment qu*'il va s'en sortir.
'I wonder how (that) he'll get out of it.'
(*b*) *Je me demande *si qu*'il va s'en sortir.
'I wonder if (that) he'll get out of it.'
(*c*) *Je me demande *comment quand* il va s'en sortir.
'I wonder how when he'll get out of it.'

In addition, a wh-word of an appropriate category (e.g. a wh-pronoun) may occur as the complement of another constituent, whereas a complementizer may not. For example, the relative pronoun *qui* 'who' may serve as the complement of a preposition like *à* 'to', whereas the relative complementizer *que* 'that' may not: cf.

(34) l'homme *à qui*/**à que* tu parlais
'the man to whom/*to that you spoke'

And conversely, a wh-word of an appropriate category may take a following phrasal complement, whereas a complementizer may not (since complementizers only have clausal complements). Thus, whereas the interrogative wh-pronoun *combien* 'how much/many?' can take a partitive prepositional phrase complement introduced by *de* 'of', the interrogative complementizer *si* cannot: cf.

(35) Je me demande *combien*/**si de bouquins* il achète.
'I wonder how many books/if (of) books he buys.'

A further criterion which we might propose for differentiating wh-expressions from complementizers is that wh-expressions can generally occur freely in any kind of clause, whereas complementizers are usually subject to heavy restrictions about the kind of clause they can occur in. For example, the interrogative wh-pronoun *combien* 'how much?' can occur freely in main clauses or complement clauses, as we see from:

(36*a*) *Combien* ça coûte?
'How much does it cost?'
(*b*) Je me demande *combien* ça coûte.
'I wonder how much it costs.'

By contrast, complementizers are typically subject to complex distributional restrictions concerning the types of clause(s) they can occur in. For example, declarative *que* 'that' in French can introduce complement clauses, but not main clauses: cf.

(37*a*) Je crois *que* Jean va gagner.
'I think that John will win.'
(*b*) **Que* Jean va gagner.
'That John will win.'

And the homophonous subjunctive *que* 'that' complementizer appears in main clauses only in archaic hortatives such as:

(38) *Que* Dieu ait pitié de son âme!
'May God take pity on his soul!'

Similar restrictions also hold for the interrogative complementizer *si* 'if'. Firstly, unlike wh-expressions, it cannot occur in infinitival clauses:

(39*a*) Je ne savais pas *quand* partir. (wh-expression)
'I didn't know when to leave.'
(*b*) *Je ne savais pas *si* partir.
'I didn't know if to leave.'

Moreover, unlike wh-expressions, the complementizer *si* 'if' is (except in the case of echo questions[2]) restricted to occurring in

[2] Echo questions in French can be introduced by the complementizer *si* 'if': cf.

(i) SPEAKER A: T'as une Porsche?
'Have you got a Porsche?'
SPEAKER B: *Si* j'ai une Porsche? Pourquoi?
'Have I got a Porsche? Why d'you ask?'

What may be going on here is that echo questions can be treated either as independent complement clauses, so that only indirect (and not direct) yes–no questions can be introduced by *si*: cf.

(40*a*) Je ne sais pas *si* elle va revenir.
'I don't know if she's coming back.'
(*b*) **Si* elle va revenir?
'If she will return?'

The exact conditions governing the use of complementizers like *que* 'that' and *si* 'if' are not at issue here: the main point that we want to establish is that complementizers tend to be subject to complex restrictions on their distribution, whereas wh-expressions are not usually subject to such conditions.

An additional syntactic property differentiating complementizers from wh-expressions is that complementizers are *bounded* in scope, in the sense that they are uniquely bound to (i.e. associated with) the immediate clause they introduce. By contrast, wh-expressions are *unbounded* in scope, in the sense that a wh-word may 'belong to' a clause other than that which it introduces. To see this, consider the contrast between:

(41*a*) Je ne me rappelle plus *si* elle pensait qu'il allait partir.
'I can't remember any more if she thought he was going to go.'
(*b*) Je ne me rappelle plus *où* elle pensait qu'il allait partir.
'I can't remember any more where she thought he was going to go.'

In (41*a*), the complementizer *si* clearly 'belongs to' (i.e. determines the nature of) the *pensait* 'thought' clause, and cannot be construed as connected in any way with the *partir* 'go' clause. But conversely, in (41*b*) the wh-word *où* 'where' is clearly a Goal complement of *partir* 'leave', so that the *où* is syntactically linked not to the immediate clause it introduces, but rather to the subordinate clause. In other words, the 'influence' of a complementizer is strictly

clauses, or as complement clauses (i.e. clauses which function as the complement of some predicate which is 'understood from the context', so that speaker B's utterance in (i) above would be analysable as an elliptical form of *Tu me demandes si j'ai une Porsche?* 'You're asking me if I've got a Porsche?'). If this is so, then it may be that when they are introduced by complementizers they are being analysed as 'elliptical' complement clauses. At any rate, the precise analysis of echo questions does not affect the general point made here, which is that complementizers are typically subject to complex restrictions on their use.

bounded, whereas a wh-word can be linked to some other element across a potentially *unbounded* domain.

Finally, we might point out that wh-phrases differ from complementizers in that only the former (and never the latter) can occur internally within clauses: thus, for example, the interrogative wh-word *où* 'where?' can occur clause-internally in popular questions such as:

(42) T'es allé *où*?
'Where did you go?'

Complementizers, by contrast, can only occur initially in their clause, never internally: cf.

(43) SPEAKER A: T'es allé au super?
'Did you go to the supermarket?'
SPEAKER B: *Si* je suis allé au super?
'Did I go (lit.: if I went) to the supermarket?'
*Je suis allé au super *si*?
'I went to the supermarket if?'

At this point, let's recapitulate briefly the criteria which we have suggested for differentiating between wh-expressions on the one hand and complementizers on the other. The relevant criteria are listed below:

(44*a*) Complementizers tend to be monomorphemic and uninflected, whereas wh-words may be polymorphemic and inflected;
(*b*) Wh-expressions play a grammatical or thematic role internally within the proposition they introduce, but complementizers do not;
(*c*) Wh-expressions leave a 'gap' within the clause containing them, complementizers do not;
(*d*) Wh-expressions show co-occurrence restrictions with elements within the clause containing them but complementizers do not;
(*e*) Wh-expressions are sensitive to island constraints but complementizers are not;
(*f*) Wh-expressions permit Stylistic Inversion, but complementizers do not;
(*g*) Complementizers block Subject Clitic Inversion, but wh-expressions do not;

(*h*) Wh-expressions can occur in elliptical phrasal constructions, complementizers cannot;

(*i*) A wh-expression can be combined with an adjacent complementizer but not with another wh-expression, nor one complementizer with another;

(*j*) Wh-expressions (of an appropriate type) can occur as complements of other categories, but complementizers cannot;

(*k*) A wh-word (of an appropriate category) may take a phrasal complement, a complementizer may not;

(*l*) Complementizers may be subject to distributional restrictions on the types of clause they can occur in, but wh-expressions are not so restricted;

(*m*) Complementizers are *bounded* in scope, whereas wh-expressions are potentially *unbounded* in scope;

(*n*) Wh-expressions may occur clause-internally, but complementizers never do.

Having established fourteen criteria for differentiating wh-expressions from complementizers, we now turn in subsequent sections to apply each of these criteria to the five exclamative expressions that we are interested in here—namely *comme* 'how', *que* 'that/what', *comment que* 'how that', *ce que* 'it that', and *qu'est-ce que* 'what-is-it that'.

3. The status of exclamative *comme*

We begin by distinguishing two different exclamative uses of *comme* 'how'. The first of these is as a manner adverb, and is illustrated by sentences such as the following (from Milner 1978: 266):

(45*a*) Comme tu y vas!
'How you go at it!'

(*b*) Comme tu me traites!
'How you treat me!'

In this manner use, there seems little doubt that *comme* is in fact a wh-word (more precisely, a wh-adverb of manner). The decisive factor here is that (as Milner notes) verbs like *y aller* (in the idiomatic sense of 'go at it') and *traiter* 'treat' (in the sense of 'behave towards') cannot be used without a manner complement: cf.

(46*a*) *Tu y vas. (* in idiomatic sense)
'You go at it.'
(*b*) *Tu me traites. (* in behaviour sense)
'You treat me.'

Given that (in the appropriate senses) *y aller* 'go at it' and *traiter* 'treat' are subcategorized as taking an obligatory manner complement, it is clear that *comme* in (45) must function as a manner complement, and hence that *comme* must be a wh-adverb of manner (by criterion (44*b*)). I take this to be an uncontroversial conclusion—and it is one which will be presupposed in subsequent discussion. What is more problematic is the status of non-manner uses of *comme* 'how' in sentences like:

(47*a*) Comme il est maso, ton pote!
'How crazy he is, your mate!'
(*b*) Comme elle roule lentement, cette bagnole!
'How slowly it goes, this old banger.'

In these non-manner uses, is *comme* an exclamative complementizer (as Gérard claims), or is it a wh-word (as Milner claims)? To answer this question, we shall look at how non-manner *comme* behaves with respect to our fourteen criteria for differentiating complementizers from wh-words given in (44) above.

Our morphological criterion (44*a*) proves fruitless here: for although *comme* is monomorphemic and uninflected, the same is true not only of complementizers, but also of many other categories—for example, many adverbs (e.g. *bien* 'well', *mal* 'badly', *vite* 'quickly', *tard* 'late', etc.), and quantifiers (e.g. *très* 'very', *peu* 'little', *trop* 'too', *assez* 'fairly', etc.). Criterion (44*b*) poses the question of whether or not *comme* 'how' plays a grammatical or thematic role within the proposition it introduces. Gérard implicitly claims that it does not, whereas Milner by contrast argues that *comme* in sentences like (47) functions as a quantifier: more precisely, *comme* quantifies the adjective *maso* 'crazy' in (47*a*), and the adverb *lentement* 'slowly' in (47*b*). Under Milner's quantifier analysis, *comme* in (47) would have essentially the same grammatical function as the italicized quantifiers in (48) below:

(48*a*) Il est *très/assez/extrêmement/particulièrement* maso.
'He is very/fairly/extremely/particularly crazy.'

(*b*) Elle roule *très/assez/extrêmement/particulièrement* lentement.
'It runs very/fairly/extremely/particularly slowly.'

The only difference between (47) and (48) under Milner's analysis would be in the position of the quantifier: in (47), *comme* 'how' (being a wh-word in Milner's analysis) is positioned clause-initially, like other wh-expressions; whereas in (48) the quantifiers are positioned immediately to the left of the head adjective or adverb that they modify. Looked at in this light, the wh-quantifier analysis might seem to have some initial plausibility.

However, there are a number of reasons for doubting the viability of the wh-quantifier analysis. To see why, it is instructive to compare *comme* with the wh-exclamative quantifier *combien* 'how (much)', whose use can be illustrated by the following examples from Milner 1978: 272:

(49*a*) *Combien heureux* j'aurais été si vous étiez venu!
'How happy I would have been if you had come.'
(*b*) *Combien* j'aurais été *heureux* si vous étiez venu!
'How I would have been happy if you had come.'

(50*a*) *Combien souvent* j'eus à l'entendre répéter!
'How often I heard it repeated!'
(*b*) *Combien* j'eus à l'entendre répéter *souvent*!
'How I heard it repeated often!'

Now if (as seems beyond dispute, and as is agreed by Milner and Gérard) *combien* functions as a quantifier in the (*a*) examples above (whatever its status in the (*b*) examples might be), then this suggests that a typical wh-quantifier behaves just like its non-wh counterparts italicized in (48) above in being able to be positioned immediately to the left of the head adjective or adverb which it modifies. But this is not at all the case with *comme* 'how', since this cannot be positioned immediately adjacent to the adjective or adverb which it allegedly quantifies: cf.

(51*a*) **Comme maso* il est, ton pote!
'How crazy he is, your mate.'
(*b*) **Comme lentement* elle roule, cette bagnole!
'How slowly it runs, this old banger.'

Thus, a wh-quantifier analysis for *comme* seems problematic, to say the least.

Moreover, its plausibility is further diminished by examples such as the following (from Milner 1978: 275):

(52) *Comme* vous habitez dans une belle maison!
'What a beautiful house you live in!'

If we try to argue that *comme* here functions as a wh-quantifier which modifies the adjective *belle*, then we run into the serious problem that such an analysis violates the Prepositional Island Constraint (22), which specifies that 'No constituent outside a prepositional phrase can be syntactically related to a constituent inside a prepositional phrase'. For, since *comme* lies outside and *belle* lies inside the prepositional phrase *dans une belle maison* 'in a beautiful house', it is clear that the constraint precludes us from arguing that *comme* has the syntactic function of modifying *belle*. Or, to put it another way, the wh-quantifier analysis wrongly predicts that sentences such as (52) are ungrammatical, because they violate the Prepositional Island Constraint (22). While this prediction is entirely correct in the case of the wh-quantifier *combien*—cf.

(53) **Combien* vous habitez dans une belle maison!
'How you live in a beautiful house!'

it is false in the case of exclamative *comme*, as the grammaticality of Milner's example (52) illustrates. In other words, the wh-quantifier analysis of *comme* seems implausible.

But if *comme* is not a wh-quantifier, can we then conclude that it is not a wh-word, but rather is a complementizer? The answer is of course 'No', since there are a variety of other wh-analyses which might be suggested. Perhaps the most plausible of these is that *comme* functions as some kind of wh-adverb, perhaps modifying the verb phrase, or perhaps modifying the whole clause. The latter analysis seems the more plausible of the two, given that in a sentence such as the following (from Milner 1978: 275):

(54) Comme des efforts gigantesques étaient nécessaires pour en arriver là!
'What gigantic efforts were needed to get there!

the subject noun phrase *des efforts gigantesques* 'gigantic efforts' seems to be included within the semantic scope of *comme* 'how'. If *comme* were analysed as a *sentential wh-adverb* (i.e. as a wh-adverb modifying a sentence or clause as a whole), sentences such as (54) could be accounted for straightforwardly. Indeed, such an analysis seems to be hinted at by Milner's remark (ibid.) that in examples like (54) it is plausible to take *comme* 'pour un adverbe de phrase portant sur la proposition toute entière' (i.e. as a sentential adverb having scope over the entire clause). Under this sentential-wh-adverb analysis, *comme* would have the same status as other sentential adverbs like *décidément* 'decidedly', so that (47) above would have a similar structure to (55) below:

(55*a*) Décidément il est maso, ton pote.
'He really is crazy, your mate.'
(*b*) Décidément elle roule lentement, cette bagnole.
'It goes really slowly, this old banger.'

Of course, the 'sentential' scope of *comme* might equally be accounted for by Gérard's complementizer analysis, on the assumption that complementizers have scope over all the constituents contained within the clause they introduce. So it would seem as if we are faced with two plausible alternatives to Milner's wh-quantifier analysis: on the one hand, *comme* might be a complementizer (as Gérard claims), while on the other hand it might be (as we have suggested here) a sentential wh-adverb.

Let us see how these three competing analyses fare with respect to our 'gap' criterion (44*c*), which tells us that wh-expressions (but not complementizers) typically leave a 'gap' within the proposition they introduce. It is interesting (as a standard of comparison) to note the behaviour of the wh-quantifier *combien* 'how many' in this respect, since it leaves a 'gap' (marked by ——) in sentences such as the following (from Milner 1978: 268):

(56) *Combien* j'ai perdu —— d'occasions!
'What a lot of chances I've missed!'

That there is a 'gap' of some sort immediately in front of *d'occasions* 'of chances' in (56) can be seen from two facts: firstly, the ungrammaticality of:

(57) *J'ai perdu *d'occasions*.
'I've missed of chances.'

which suggests that *combien* in (56) cannot be a complementizer or sentential adverb, since if it were we'd expect (57) to be well formed. On the other hand, if we (correctly) assume that *combien* is a wh-quantifier, then (57) is ungrammatical precisely because it contains an unquantified partitive expression *d'occasions*, whereas (56) is grammatical precisely because the partitive expression is quantified by *combien*. The second fact which argues in favour of positing a 'gap' in (56) is that this 'gap' cannot be filled by another quantifier like *énormément* 'loads', cf.

(58) **Combien* j'ai perdu *énormément* d'occasions!
'What a lot I've missed loads of chances.'

If we follow Milner and Gérard in positing that *combien* is a wh-quantifier, then we have a simple account of the ill-formedness of (58), since the partitive expression *d'occasions* would be doubly quantified; and doubly quantified expressions lead to ungrammaticality, as we see from:

(59) *J'ai *énormément* perdu *beaucoup* d'occasions.
'I've missed loads lots of chances.'

So, if *comme* is a wh-quantifier, then we would expect it to pattern just like *combien* in these respects.

However, this is not the case at all. For, on the one hand, *comme* cannot occur in 'gap' sentences parallel to (56): cf.

(60) **Comme* j'ai perdu —— d'occasions!
'How I've missed —— of chances!'

while on the other hand it can freely occur in sentences parallel to (58) where the 'gap' has been filled by a quantifier such as *énormément* 'loads': cf.

(61) *Comme* j'ai perdu *énormément* d'occasions!
'How I've missed loads of chances!'

Can we therefore follow Gérard (1980: 36) in concluding that these facts show that *comme* cannot be a wh-word like *combien*, but rather must be a complementizer?

The answer is emphatically 'No'. All that examples like (60) and (61) show us is that *comme* never leaves a quantifier gap within its clause. But from this fact it follows only that *commè* cannot be a quantifier, not that it must therefore be a complementizer. The facts of (60) and (61) would in fact be equally compatible with the alternative sentential-wh-adverb analysis which we suggested above. For note that the behaviour of *comme* in (60) and (61) is exactly parallel to that of a typical sentential adverb like *décidément* 'decidedly': cf.

(62*a*) **Décidément* j'ai perdu —— d'occasions!
'I've really missed —— of chances'
(*b*) *Décidément* j'ai perdu *énormément* d'occasions!
'I've really missed loads of chances!'

The most significant 'gap' here seems to be in the logic of Gérard's argumentation! The facts of (60) and (61) clearly have no bearing on the issue of whether *comme* is a complementizer or an adverb: they are 'neutral' between the two analyses.

So far, the evidence we have considered seems to discount Milner's wh-quantifier analysis, but to be neutral as between Gérard's complementizer analysis and our own sentential-wh-adverb analysis. However, our fourth criterion (44*d*) seems to lend some support to the adverbial analysis at the expense of the complementizer analysis. For, it would seem as if *comme* behaves very differently from typical complementizers like declarative *que* 'that' and interrogative *si* '*if*' in that unlike the latter it is subject to quite complex co-occurrence restrictions with constituents within the proposition it introduces. In this respect, its behaviour is more typical of a sentential adverb like *décidément* 'decidedly', as the following sentences show:

(63*a*) Je ne savais pas *que/si* Dieu était *éternel.*
'I didn't know that/if God was eternal.'
(*b*) **Comme*/**Décidément* Dieu est *éternel*!
'How/Decidedly God is eternal!'

(64*a*) Je ne savais pas *que/si* elle était *normale.*
'I didn't know that/if she was normal.'
(*b*) **Comme*/**Décidément* elle est *normale*!
'How/Decidedly she is normal!'

(65*a*) Je ne savais pas *que/si* elle était *assez* intelligente.
'I didn't know that/if she was fairly intelligent.'
(*b*) **Comme*/**Décidément* elle est *assez* intelligente!
'How/Decidedly she is fairly intelligent!'

The exact nature of such restrictions (discussed at length in Milner 1978: 269 ff. and Gérard 1980: 54 ff.) is not at issue here. The essential point is that complementizers are not typically subject to such restrictions, whereas sentential adverbs are. Our fourth criterion thus seems to favour the sentential-wh-adverb analysis of *comme*.

But what of our island-sensitivity criterion (44*e*)? Here, it seems clear from the contrast between (52) and (53), namely *Comme*/**Combien vous habitez dans une belle maison!*, that in such sentences *combien* is island-sensitive (in particular, subject to the Prepositional Island Constraint (22)), whereas *comme* is not. Given that complementizers are not island-sensitive, does this therefore support a complementizer analysis of *comme*? The answer is that it does not: for all that (52) shows us is that *comme* is not syntactically linked to any element such as *belle* within the prepositional phrase. However, this observation would be equally compatible with a sentential-adverb analysis, given that not only complementizers, but also sentential adverbs, have scope over all the constituents contained within the clause they introduce: thus, in place of *comme* in (52) we can have a typical sentential adverb such as *décidément* 'decidedly': cf.

(66) Décidément vous habitez dans une belle maison!
'You really to do live in a beautiful house!'

Thus, while island-sensitivity facts seem to exclude a quantifier analysis, they are neutral between the complementizer analysis and the wh-adverb analysis.

Let us now turn to consider criterion (44*f*), which tells us that wh-expressions permit Stylistic Inversion, but complementizers do not. At first sight, this criterion might seem to favour the complementizer analysis, given that (as Gérard 1980: 37 observes) *comme* never triggers Stylistic Inversion—hence the ungrammaticality of her examples:

(67*a*) **Comme* est singulière **la vie!**
'How is peculiar life!'
(*b*) **Comme* a l'air vicieux **cet individu!**
'How seems nasty this individual'

And indeed, this is the conclusion which Gérard draws. However, her argument is only valid if it turns out that *all* wh-words allow Stylistic Inversion: but this is not the case at all. For example, interrogative *pourquoi* 'why?' blocks inversion (as noted by Kayne 1972): cf:

(68) **Pourquoi* est parti **Jean?**
'Why has left Jean?'

Thus, since there are some wh-words like *pourquoi* which block inversion, it is not by any means beyond the bounds of plausibility to argue that exclamative *comme* is another such wh-word. What lends additional plausibility to this claim is the fact that, even when used as a wh-adverb of manner, *comme* still does not permit inversion: cf.

(69) **Comme* le traite **sa mère!**
How him treats his mother
'How his mother treats him!'

Thus, the claim that *comme* is a wh-adverb which (for reasons which need not concern us here) blocks Stylistic Inversion seems to have some empirical plausibility.

Our seventh criterion in (44) relates to the fact that wh-expressions permit Subject Clitic Inversion whereas complementizers do not. However, there is one complication which we should point out here—namely that Subject Clitic Inversion is found only in *negative* exclamatives, as the following paradigm illustrates:

(70*a*) Que de fois *ne s'était-il pas* plaint de son patron!
'How many times hadn't he complained of his boss!'
(*b*) *Que de fois *s'était-il* plaint de son patron!
'How many times had he complained about his boss!'

(Note that (70) must be exclamative rather than interrogative, since *que de* . . . is never used in interrogatives.) Interestingly, we find that *comme* cannot trigger this negative clitic inversion: cf.

(71) *Comme *ne s'était-il pas* plaint de son patron!
'How hadn't he complained about his boss!'

On the face of it, this would seem to support a complementizer analysis of *comme*, given our earlier observation that complementizers block clitic inversion. However, any such conclusion would be hasty; for it turns out that even when used as a manner wh-adverb, *comme* still does not permit negative clitic inversion: cf.

(72) *Comme *ne l'aurait-il pas* traitée s'il l'avait pu!
'How wouldn't he have treated her if he could have!'

There seems to be no 'semantic' reason why (72) should be illformed, since alongside (72) we find:

(73) Combien cruellement *ne l'aurait-il pas* traitée s'il l'avait pu.
'How cruelly wouldn't he have treated her if he could have!'

Rather, it seems that there is some *lexical* restriction on the class of items which permit clitic inversion in exclamatives. The existence of such lexical restrictions is further suggested by contrasts such as the following:

(74) *Tellement*/**Tant* était-elle jolie que tout le monde la regardait.
'So pretty was she that everyone looked at her.'

Given the existence of complex lexical restrictions on clitic inversion of a poorly understood nature, it would seem that this phenomenon does not lead us to any firm conclusions about the nature of *comme*.

We now turn to criterion (44*h*)—namely that wh-expressions can be used as elliptical phrases, whereas complementizers cannot. In this respect, it is interesting to note the contrast between the wh-quantifier *combien* 'how (much/many)' and the particle *comme* 'how':

(75*a*) *Combien*/**Comme* de crimes qui n'ont pas été punis!
'How many crimes haven't been punished!'
(*b*) Deux races différentes, et *combien*/**comme* différentes!
'Two different breeds, and how different!'

Thus, we see that *combien* but not *comme* can be used to introduce a noun phrase in (75*a*), and an adjectival phrase in (75*b*). Are we to follow Gérard (1980: 37) in concluding that this shows that *combien* is a wh-word, but that *comme* is a complementizer? The answer is surely 'No'. For all (75) shows us is that *combien* can be used to quantify a partitive or adjectival expression, whereas *comme* never functions as this type of quantifier. In other words, (75) tells us what we already knew—namely that whatever *comme* is, it is not a wh-quantifier. But (75) is equally compatible with Gérard's complementizer analysis, or with our own sentential-wh-adverb analysis. More significant here might have been the contrast in:

(76) Il l'avait toujours aimée, et *combien*/**comme*!
'He had always loved her, and how much/how!'

At first sight, given our assumption that wh-words can be used elliptically but not complementizers, it might seen as if (76) supports the conclusion that *combien* is a wh-word, whereas *comme* is a complementizer. However, the assumption that all categories other than complementizers can be used in this type of elliptical construction is false, since we see from (77) below that sentential adverbs like *décidément* 'decidedly' are subject to a similar restriction: cf.

(77) *Il l'avait toujours aimée, et décidément!
'He had always loved her, and really!'

So, in this respect, *comme* might equally be said to behave like a sentential adverb, rather than a complementizer.

Consider next criterion (44*i*), according to which a wh-word can combine with a complementizer, but not with another wh-word, nor one complementizer with another. The fact that *comme* cannot combine with the finite-clause complementizer *que* 'that'—cf.

(78) **Comme qu*'elle est mignonne!
'How that she is cute'

might at first sight seem to argue in favour of a complementizer analysis, since we could then account for the ungrammaticality of (78) in terms of a restriction that French does not allow two complementizers to combine. However, any such argument would be fatally flawed. For one thing, in its use as a wh-adverb of manner, *comme* does not combine with *que* either: cf.

(79) **Comme* que tu me traites!
'How that you treat me!'

Moreover, if *comme* were a complementizer, we might expect it to be able to combine with an exclamative wh-expression; but as (80) below indicates, this is not possible:

(80) **A combien de ces idéologies comme* il a dû croire passionément!
'How many of those ideologies how he must have believed in passionately.'

It seems, then, that the restriction in (78) is lexical in nature, and thus is not decisive in helping us decide whether *comme* is a complementizer or not. It is interesting to note in this respect that sentential adverbs appear to be subject to similar lexical restrictions on their combinability with *que*: even apparently related adverbs may differ in this respect: cf.

(81*a*) *Heureusement* (*qu*')il est parti.
'Fortunately (that) he has left.'
(*b*) *Malheureusement* (**qu*')il est parti.
'Unfortunately (that) he has left.'

Our tenth criterion (44*j*) tells us that wh-expressions belonging to an appropriate category can occur as the complements of (e.g.) prepositions, whereas complementizers cannot. In this respect, it is interesting to note the contrast between *combien* and *comme* in:

(82) A *combien*/**comme* il a acheté sa liberté!
'What a price he paid for his liberty!'

Are we to conclude from (82) that *combien* is a wh-word whereas *comme* is a complementizer? This would indeed be a rash conclusion: for, given that only (pro)nominal constituents generally occur as the complements of prepositions in French, then all (82) shows us is that *combien* can function as a wh-pronoun, whereas *comme* cannot. But from the fact that *comme* is not a pronoun, it does not follow that it must be a complementizer: after all, given that adverbs don't occur as the complements of prepositions, (82) would be equally compatible with an analysis of *comme* as a sentential wh-adverb.

Criterion (44*k*) specifies that wh-words (but not complementizers) may take phrasal complements. However, it is quite clear that *comme* cannot take a nominal, adjectival, adverbial, or even prepositional complement: cf.

(83*a*) **Comme* (*de*) *copines* il a!
'How (of) girlfriends he has!'
(*b*) **Comme gentille* elle est!
'How kind she is!'
(*c*) **Comme vite* elle roule!
'How quickly it goes!'
(*d*) **Comme à l'aise* elle se sentait!
'How at ease she felt!'

We might follow Gérard (1980: 37) in taking this to be a telling argument in favour of the complementizer analysis. In fact, it is nothing of the sort, since all (83) tells us is that *comme* cannot act as a nominal/adjectival/adverbial/prepositional quantifier. But from this we cannot deduce anything about whether *comme* is a complementizer or a sentential wh-adverb.

Criterion (44*l*) tells us that complementizers may be subject to distributional restrictions on the type of clause they can occur in, whereas wh-expressions tend not to be so restricted. In this connection, note the contrast between *combien* and *comme* in:

(84*a*) *Combien* à dépenser pour un projet si peu viable!
'What a lot to spend on such an unviable project!'
(*b*) **Comme* rouler lentement!
'How slowly to go!'

This appears to suggest that *comme*, unlike *combien*, cannot occur in infinitival exclamatives—a fact which could be easily accounted for by positing that *comme* (like declarative *que* 'that' and interrogative *si* 'whether') is a finite-clause complementizer. But again, this would be a hasty conclusion: a wider look at infinitival exclamatives in French reveals the following pattern:

(85*a*) *Que de bouches* à nourrir!
'What a lot of mouths to feed!'
(*b*) **Combien belle* à paraître.
'How beautiful to appear!'
(*c*) **Combien lentement* à rouler!
'How slowly to go!'
(*d*) **De quelle façon* à se comporter!
'In what a way to behave!'

In (85*a*) we have a nominal expression heading the infinitive, in (*b*) an adjectival, in (*c*) an adverbial, and in (*d*) a prepositional expression. The relevant generalization is thus that only *nominals* can head infinitival exclamatives (this is arguably because the infinitives here are infinitival relative clauses, and relative clauses of this type can only modify nominals: cf. Radford 1982 for some discussion of the parallel construction in Italian). Thus, the contrast in (84) shows nothing more than that *combien* can function as a (pro)nominal, whereas *comme* cannot: in other words, (84) is equally compatible with a wh-adverb analysis as with a complementizer analysis. Predictably, *comme* in its use as a manner adverb is subject to the same restriction against being used in an infinitival exclamative: cf.

(86) **Comme* à se comporter!
'How to behave!'

Criterion (44*m*) tells us that complementizers have scope over a *bounded* domain, whereas wh-expressions are not similarly restricted. Hence, we might conclude from the contrast in:

(87*a*) *Combien étrange* il a dit que ça lui semblait!
'How strange he said it seemed to him!'
(*b*) **Comme* il a dit que ça lui semblait *étrange*!
'How he said that it seemed strange to him!'

that *combien étrange* is a wh-expression (since it is syntactically linked to the subordinate clause verb *semblait* 'seemed', and hence is not clause-bound), whereas *comme* is a clause-bound complementizer which therefore cannot be associated with any element in the subordinate clause (e.g. *étrange* 'strange'). But once again, this is a hasty conclusion: for as Milner (1978: 263–4) notes, even the wh-word *combien* seems to be bounded in scope when separated from the expression it quantifies: cf.

(88) **Combien* il a dit que ça lui semblait étrange!
'How he said that it seemed strange to him!'

Since Milner and Gérard both agree that *combien* is a wh-word in structures such as (88), then there is clearly no reason not to treat *comme* as a wh-word in sentences such as (87). Indeed, the fact that when used as a manner adverb, *comme* is subject to the very same restriction: cf.

(89) **Comme* il a dit qu'elle le traitait!
'How he said that she treated him!'

makes the analysis of *comme* as a wh-word all the more plausible. Of course, such an analysis leaves open the question of what kind of restriction might be operating in sentences such as (87)–(89). It would appear that (for reasons which are unclear) exclamative wh-words cannot generally extend their scope across a finite-clause boundary. Some weak evidence that this *bounding* restriction holds only for finite clauses and not for infinitives comes from sentences like:

(90*a*) *Comme* la vieillesse la faisait *devenir irritable*!
'How old age made her become irritable!'
(*b*) *Comme* elle se faisait *mépriser par son entourage*!
'How she made herself despised by her entourage!'

If *comme* here is associated with the italicized subordinate infinitive clause, then it does indeed seem that *comme* is not clause-bound, and hence is not a complementizer. The evidence is 'weak', however, to the extent that it is not clear exactly what *comme* does modify in (90), or indeed what we mean by 'modify'. It seems safer to say that we are dealing with restrictions of a presently unknown nature here, and that until they are clarified, the question of whether or how *comme* (and other exclamative particles) is bounded should be left in abeyance.

Our final criterion (44*n*) tells us that wh-phrases can generally occur internally within clauses, whereas complementizers never can. In this respect, *comme* seems at first sight to pattern like a typical complementizer, since it cannot be positioned clause-internally: cf.

(91) *Elle m'énerve *comme*!
'She gets on my nerves how!'

However, this fact is not as decisive as it first seems, since it turns out that even wh-words like *combien* are similarly restricted:

(92) *Il dépense *combien* comme fric!
'He spends what a lot by way of money.'

What is going on here? The answer appears to be that we are dealing with a restriction which requires wh-exclamatives to be introduced by (i.e. have as their leftmost constituent) an 'exclamative expression'. The ungrammaticality of both (91) and (92) follows from this restriction, but has no bearing on the question of whether *comme* is a complementizer or a wh-adverb.

However, with a little imagination, we can 'rescue' our apparently abortive test (44*n*). For it turns out that in multiple wh-exclamatives we can conspire to show that wh-phrases can indeed occur clause-internally, as with the italicized wh-expression in:

(93) Les ravages du SIDA aux USA ne m'étonnent pas, car combien de garçons couchent avec *combien de filles*!
'The ravages of AIDS in the USA don't surprise me at all, because how many boys sleep with how many girls!'

But as the following (admittedly artificial) pair shows, this is not possible with *comme*:

(94*a*) *Comme* il a dû croire passionément à combien de ces idéologies!

'How he must have believed passionately in how many of those ideologies.'

(*b*) *A combien de ces idéologies il a *comme* dû croire passionément.
'How many of those ideologies he must how have believed in passionately!'

This might seem to clinch the argument in favour of a complementizer analysis of *comme*: but this is not in fact the case at all, for two reasons. Firstly, because even when used as a manner wh-adverb *comme* is subject to the same restriction against being positioned clause-internally, as we see from the following (inevitably somewhat contrived) pair of examples:

(95*a*) *Comme* il y allait avec combien d'accusations contre ses collègues!
'How he went at it with how many accusations against his colleagues!'

(*b*) *Avec combien d'accusations contre ses collègues il y allait *comme*!
'How many accusations against his colleagues he went at it with how!'

And secondly, because a similar restriction holds for some other wh-words—for example, for interrogative *pourquoi* 'why?', though not for interrogative *où* 'where?'—hence the following contrast:

(96) Tu les a vendus *où*/**pourquoi*, tes bouquins?
'You sold them where/why, your books?'

Clearly, then, there are lexical factors at work here which mean that the non-occurrence of *comme* clause-internally does not help us choose between whether to analyse it as a complementizer (like declarative *que* 'that'), or as a wh-adverb (like interrogative *pourquoi* 'why?').

Overall, then, the case in favour of a complementizer analysis of *comme* is far from proven: we have seen that every single piece of evidence which might be adduced in support of such an analysis is in fact equally compatible with a 'sentential-wh-adverb' analysis; and indeed, at least one piece of evidence (the existence of co-occurrence relations between *comme* and elements of the clause it introduces) seems to point quite strongly in favour of the adverb analysis rather than the complementizer analysis.

4. The status of exclamative *que*

The origins of exclamative *que* 'that/what' (a descendant of the Latin wh-quantifier *quam* 'how') can be seen in the 'classical' use of *que* to quantify adjectival, adverbial, prepositional, and partitive-nominal expressions—as the following examples from Gérard (1980: 12–15) illustrate:

(97*a*) *Que courte* est la vie! (Augier)
'How short is life.'

(*b*) *Que bien plus aisément* j'en saurais triompher! (Corneille)
'How much more easily I could triumph over it!'

(*c*) *Qu'en termes galants* ces choses-là sont mises! (Molière)
'In what gallant terms those things are put!'

(*d*) *Que d'eau* a coulé sous le pont depuis notre jeunesse! (Carco)
'What a lot of water has flowed under the bridge since our youth.'

And its use as a partitive-nominal quantifier in sentences such as (97*d*) survives into modern French. We take it for granted here (given the numerous arguments to this effect presented by Milner and Gérard alike) that *que* in this quantifier use is indeed a wh-word. What we are more interested in is other uses of exclamative *que*, exemplified by sentences such as:

(98*a*) *Que* la vie est dure!
'How life is hard!'

(*b*) *Que* je me sens bien!
'How well I feel!'

(*c*) *Qu*'elle est à l'aise!
'How at ease she is!'

(*d*) *Qu*'il a de la chance!
'How lucky he is.'

What is the status of *que* in sentences such as (98)? One possibility (advocated by Gérard) is that *que* is an exclamative complementizer. Another (suggested by Milner 1978: 268–75) is that it is a wh-quantifier. A third possibility would be to analyse *que* in the same way that we proposed to analyse *comme*, namely as a sentential wh-adverb. Let us see how each of these three analyses fares in respect of the fourteen criteria which we outlined in (44) above.

We discount the morphological criterion (44*a*) here as inconclusive (for the same reasons as with *comme*), and pass instead to consider (44*b*)—namely the question of what grammatical role (if any) *que* plays within the proposition it introduces. Clearly, *que* cannot be used e.g. in a pronominal function, as the ungrammaticality of (99) below shows:

(99) **Qu*'il gaspille comme fric pour les nanas!
'What he spends by way of bread on chicks!'

If indeed *que* does play a grammatical role within its clause, it seems more likely to be that of a quantifier, or a sentential adverb. Milner (ibid.) argues in favour of a quantifier analysis, pointing out (1978: 271) that *que* leaves a 'quantifier gap' internally within its clause (criterion (44*c*)), thereby excluding the presence of another (unquantifiable) quantifier, as in his example:

(100) **Qu*'il est *très* gentil!
'How he is very kind!'

However, if we look more carefully at examples like (100), we find that the argument is not as decisive as it would seem. To see this, we must first draw a distinction between two different types of quantifier in French—*quantifiable* and *unquantifiable*. Some quantifiers in French (including *peu* 'little', *trop* 'too', and *assez* 'enough') can themselves be quantified by another quantifier (hence *très peu* 'very little', *beaucoup trop* 'much too', *bien assez* 'quite enough') and hence might be called *quantifiable quantifiers*. But other quantifiers (e.g. *très* 'very', *beaucoup* 'lots', *énormément* 'loads') cannot be so quantified (cf. **bien très* 'extremely very', **très beaucoup* 'very lots', **assez énormément* 'pretty loads') and hence are *unquantifiable* quantifiers. Given this distinction, a quantifier analysis of *que* would make two predictions: (i) that *que* excludes the presence of an unquantifiable quantifier (like *très* 'very') in (100); but that (ii) it does not exclude the presence of a quantifiable quantifier. In the event, neither prediction is correct: thus, (i) is falsified by examples like the following (from Gérard 1980: 59):

(101) *Qu*'il a *beaucoup* de chance!
'How he has (= He really has) lots of luck!'

(where *que* occurs with the unquantifiable *beaucoup* 'lots'); while (ii) is falsified by Gérard's (1980: 59) example:

(102) **Qu*'il a *trop* d'ennuis!
'How he has too many troubles!'

(where the quantifiable *trop* 'too many' nonetheless excludes *que*). A quantifier analysis thus seems somewhat problematic.

The plausibility of the quantifier analysis is further reduced by the fact that *que* in cases like (98) can never immediately precede the expression it supposedly quantifies—i.e. in contemporary French we do not find:

(103*a*) **Que dure* est la vie!
'How hard is life!'

(*b*) **Que bien* je me sens!
'How well I feel!'

(*c*) **Qu'à l'aise* elle est!
'How at ease she is!'

(*d*) **Que de la chance* il a!
'How lucky he is!'

Now, we have already seen that it is a general property of quantifiers that they can always precede the expressions they quantify (cf. examples (48), (49*a*), and (50*a*) above)—hence *que* is clearly not like a typical quantifier in this respect. Moreover, a quantifier analysis would seem to be excluded for a sentence such as the following (from Milner 1978: 273):

(104) *Que* vous êtes un garçon serviable!
'How you are a helpful boy!'

It is hard to see how *que* could be seen as quantifying the expression *un garçon serviable* 'a helpful boy' here, since this expression is already quantified by the article *un* 'a/one'. Moreover, any analysis of *que* as a nominal quantifier (hence as a determiner) here would be flawed by the fact that typical wh-determiners cannot be separated from the nominal expressions which they qualify—hence the ungrammaticality of:

(105) **Quel* vous êtes *garçon serviable*!
'What you are a helpful boy!'

where *quel* 'what/which' has been separated from the italicized nominal which it qualifies. Much the same point could be made about examples like (98*d*) *Qu'il a de la chance!* Any analysis of *que* as quantifying the nominal *de la chance* here is precluded by the fact that *de la chance* is already properly quantified (by the partitive quantifier *de* 'some/of'), and so can be used independently without *que*: cf.

(106) Il a *de la chance*.
'He has some luck.' (i.e. 'He is lucky.')

Precisely because the italicized nominal in (106) is already properly quantified, it cannot be premodified by a nominal quantifier—cf.

(107) *Il a *énormément* de la chance.
'He has loads of some luck.'

Thus, if *que* were a quantifier in structures such as (98*d*), we should wrongly expect the sentence to be ill formed, because it contains a doubly quantified nominal, and such structures are ungrammatical, as (107) shows. In other words, sentences such as (98*d*) and (104) seem to preclude the possibility of *que* functioning as a wh-quantifier.

If we reject the analysis of *que* as a wh-quantifier, this leaves us with two major alternative analyses—Gérard's complementizer analysis, and our own sentential-wh-adverb analysis. Now, at first sight, the adverbial analysis might seem to be called into question by the ungrammaticality of Milner's (1978: 237) example:

(108) *Que des efforts gigantesques étaient nécessaires pour en arriver là!
'How some enormous efforts were needed to get there!'

We might conclude from the ungrammaticality of (108) that *que* cannot have within its 'scope' (any part of) the subject of its clause—and indeed both Milner (1978: 272) and Gérard (1980: 25) posit such a restriction. However, I would venture to suggest that their proposed restriction is purely chimerical: more precisely, it is the artefact of a bad choice of example in (108). What is wrong with (108) is that alongside it we find the highly preferred alternative (109) below, in which *que* is used to quantify a partitive nominal:

(109) *Que d'efforts gigantesques* étaient nécessaires pour en arriver là!
'What a lot of gigantic efforts were needed to get there!'

The existence of the more idiomatic and less archaic (109) thus accounts for the rejection of (108), which may well be interpreted as a mistaken attempt at producing (109). If we eliminate this 'preferred alternative' factor by taking a sentence such as:

(110) *Qu'un travail titanique* a dû être fourni pour construire les pyramides!
'What a titanic enterprise it must have been to build the pyramids!'

then we see that the 'restriction' spoken of by Milner and Gérard disappears. Given the non-existence of the supposed 'never-on-a-subject' restriction, there seems no reason not to continue to envisage the possibility of a sentential-wh-adverb analysis for *que* (on which *que* might mean something like 'How true it is that . . .').

Given that we have already touched upon the possibility of *que* leaving a 'gap' internally within its clause in relation to examples such as (100), we leave aside criterion (44*c*) and proceed to (44*d*), which relates to co-occurrence restrictions. As both Milner and Gérard observe, there are in fact severe co-occurrence restrictions between *que* and the types of elements which can occur with it in its clause: some of these restrictions are illustrated below:

(111*a*) **Que* Dieu est *éternel*! (Milner 1978: 270.)
'How God is eternal!'
(*b*) **Que* cet ensemble est *dénombrable*! (ibid.)
'How this set is enumerable!'
(*c*) **Que* la pluie a *cessé*! (Milner 1978: 271.)
'How the rain has stopped!'
(*d*) **Qu*'il a *commencé* à pleuvoir! (Gérard 1980: 54.)
'How it has begun to rain!'
(*e*) **Qu*'il a *énormément* de chance! (Gérard 1980: 59.)
'How he has loads of luck!'
(*f*) **Qu*'il a *trop* mangé! (ibid.)
'How he has eaten too much!'

This seems to be a telling argument against the complementizer analysis, since we have already shown in (63)–(65) above that neither of the two 'classic' complementizers in French (declarative *que* 'that' and interrogative *si* 'if') is subject to such restrictions; whereas by contrast (as the same examples illustrate) at least some sentential adverbs typically are subject to similar restrictions.

Turning now to the island-sensitivity criterion (44*e*), it is interesting to note in this connection the observation by Milner (1978: 273) that *que* cannot 'modify' material contained within a prepositional phrase—e.g. it cannot modify *belle* in his example:

(112) **Que* vous habitez dans une *belle* maison!
'How you live in a beautiful house!'

Given that prepositional phrases are islands in French (cf. (22) above), and that wh-words but not complementizers are island-sensitive, we might follow Milner and conclude from the ungrammaticality of (112) that *que* cannot be a complementizer, but rather must be a quantifier which (illicitly) modifies *belle*, in violation of the Prepositional Island Constraint (22), which prevents a constituent inside a prepositional phrase from being syntactically linked to one outside the same prepositional phrase. However, this is a conclusion which is somewhat difficult to defend in the face of Milner's example (ibid.):

(113) Que tu me traites de manière révoltante!
'How you treat me in a revolting manner!'

and in the face of parallel examples such as:

(114*a*) Que tu es de mauvaise humeur!
'How you are in a bad mood!'
(*b*) Que tu es en pleine forme!
'How you are on good form!'
(*c*) Que tu es tombée sur un salaud de mari, ma pauvre!
'What a bastard of a husband you got landed with, you poor thing!'
(*d*) Qu'elle était dans une situation désespérée!
'What a desperate situation she was in!'

Clearly a wh-quantifier analysis of *que* as modifying some constituent (e.g. an adjective) contained within a prepositional phrase would not be tenable, since it would violate the Prepositional Island Constraint, so that we would wrongly predict that examples such as (113) and (114) were ungrammatical. By contrast, neither the complementizer analysis nor the sentential-wh-adverb analysis would run into such problems, since in both cases *que* would stand 'outside' the clause as a whole and not be syntactically linked to any specific element within the clause (It is interesting to note that *que* in examples such as (113) and (114) can freely be replaced by a sentential adverb such as *décidément* 'decidedly').

Gérard (1980) argues that exclamative *que* does not permit Stylistic Inversion—hence the ungrammaticality of her example:

(115) **Que* me plaisait **le silence!**
'How pleased me silence!'

and she maintains that this fact provides 'confirmation' of its complementizer status, given (44*f*). However, even if we accept her (questionable) grammaticality judgement, the argument still fails, for two reasons. Firstly, not all wh-words permit inversion, as we have already seen in relation to (69). And secondly, not all complementizers block inversion: thus, as Kayne and Pollock (1978) note, inversion occurs after the subjunctive complementizer *que* 'that': cf.

(116) La loi exige *que* soient exécutés **tous les traitres.**
'The law requires that be executed all traitors.'

Thus, inversion facts in (115) would be equally compatible with a wh-word or complementizer analysis.

Turning now to our Clitic Inversion criterion (44*g*), we find that there are indeed cases of negative clitic inversion after *que*: cf.

(117*a*) Que *n'aurait-il pas* fait pour elle!
'What wouldn't he have done for her!'
(*b*) Que *ne l'ai-je pas* su avant!
'Why didn't I find out beforehand!'

But the problem we face here is whether *que* is indeed an *exclamative* particle in such uses. An alternative possibility would be to say that sentences like (117) are in fact *rhetorical questions.* Distinguishing between exclamatives on the one hand and interrogatives on the other is by no means an easy matter. For example, the phenomenon of negative clitic inversion is found not only in exclamatives but also in interrogatives like:

(118*a*) Qui *n'aurait-il pas* invité s'il l'avait pu?
'Who wouldn't he have invited if he could have?'
(*b*) Où *ne serait-il pas* allé s'il en avait eu l'occasion?
'Where wouldn't he have gone if he had had the chance to?'

Moreover, negative exclamatives and negative interrogatives have much the same *illocutionary force* (i.e. they produce a similar rhetorical effect), and hence it is difficult to distinguish between the two on pragmatic grounds (i.e. in terms of their 'use'). And even many of the supposed lexical differences between the two described in traditional grammars are of doubtful validity: for example, the traditional claim that *qui* 'who?', *où* 'where?', *quand* 'when?', and *quoi* 'what?' are exclusively interrogative particles is called into question by an apparently exclamative use in sentences such as:

(119*a*) Qu'est-ce qu'elle a comme copains, et *qui* elle fréquente!
'What a lot of friends she's got, and who she mixes with!'
(*b*) Les Dubois sont partis en croisière. Et *où* il sont allés!
'The Dubois went on a cruise. And where they went!'
(*c*) Ils sont sortis ensemble. Et jusqu'à *quand* il sont restés dehors!
'They left together. And until when they stayed out!'
(*d*) Elle a été assaillie dans le rue. Et avec *quoi* on l'a frappée!
'She was attacked in the street. And what they hit her with!'

For such reasons, then, deciding whether the sentences in (117) are syntactically exclamative or interrogative is by no means unproblematic.

However, it seems clear that at least in (117*a*) *que* must be interrogative. For, here *que* plays an apparently pronominal role as the direct object of *fait* 'done'; and yet we have already seen in relation to the ungrammaticality of (99) **Qu'il gaspille comme fric pour les nanas!* that exclamative *que* cannot be used in this pronominal function. But by contrast, interrogative *que* can be used pronominally: cf.

(120) *Que* gagne-t-il comme fric?
'What does he earn by way of money?'

Hence, in its 'pronominal' use in (117*a*), *que* must be interrogative, and not exclamative. We shall likewise assume that *que* in (117*b*) is also interrogative, and marks an archaic (non-productive) use of *que* in the sense of 'why?' which now survives only in stereotyped formulae.

Criterion (44*h*) suggests that wh-expressions, but not complementizers, can occur in elliptical phrasal exclamatives. Certainly, it is beyond question that *que* (in its non-quantifier use) cannot be used in this way: cf.

(121) *Il l'a toujours admiré, et *que*!
'He has always admired him, and how!'

At first sight, this behaviour would appear to be consistent with a complementizer analysis for *que*, and inconsistent with a wh-word analysis. If we are to maintain the wh-word analysis, we must be able to provide a principled account of the ungrammaticality of (121). One initially attractive possibility would be to analyse *que* as a *clitic* particle which requires a verbal host, and hence to rule out (121) in terms of the same restriction that rules out co-ordinate clitic sequences such as **te et me* 'you and me'. However, while a clitic analysis of interrogative *que* 'what' seems plausible (because e.g. it cannot be separated from the verb by a subject noun phrase), such an analysis does not seem feasible for exclamative *que*, as the following contrast illustrates:

(122*a*) **Que* ta sœur a(-t-elle) fait?
'What has your sister done?'
(*b*) *Que* ta sœur est moche!
'How your sister is ugly!'

For while interrogative *que* in (122*a*) cannot be separated from the verb *a* 'has' by the intervening subject *ta sœur* 'your sister', the same is not true of exclamative *que* in (122*b*). Thus, it is clear that exclamative *que* cannot be a clitic, and hence that we shall have to look elsewhere for an account of the ungrammaticality of (121). Perhaps the answer might lie in the restriction already noted in relation to (73) to the effect that sentential adverbs like *décidément* 'decidedly' cannot be used as independent phrases.

Criterion (44*i*) leads us to expect that a wh-word can combine with the finite-indicative complementizer *que* 'that', but a complementizer cannot. As Gérard (1980: 24) notes, exclamative *que* 'how' cannot in fact combine with indicative *que* 'that' in this way—as the ungrammaticality of the following example of hers illustrates:

(123) **Que que* la vie est courte!
'How (that) life is short!'

She argues that this provides further evidence in support of the complementizer analysis, since (123) would then be ruled out by the constraint against having two complementizers introducing the same clause. However, this is a somewhat hasty conclusion, since we might argue that (123) would be ruled out by a far more general constraint, which Gross (1968) terms the Cacophony Constraint, and Radford (1979) the Like Form Constraint. This constraint rules out a sequence of two identical morphemes within the same tone group, and hence rules out (*inter alia*) other 'double *que*' sequences such as those in:

(124*a*) *Je n'ai dit *que que* je voulais partir.
'I only said that I wanted to leave.'

(*b*) *Je préfère que tu restes, plutôt *que que* tu t'en ailles.
'I prefer that you stay, rather than that you go.'

It seems natural therefore to conclude that the restriction in (123) is an independent one which has no bearing whatever on the question of the status of exclamative *que* as a complementizer or a wh-word.

Criterion (44*j*) suggests that only wh-expressions and not complementizers can occur as the complement of e.g. a preposition. However, while it is true that we do not find sentences such as:

(125) *A *que* il a acheté sa liberté!
'At what price he bought his liberty!'

this shows only that exclamative *que* cannot be used in a pronominal function (which we had already established in relation to (99) above), and has no bearing on whether *que* is a complementizer or a wh-word. Moreover, as Milner (1978: 265) notes, the same restriction is found for the wh-quantifier use of *que*: cf.

(126) *A *que de personnes* j'ai dû m'adresser!
'What a lot of people I had to address myself to!'

So the criterion proves inconclusive.

Much the same is true of criterion (44*k*); for while it is true—as we have already seen in relation to the ungrammaticality of (103*a–c*)—that in Modern French *que* cannot take an immediately following adjectival, adverbial, or prepositional complement, this shows only that *que* is no longer used as an adjectival/adverbial/prepositional quantifier, and does not in any way help us choose between a complementizer or a wh-adverb analysis.

In relation to (44*l*), an obvious question to ask is whether *que* (in its non-nominal-quantifier use) is subject to distributional restrictions. The answer is that it is: firstly, it cannot occur in non-finite exclamatives—cf.

(127) **qu'*à/*que* souffrir pour une cause perdue!
'What to suffer for a lost cause!'

and secondly (unlike *comme* 'how'), it cannot be used to introduce embedded (i.e. complement-clause) exclamatives: cf.

(128) T'as pas remarqué *comme*/≠*que* c'est mignon!?
'Haven't you noticed how cute it is!'

(The symbol ≠ is used to indicate that *que* here cannot be used in the intended exclamative sense.) The first restriction here is not particularly significant—it follows from our earlier observation in relation to (85) that only (*pro*)*nominal* expressions can head infinitival exclamatives, and thus shows only that *que* is not pronominal in (127). Likewise, the second restriction may be equally unhelpful in determining the status of exclamative *que*, since such examples prove problematic for both the wh-word and the complementizer analysis: it may be that the desire to avoid 'unacceptable ambiguity' (in the sense of Hankamer 1973) has led to a restriction whereby the only use of *que* accepted in complement clauses is that of the indicative/subjunctive complementizer *que* found in sentences such as:

(129*a*) Je crois *que* tu as raison.
'I think that you're right.'

(*b*) J'aurais voulu *qu'*elle reste.
'I would have prefered that she stay.'

Thus the more frequent use of *que* as a declarative particle vitiates its use as an exclamative particle.

In relation to the clause-boundedness (or otherwise) of *que*—cf. criterion (44*m*)—we shall have nothing to say here, since the behaviour of *que* in this respect is very similar to that of *comme*, and there is little point in repeating our earlier discussion. Suffice it to remark that there are restrictions on *que* in this respect, but the extent and nature of these restrictions is at present unclear.

Let us turn, therefore, to our last criterion (44*n*): in this respect, it seems clear that exclamative *que* can never occur internally within a clause, even in multiple exclamatives like:

(130) *A combien de ces idéologies il a dû *que* croire passionément!
'How many of those ideologies he must have how believed in passionately!'

Clearly, a complementizer analysis would provide a principled account of the ill-formedness of (130). However, it is also significant that, even when used as a wh-word (i.e. in its nominal-quantifier function), *que* likewise cannot be positioned internally within its clause—cf.

(131) *Que de gens payent *que d'impôts* en Angleterre!
'What a lot of people pay what a lot of taxes in England!'

(to be contrasted with the sentence-internal position of *combien* in (93) above). So yet again we cannot draw any firm conclusion about the status of (non-quantifier) *que* as complementizer or wh-word in examples like (130).

What conclusions are we to draw from our discussion of *que*? While it seems clear that (except in the case of *que de + nominal* structures) *que* does not function as a wh-quantifier, it is much less clear whether (in its non-quantifier uses) it should be analysed as a complementizer or as a wh-adverb. Contrary to Gérard's claims, a complementizer analysis is *not* required in order to account for the behaviour of non-quantifier *que*: and at least one set of facts (the existence of strong co-occurrence restrictions on the use of *que*) seems to favour a wh-word analysis (e.g. as a sentential wh-adverb).

5. The status of exclamative *comment que*

In many respects, *comment que* 'how that' can be seen as a more popular counterpart of *comme* 'how': for this reason, we shall not run through the full range of criteria presented in (44), since this would involve much tedious repetition. Instead, we shall concentrate on the arguments presented by Gérard in favour of a complementizer analysis for *comment que*, and see just how (un)convincing they are.

First of all, however, we should point out that (as with *comme* 'how') there are two distinct uses of *comment que*: on the one hand, we have a *manner* use illustrated by sentences such as:

(132*a*) *Comment que* tu traites ce pauvre animal!
'How you treat this poor animal!'

(*b*) *Comment qu*'elle y va pour les dépenses!
'How she goes at it with spending money!'

Given that (as we saw earlier) *traiter* 'treat' and (the idiomatic use of) *y aller* 'go at it' require a manner complement, there can be little doubt that *comment* (*que*) here functions as a manner wh-adverb. What is of more direct concern to us here is the status of *comment que* in its non-manner use, as in the following examples from Gérard (1980: 50–1):

(133*a*) *Comment que* c'est grand, chez vous!
'How big it is where you are!'
(*b*) Et sa tire, *comment qu*'elle roule bien!
'And his old banger, how well it's running!'
(*c*) *Comment qu*'il est peu bavard, ton pote!
'How quiet he is, your mate!'
(*d*) Regarde *comment qu*'il a du pot!
'Look how lucky he is!'

Gérard (1980: 51) gives three main arguments in support of a complementizer analysis of non-manner uses of *comment que*. Firstly, she notes, *comment que* behaves like a complementizer in not permitting complements—cf.

(134*a*) **Comment que belle* elle est!
'How that pretty she is!'
(*b*) **Comment que de fric* il a!
'How (much) that of money he has!'

Secondly, it never leaves a 'gap' internally within its clause: cf.

(135) **Comment qu*'il a —— de chance!
'How much that he has —— of luck!'

And lastly, it cannot occur in non-clausal exclamatives: cf.

(136*a*) *Une belle journée que nous avons là, et *comment qu*'ensoleillée!
'A nice day we've got there, and how (that) sunny!'
(*b*) **Comment que* du pot!
'How (that) of luck!' (i.e. 'What luck!')

By now, these arguments should have a familiar ring to them, and the reader should be equally familiar with our reply to this kind of argumentation. Thus, the obvious response is that (134*a*) and (136*a*) show only that *comment que* cannot function as an adjectival quantifier; while (134*b*), (135), and (136*b*) show only that *comment* *que* cannot function as a nominal quantifier either. Even if we were to seek to generalize these two observations, the most sweeping conclusion that would be justified is that *comment que* never functions as a quantifier. But from this fact, we cannot conclude anything about whether it functions as (e.g.) a complementizer or sentential adverb. There is a fundamental flaw in the logic here.

Moreover, there is something strange about examples like (134)–(136): for it seems that Gérard is treating *comment que* as some kind of indivisible unit. But this cannot be the case—for two reasons. Firstly, *comment* can occur without *que* in both manner and non-manner uses: cf.

(137*a*) *Comment* elle y va pour les dépenses!
'How she goes at it with spending money!'
(*b*) *Comment* c'est grand, chez vous!
'How big it is where you are!'

And secondly, *que* can be separated from *comment* in co-ordinate structures, again in both manner and non-manner uses: cf.

(138*a*) Regarde *comment qu*'il s'est comporté envers ses invités, et *qu*'il les a traités!
'Look how he behaved towards his guests and how (lit.: that) he treated them!'
(*b*) Regarde *comment qu*'il est mignon et *qu*'il est potelé, ce bébé!
'Look how cute he is, and how (lit.: that) chubby he is, this baby!'

It seems beyond doubt, then, that *comment que* 'how that' is not an indivisible unit, but rather comprises two separate words, namely *comment* 'how' and *que* 'that'. But what is *comment* here, and what is *que*? In the case of the manner use of *comment que*, it seems clear that *comment* must be an exclamative wh-adverb, just like interrogative *comment* 'how'; and *que* 'that' seems to be the same finite-clause complementizer which is found in popular interrogative structures after wh-expressions—cf. e.g.

(139*a*) Où *que* tu vas?
'Where (that) are you going?'
(*b*) Comment *que* tu l'as eu?
'How (that) did you get it?'

Thus, it seems plausible to conclude that the *que* of exclamative *comment que* must also be the same finite-clause complementizer *que* 'that'. Moreover, if *que* is a complementizer, then it follows that *comment* must be a wh-word and cannot itself be a complementizer, since criterion (44*i*) tells us that two complementizers can never be combined in French (though a wh-word can be combined with a following complementizer).

Once we accept that in the sequence *comment que* 'how that' *comment* is a wh-word and *que* is an optional finite-clause complementizer, then the 'oddity' of examples like (134) becomes immediately apparent. For if in fact *comment* had been a wh-quantifier, then we should have expected the expression being quantified to have been positioned immediately after *comment* (and *not* after the complementizer *que*), giving us:

(140*a*) **Comment belle* (qu')elle est!
'How beautiful (that) she is!'
(*b*) **Comment de fric* (qu')il a!
'How of money (that) he has!'

But, as we see, (140) is not grammatical either. Why? The obvious answer is that *comment* (like *comme*) cannot be used to quantify an adjectival or partitive nominal expression, since it is not in fact a quantifier of any sort. Moreover, a further anomaly arises in relation to Gérard's examples (136): here, given that we are dealing with a non-clausal exclamative, it is scarcely surprising to find that we can't have *comment que*, since *que* is a finite-clause complementizer, and hence can only be used in finite clauses (not in phrases). Moreover, given that *comment* cannot function as a quantifier either, it follows that even if we omit *que* in (136), the resultant sentences will still be ungrammatical: cf.

(141*a*) *Une belle journée que nous avons là, et *comment ensoleillée*!
'A nice day we've got there, and how sunny!'
(*b*) **Comment de pot*!
'How of luck!'

Thus, all the relevant facts follow from our twin assumptions that (i) *que* is a finite-clause complementizer, and (ii) *comment* is a wh-word which cannot function as a quantifier. What kind of wh-word is *comment*? Since in its manner use it is an adverb, an obvious suggestion would be that in its non-manner use it also has an adverbial function: more precisely, like *comme*, it functions as a sentential wh-adverb.

Our rejection of the complementizer analysis of *comment* in favour of a wh-word analysis has interesting consequences for Gérard's hypothesis that a major historical change has been taking place in Modern French under which the 'old' wh-exclamatives have been replaced by the 'new' complementizer-exclamatives. But given our conclusion that exclamative *comment* is not a complementizer but rather a wh-word, then the recent appearance of *comment* as an exclamative particle suggests *precisely the opposite*—namely that Modern French has strengthened its armoury of wh-exclamatives by the addition of an additional exclamative wh-word, *comment*. Moreover, it is interesting to note that in expanding from an interrogative to an exclamative use, the wh-adverb *comment* has followed the well-worn path previously trodden by the wh-adverb *comme* 'how', since the latter too originated as an interrogative adverb, and subsequently became used as an exclamative adverb (ultimately to the exclusion of its interrogative use). Contrary to Gérard's claim of a radical restructuring of exclamatives, it seems more probable that exclamative *comment* presents us with a case of 'Plus ça change, et plus c'est la même chose.'

6. The status of exclamative *ce que*

The use(s) of exclamative *ce que* 'it that' in Modern French can be illustrated by the following examples (from Gérard 1980: 43–54):

(142*a*) Ce qu'on peut s'emmerder ici!
'How cheesed off you can get here!'

(*b*) Ce qu'il est enquiquinant!
'What a pain in the neck he is!'

(*c*) Ce qu'on mange bien ici!
'How well you eat here!'

(*d*) Ce qu'il a dépensé du fric!
'What a load of bread he spent!'

(*e*) C'est fou ce qu'il a comme courage!
'It's unbelievable what courage he has!'

(*f*) Ce qu'il s'est conduit avec lâcheté!
'What cowardice he behaved with!'

Gérard (1980: 45) maintains that in all these uses 'l'exclamatif *ce que* se comporte comme un complémenteur' (='the exclamative *ce que* behaves like a complementizer'): this is reaffirmed in her 'Conclusion' (1980: 131). But how convincing a 'conclusion' is it?

Our morphological criterion (44*a*) casts doubt on the validity of the complementizer analysis. For one thing, it seems clear that *ce que* 'it that' is not an indivisible monomorphemic unit, since (e.g.) *que* can occur without *ce* in co-ordinate structures like:

(143) *Ce qu*'il descend comme pâtes et *qu*'il sirote comme vin!
'What he guzzles by way of pasta and swigs by way of wine!'

Note particularly that the second *que* here cannot be our familiar 'exclamative *que*' discussed in section 4, since the latter does not occur in sentences such as:

(144) **Qu*'il sirote comme vin!
'What he swigs by way of wine!'

In other words, *que* in (143) must be an 'elliptical' form of *ce que*; but the fact that *que* occurs without *ce* in the second conjunct shows that we are dealing with a sequence of two different morphemes—*ce* 'it' on the one hand, and *que* 'that' on the other. Hence, if indeed *ce que* is a complementizer, it must represent a new breed of 'compound complementizer' previously unheard of in the history of French.

However, not only does *ce que* not satisfy the criterion (44*a*) of being monomorphemic, but it also fails to satisfy the second condition in (44*a*)—that of being *invariable*. For it turns out that in place of *que* in *ce que* exclamatives we can have (in an appropriate context) *qui* 'which/who' or even *dont* 'of which/whom': cf.

(145*a*) *Ce qui* est descendu comme pluie!
'What came down by way of rain!'

(*b*) *Ce dont* on l'accuse comme crimes!
'What they're accusing him of by way of crimes!'

Now since *qui* 'which' and *dont* 'of which' (and indeed *que* 'that') are all used as relative 'particles', it becomes apparent that *ce que* exclamatives are essentially of the form *ce + restrictive relative clause*. *Ce* here is arguably a demonstrative pronoun which heads the overall structure, and is itself modified by a relative clause. This analysis is made all the more plausible by the fact that demonstrative *ce* 'this/that' in French is not infrequently used with 'exclamative force' (like English *the*), as in the following examples (from Milner 1978: 360):

(146*a*) *Ce vacarme*! Impossible de s'entendre!
'The din! Impossible to hear yourself!'

(*b*) Jean m'a dit qu'il t'avait soutenu. —— *Ce culot*!
'Jean told me that he'd supported you. —— The cheek!'

(*c*) Jean a joué la Sonate au clair de lune. Vous imaginez *ce massacre*!
'Jean played the Moonlight Sonata. You can imagine the mess!'

What is even more significant is the fact that demonstrative nominals of the form *determiner* + *noun* can be used to head a relative clause, with the whole resultant structure having the illocutionary force of an exclamation, as in:

(147*a*) *Ce respect* qu'il a pour son patron!
'The respect which he has for his boss!'

(*b*) *Cette dévotion* qu'elle a pour ses enfants!
'The devotion she shows to her children!'

(*c*) *Ces crimes horribles* dont on l'accuse!
'The horrible crimes they're accusing him of!'

(*d*) *Ces rumeurs* qui courent sur elle!'
'The rumours which are going round about her!'

The only difference between 'standard' relative clauses like (147) above and *ce que* exclamatives lies in the simple fact that *ce que* exclamatives have a pronominal head rather than a nominal one. But, of course, relative structures can perfectly well have a pronominal head, as the following (non-exclamative) examples show:

(148*a*) *ce qui* m'est arrivé
'what (lit.: that which) happened to me'

(*b*) *ce que* tu fais
'what (lit.: that which) you are doing'

(*c*) *ce dont* il a parlé
'what he talked about' (lit.: that about which)

I therefore see no reason not to treat *ce que* exclamatives as ordinary relative-clause structures, their exclamative force lying in the use of the 'emphatic' demonstrative *ce*.

One interesting consequence of a relative-clause analysis for *ce que* exclamatives is that, since relative clauses are used to modify nominals, the overall nominal + relative structure has the status of a noun phrase—so that it would follow that we should expect exclamative *ce que* . . . structures to behave like noun phrases. And indeed—as Gérard 1980: 106–11 shows—they do have the same distribution as noun phrases. For example, like noun phrases they can be used as the object of a preposition: cf. e.g.

(149) Tu ne peux pas te faire une idée *de ce qu'il a été gentil.*
'You've got no idea about how kind he was!'

Moreover, like other noun phrases, *ce que* exclamatives can be used as the subject (or indeed object) of a verb: cf.

(150) *Ce qu'il a dit comme bêtises* m'a sidérée!
'What stupid things he said floored me.'

And, like other noun phrases, *ce que* exclamatives can occur as the topic of a sentence—cf.

(151) *Ce qu'il a commis comme bourdes*, j'ai encore du mal à le réaliser!
'What blunders he made, I still have difficulty in imagining it.'

(examples (149)–(151) are from Gérard, loc. cit.). The 'relative-clause' analysis thus seems to have considerable plausibility.

Moreover, a relative-clause analysis also accounts for many other aspects of the behaviour of *ce que* exclamatives with respect to the criteria in (44): a few examples should suffice to illustrate this (hence I shall not try the patience of the reader by going through the complete list!). Consider, for example, how we might account for the fact that *ce que* appears to play a grammatical role internally within its clause (criterion (44*b*)) in sentences such as:

(152) *Ce qu*'il a descendu comme vin!
'What he swigged down by way of wine!'

where it appears to act as the object of *descendu*. Under our proposed relative-clause analysis, this is easily accounted for if (e.g.) *que* is a relative pronoun and hence able to function as the object of *descendu.*[3] Likewise, the fact that we find Stylistic Inversion (criterion (44*f*)) in *ce que* exclamatives—cf.

(153*a*) Ce qu'a siroté *ton père* comme vin!
'What your father swigged by way of wine!'
(*b*) C'est incroyable ce qu'a gémi *ce pauvre malade* hier soir.
'It's incredible how much the poor patient groaned last night.'

follows from the fact that the same inversion is found in 'ordinary' relative clauses—cf.

(154) la quantité de vin qu'a siroté *ton père*
'the quantity of wine that your father swigged'

Conversely (cf. 44(*g*)), the fact that Subject Clitic Inversion is not found in *ce que* exclamatives—cf.

(155) *Ce que n'*aurait-il* pas fait pour se payer une Porsche!
'What wouldn't he have done to buy a Porsche!'

follows from its exclusion in relative clauses:

(156) *La voiture que *veut-il* se payer est une Porsche.
'The car that he wants to buy is a Porsche.'

No less significant (criterion (44*j*)) is the fact that *ce* can be modified by *tout*:

(157*a*) *Tout* ce qu'il claque comme fric!
'All that he earns by way of bread!'
(*b*) *Tout* ce qu'il est mignon, ce petit *bébé*!
'He really is cute (lit.: All that he is cute), this little baby.'

This of course would be entirely consistent with the relative analysis proposed here, under which *ce* 'it/this/that' would be modified by *tout* 'all' in the same way as other demonstrative pronouns in 'ordinary' relatives such as:

(158) *Tout* ce qui brille n'est pas de l'or.
'All (it) that glitters is not gold.'

[3] A technical complication here is posed by the possbiility that relative *que* is a complementizer (as Kayne 1976 claimed) rather than a relative pronoun; in such a case, we would say that the relative clause contains an abstract 'empty' relative pronoun operator which itself functions as the object of the relevant verb: however, this technical complication does not destroy the force of the argument here.

I see no plausible way of handling structures such as (157) under a complementizer analysis, since complementizers cannot be modified by quantifiers like *tout* 'all'. And finally, the clearly unbounded character of *ce que* in cases like:

(159) *Ce que* l'on dit qu'il gagne comme fric!
'What people say he earns by way of bread!'

(where *ce que* is 'associated with' the expression *comme fric* in the subordinate clause) again seems hard to square with a complementizer analysis (cf. (44*n*)), but is simply accounted for on a relative analysis, given that relative pronouns are not clause-bound: cf.

(160) la quantité de vin *qu*'on dit qu'il sirote
'the quantity of wine that people say that he swigs'

where *que* appears to function as the object of the subordinate verb *sirote* (with the proviso made in n. 3). For reasons such as these, then, it seems clear that *ce que* exclamatives are simply thinly disguised relative-clause structures.

At this point it is perhaps opportune to recall that Gérard's central thesis is that Modern French has seen the creation of a new series of 'exclamative complementizers' (namely *comment que*, *ce que*, and *qu'est-ce que*) which have largely ousted more traditional wh-constructions. However, if our 'relative' analysis of *ce que* exclamatives is correct, then far from being a radically new type of exclamative structure involving a compound *ce que* complementizer, *ce que* exclamatives turn out to be nothing more spectacular than a traditional relative-clause structure comprising a demonstrative pronoun modified by a restrictive relative clause—a pattern which is as old as the French language itself. So, once again we have a case of 'Plus ça change, et plus c'est la même chose.'

7. The status of exclamative *qu'est-ce que*

The uses of exclamative *qu'est-ce que* 'what is it that' can be illustrated by the following examples (from Gérard 1980: 47–8):

(161*a*) Qu'est-ce qu'ils trimbalent!
'How daft they are!'

(*b*) Qu'est-ce qu'elle est mignonne, cette petite!
'How cute she is, this little girl!'

(*c*) Qu'est-ce qu'elle parle mal!
'How badly she speaks!'

(*d*) Qu'est-ce qu'elle a du fric!
'What a lot of dough she has!'

Gérard argues (1980: 50) that '*qu'est-ce que* n'est pas un élément +wh, mais un complémenteur' ('*qu'est-ce que* isn't a wh-element, but a complementizer'). We shall see, however, that this conclusion is far from convincing.

Given that (by criterion (44*a*)) complementizers tend to be invariable, an obvious question to ask is whether or not *qu'est-ce que* can be regarded as an 'indivisible' unit in Modern French. It is interesting to note in this connection that there is an important contrast between *ce que* and *qu'est-ce que*: for whereas the final *que* of *ce que* can be replaced by the genitive relative pronoun *dont* 'of whom' (as we saw in (145) above), this is not possible with *qu'est-ce que*: cf.

(162) *Qu'est-ce dont on l'accuse comme crimes!
'What people accuse him of by way of crimes!'

Thus, if the final *que* of *qu'est-ce que* is indeed an independent morpheme, it seems clear that it is not a relative-clause particle of any sort. So what else could it be? Well, it might of course be the finite-clause complementizer *que* 'that' (which, as we have already seen, can combine with exclamative wh-expressions like *comment* 'how'). In connection with this possibility, it is interesting to note that (as Kayne 1976 observes) the complementizer *que* has the allomorph *qui* when it immediately precedes a finite verb:[4] hence contrasts such as:

(163*a*) Tu crois *que* laquelle va gagner?
'You think that which one will win?'

(*b*) Laquelle crois-tu *qui* va gagner?
'Which one do you think that will win?'

It is interesting to note that the final *que* of the interrogative expression *qu'est-ce que* 'what is it that' shows the same *qui* allomorph under appropriate conditions: cf. the contrast below:

[4] More technically, *que* absorbs the Nominative Case of the trace of a preposed Nominative subject; however, this technical complication need not concern us here, since it does not affect that validity of the argumentation in any way.

(164*a*) Qu'est-ce *que* tu vas faire?
'What is it that you are going to do?'
(*b*) Qu'est-ce *qui* sera fait?
'What is it that will be done?'

This suggests that the final *que* of interrogative *qu'est-ce que* is an independent morpheme, probably to be identified with the complementizer *que* 'that'. However, what is of more immediate relevance for our purposes here is the fact that, in the exclamative sequence *qu'est-ce que*, the final *que* cannot have the *qui* allomorph, as we see from the ungrammaticality of:

(165) *Qu'est-ce *qui* est descendu comme pluie!
'What fell by way of rain!'

Interestingly, the only way of expressing (165) using *qu'est-ce que* would be in terms of the corresponding impersonal construction:

(166) *Qu'est-ce qu*'il est descendu comme pluie!
'What there fell by way of rain!'

and the interesting point to note about the construction in (166) is that it allows the form *qu'est ce que* to be used. Thus we are beginning to see evidence which suggests that exclamative *qu'est-ce que* may have become a 'fossilized formula' in Modern French.

If indeed this is the case, then we should expect that the remainder of the exclamative formula (i.e. the *qu'est-ce* sequence) should also be invariable: and, indeed, there is strong evidence to suggest that this is the case. For one thing, the initial *qu'* element cannot be replaced by another exclamative wh-expression, as we see from the ungrammaticality of:

(167) **Que de bonbons* est-ce qu'il a mangés!
'How many sweets he has eaten!'

In this respect, the initial *que* of exclamative *qu'est-ce que* differs from the initial *que* of interrogative *qu'est-ce que*, since the latter can indeed be replaced by other wh-expressions: cf. e.g.

(168) *Lequel* est-ce qu'il a choisi?
'Which one is it that he has chosen?'

Thus, the fact that the initial *qu'* of exclamative *qu'est ce que* cannot be replaced by another exclamative wh-expression strongly suggests that fossilization of the formula has taken place with exclamatives (though not, of course, with interrogatives).

Now, if we are right in claiming that interrogative *qu'est-ce que* is a productive four-morpheme construction whereas exclamative *qu'est-ce que* is an unproductive fossilized formula, then we should expect to find evidence that the *est-ce* sequence of *qu'est-ce que* in interrogatives is an 'inverted' form of *c'est*, whereas in exclamatives it is not (but rather is fossilized as *est-ce*). Now, although interrogative *qu'est-ce que* has the 'uninverted' counterpart *que c'est que*: cf. e.g.

(169) Que *c'est* qu'il a fait?
'What is it that he did?'

the same is not true of exclamative *qu'est-ce que*, which has no 'uninverted' *que c'est que* counterpart: cf.

(170*a*) *Que *c'est* qu'il a descendu comme vin!
'What he swigged down by way of wine!'
(*b*) *Que *c'est* qu'elle est mignonne!
'How cute she is!'

Indeed, the fact that exclamative *qu'est-ce que* cannot be analysed as a productive inverted form of *que c'est que* is hardly surprising, given that 'positive' Subject Clitic Inversion in not found in exclamatives (as we noted earlier)—hence the ungrammaticality of:

(171) *Que de bouquins *a-t-il* achetés!
'What a lot of books he bought!'

Thus, the natural conclusion to draw from our discussion is that while interrogative *qu'est-ce que* is probably best analysed as a quadrimorphemic [*qu* + *est* + *ce* + *que*] sequence, exclamative *qu'est-ce que* is probably best analysed as a 'fossilized formula'—i.e. as an invariable monomorphemic sequence.

So far, we have established only that exclamative *qu'est-ce que* is an unanalysable exclamative expression: but we have not discussed its status. Is it an exclamative *complementizer* (as Gérard would have us believe), or is it an exclamative wh-expression? Bearing in mind that (by criterion (44*b*)) wh-expressions play a grammatical role internally within their clause but complementizers do not, it is interesting to note that in sentences such as:

(172) Qu'est-ce qu'il a comme voitures!
'What he has by way of cars!'

the *qu'est-ce que* expression must clearly function as the direct object of *a* 'has', since the sentence becomes ungrammatical if this object is removed: cf.

(173) *Il a comme voitures.
He has by way of cars.

Now, since we established earlier that only a wh-expression can play a grammatical role within its clause (not a complementizer), it seems clear that *qu'est-ce que* in (172) must be a wh-expression (whose grammatical role is that of direct object of *a* 'has'). Since the verb *a* 'has' typically subcategorizes a nominal object, it follows that exclamative *qu'est-ce que* in this type of function must be analysed as a nominal expression (i.e. as a noun phrase of some sort, a wh-NP).

Some further support for the wh-NP analysis comes from the fact that, like typical wh-expressions (and unlike complementizers), exclamative *qu'est-ce que* is potentially unbounded in scope (cf. criterion (44*m*)): thus, in

(174) Qu'est-ce qu'on nous demande de lire comme bouquins dans cette maudite université!
'What they ask us to read by way of books in this damned university!'

qu'est-ce que is positioned at the front of the main *demande* 'ask' clause and yet functions as the object of the subordinate *lire* 'read' clause, showing its potentially unbounded character.

Now, if we are right in suggesting that one function of exclamative *qu'est-ce que* is as a wh-NP, then we might expect to find that (like other noun phrases), it can be used as a subject, verbal object, or prepositional object. However, this is not the case at all. For, although *qu'est-ce que* can be used to 'replace' a direct object (as in (172) above) or postposed subject (i.e. a subject postposed in an impersonal construction, as in (166) above), it cannot be used in subject or prepositional object function, as we see from the ungrammaticality of:

(175*a*) **Qu'est-ce que* descend comme neige!
'What is falling by way of snow!'

(*b*) *De *qu'est-ce que* tu rigoles!
'What you giggle about!'

Now, at first sight, this restriction of *qu'est-ce que* to object and postposed subject function might seem strange—unparalleled even—and thus might call into question the plausibility of the wh-NP analysis. However, there is an interesting parallel to be drawn between exclamative *qu'est-ce que* and the interrogative pronoun (i.e. wh-NP) *que* 'what'.[5] For interrogative *que* seems to be subject to similar restrictions: thus, as (176) below suggests, *que* can function to question a verbal object and a postposed subject, but not a preverbal subject or a prepositional object: cf.

(176*a*) *Que* fait-il? (verbal object)
'What is he doing?'
(*b*) *Que* se passe-t-il? (postverbal subject)
'What is there happening?'
(*c*) **Que* se passe? (preverbal subject)
'What is happening?'
(*d*) **De que* parlaient-ils? (prepositional object)
'About what were they talking?'

Thus, the restrictions on exclamative *qu'est-ce que* seem to be very much parallel to those on interrogative *que*. One way of describing these restrictions would be to say that both interrogative *que* and exclamative *qu'est-ce que* are restricted (in their nominal use) to Objective (or Accusative) case function. If we assume that preverbal finite-clause subjects are assigned Nominative case, prepositional objects are assigned Oblique case, and postverbal NPs (i.e. direct objects or postposed subjects) are assigned Objective case, then it follows that, if interrogative *que* and exclamative *qu'est-ce que* are intrinsically Objective, they can only be used to 'replace' a direct object or postposed subject. However, it should be noted that any such analysis raises complex issues in Case Theory which we cannot go into here. The more general point, however, is that the plausibility of a wh-NP analysis for exclamative *qu'est-ce que* is strengthened by the fact that it seems to be subject to the same restrictions as another wh-NP, namely the interrogative pronoun *que* 'what'. In other words, a wh-NP analysis of exclamative *qu'est-*

[5] I am following the traditional analysis of *que* as an interrogative pronoun, and thus implicitly rejecting Obenauer's (1976) analysis of it as a complementizer, for reasons which I lack the space to go into here.

ce que would be no less plausible than the traditional wh-NP analysis of interrogative *que*.[6]

However, although it seems clear that one function of exclamative *qu'est-ce que* is as an (Objective?) wh-NP, this cannot be its only function. For example, in sentences such as (177) below (repeated from (161) above), *qu'est-ce que* represents neither a verbal object nor a postposed subject:

(177*a*) Qu'est-ce qu'ils trimbalent!
'How daft they are!'
(*b*) Qu'est-ce qu'elle est mignonne, cette petite!
'How cute she is, this little girl!'
(*c*) Qu'est-ce qu'elle parle mal!
'How badly she speaks!'
(*d*) Qu'est-ce qu'elle a du fric!
'What a lot of dough she has!'

So what function does *qu'est-ce que* serve in such examples? The obvious suggestion to make here is that *qu'est-ce que* functions as an exclamative sentence-adverbial (i.e. it is an exclamative counterpart of adverbs such as *décidément* 'decidedly', so that, in all the examples in (177) above, *qu'est-ce que* could be replaced by *décidément*). If this is so, then it would mean that *qu'est-ce que* would serve a dual function as a wh-NP on the one hand, and a sentence adverbial on the other.

But surely such a 'dual' analysis would be unprecedented, would it not? No, of course not! After all, as we have already seen, exclamative *combien* can function both as a wh-NP in sentences such as:

(178) *Combien* il a payé!
'How much he paid!'

and as a wh-adverb in sentences such as the following (from Milner 1978: 272):

(179) *Combien* j'eus à l'entendre répéter souvent!
'How I heard it repeated often!'

Thus, our proposal to assign dual categorial status to exclamative *qu'est-ce que* is by no means unprecedented or implausible.

[6] This is not to say that there are not differences between the two: e.g. interrogative *que* is arguably a clitic whereas exclamative *qu'est-ce que* is not.

So, what we have suggested here is that, in Modern French, exclamative *qu'est-ce que* has become fossilized as an invariable monomorphemic expression which can either function as an Objective wh-NP, or as a sentential wh-adverbial. Given that *qu'est-ce que* has changed its status from being (historically) a productive phrase to becoming (synchronically) an unanalysable word, we might wonder how far down the path from *phrase* to *word* it has travelled: i.e. we might wonder what aspects of its behaviour can be accounted for under the wh-word analysis, and what aspects (if any) are anomalous under the wh-word analysis (and are in historical terms attributable to the phrasal origin of the expression).

Certainly, there are many aspects of the use of exclamative *qu'est-ce que* which are immediately consistent with its new-found status as a wh-word. For example, the fact that (in both nominal and adverbial uses) it permits Stylistic Inversion: cf.

(180*a*) Qu'est-ce qu'a bouffé *ton copain*!
'What a lot your friend guzzled!'
(*b*) Qu'est-ce qu'a rigolé *ton copain*!
'What a lot your friend laughed!'

is an automatic consequence of its wh-word status (though is inconsistent with Gérard's complementizer analysis), since we saw in (44*f*) that wh-words trigger Stylistic Inversion but complementizers do not. However, some aspects of the behaviour of *qu'est-ce que* seem more difficult to reconcile with its status as a wh-word. For example, we have already seen that wh-words can generally co-occur with the complementizer *que* (cf. 44*i*)); and yet exclamative *que* cannot be used in this way:

(181) *Qu'est-ce que *qu'*on a rigolé!
'What a lot (that) we laughed!'

Surely this fact can only be explained in terms of the historical (phrasal) origins of *qu'est-ce que*? Well, no, not at all! For the simple fact is that there are complex lexical restrictions on the set of wh-words which can co-occur with *que*: for example, we saw earlier that although the manner adverb *comment* 'how' can be followed by *que* in its exclamative use, the manner adverb *comme* cannot: hence contrasts such as:

(182*a*) Comme (**qu'*)il traite ses parents!
'How (that) he treats his parents!'

(*b*) Comment (*qu'*)il traite ses parents!
'How (that) he treats his parents!'

Thus, in this respect exclamative *qu'est-ce que* patterns like *comme* rather than *comment*—a fact which therefore in no sense undermines the wh-word analysis of *qu'est-ce que*.

Rather more problematic is the fact that exclamative *qu'est-ce que* cannot occur internally within sentences—hence the ungrammaticality of:

(183) *Combien de personnes bouffent *qu'est-ce que*!
'How many people are guzzling what a lot!'

However, in this respect, *qu'est-ce que* is no different from interrogative *que*, which likewise cannot be sentence-internal: cf.

(184) *T'as fait *que*/*T'as *que* fait?
'You did what!'

Thus whatever restriction holds for interrogative *que* also seems to operate in the case of exclamative *qu'est-ce que*, so heightening the parallels between the two expressions.

A far greater apparent problem faced by the wh-word analysis of exclamative *qu'est-ce que* is the fact that it does not allow Subject Clitic Inversion (even in negatives): cf.

(185) *Qu'est-ce que n'*aurait-il* pas bouffé s'il l'avait pu!
'What wouldn't he have guzzled if he had been able to!

Does this fact not require us to recognize that *qu'est-ce que* still behaves in part like a phrasal sequence which itself contains an instance of Subject Clitic Inversion (*est-ce* 'is it'), and thus blocks any further application of inversion? I think that, even here, the answer is 'No'. For we have already seen that clitic inversion is subject to some extremely strong syntactic restrictions in exclamatives (e.g. it occurs only in negatives) and likewise subject to some puzzling lexical restrictions (e.g. it does not occur after exclamative *comme* even when used as a manner adverb). So it would seem as if even in this respect we can continue to defend the wh-word analysis, if we argue that *qu'est-ce que* has some of the properties of exclamative *comme* (properties, it must be admitted, of a poorly understood nature).

One final problem relating to the wh-word analysis of *qu'est-ce que* arises in relation to sentences such as:

(186) Qu'est-ce qu'il sirote comme vin et *qu*'il bouffe comme pâtes!
'What he swigs by way of wine and guzzles by way of pasta!'

Now here it might at first sight seem as if the italicized (contracted) occurrence of *que* is being used as an 'elliptical' form of *qu'est-ce que*, and hence that *qu'est-ce que* must comprise at least two morphemes, namely *qu'est-ce* and *que* (with the *qu'est-ce* part being ellipsed in the second clause, and only *que* remaining). However, the assumption here that the second (italicized) *que* is an elliptical form of *qu'est-ce que* is a fallacious one: after all, in an exclamative such as:

(187) Combien de fois il est allé au cinéma et *qu*'il a raté le film!
'How many times he has been to the cinema, and (that) he has missed the film!'

it would clearly be implausible to analyse *que* as an elliptical form of *combien de fois*. Rather, what seems to be going on here is that a wh-phrase can (generally) be followed by the finite complementizer *que*, and the complementizer position is left empty in the first clause in (187), but is filled by *que* in the second clause. We might then assume that something similar is going on in (186), with the additional complication that exclamative *qu'est-ce que* cannot be immediately followed by *que*, as we saw earlier.

Overall, then, I think there is little reason to suppose that in Modern French exclamative *qu'est-ce que* retains any of its historical phrasal status. Rather, the balance of the empirical evidence clearly favours reanalysis of *qu'est-ce que* into an invariable wh-word which can function either as an Objective pronoun, or as a sentence adverbial. Our wh-word analysis deals yet another blow to Gérard's claim that Modern French has been developing a new series of exclamative complementizers: for, as we have seen, it turns out that the very opposite is the case—i.e. Modern French has seen the creation of a new wh-word with both a nominal and an adverbial function. Thus, French has strengthened its armoury of exclamative wh-words by the addition of *qu'est-ce que* (which we might write as *quesque* to symbolize its new status as an indivisible free morpheme)—a development clearly in the *opposite* direction from that envisaged by Gérard!

8. Summary

The main purpose of this paper has been to investigate the plausibility of Gérard's (1980) claim that Modern French has seen a major restructuring in the syntax of exclamations, with the replacement of wh-exclamatives by complementizer-exclamatives. More precisely, Gérard argues that whereas Classical French had both exclamative wh-words like *combien* 'how (much/many)' and *que* 'what' (in its quantifier use), and exclamative complementizers like *si* 'if', *comme* 'how', and *que* 'that' (in its non-quantifier use), Modern French by contrast has seen a contraction in wh-exclamatives and an expansion in complementizer-exclamatives. The contraction in wh-exclamatives follows (in Gérard's view) from the twin facts that (i) *combien* 'est aujourd'hui réservé à la langue littéraire et absent de la langue parlée' ('is today reserved for the literary language and absent from the spoken language'), and (ii) the wh-quantifier *que* was formerly used to quantify adjectival, adverbial, prepositional, and nominal constituents, but now survives only in the latter use. The expansion in the use of exclamative complementizers (Gérard claims) comes from the fact that Modern French has created three new 'compound complementizers', namely *comment que*, *ce que*, and *qu'est-ce que*.

Interesting though Gérard's hypothesis is, it appears from the evidence here that it is completely untenable. For one thing, the claim that *comme* and (non-quantifier) *que* are (or indeed ever were) complementizers seems (to say the least) open to doubt, given that a wh-adverb analysis is at least equally (and in some respects more) plausible. And the claim that *ce que*, *comment que*, and *qu'est-ce que* represent the emergence of a new breed of complementizer seems even less tenable. On the contrary, as we have argued here, *ce que* . . . structures are best analysed as relative Noun Phrases headed by the demonstrative pronoun *ce* 'this/that' modified by a restrictive relative clause introduced by relative *que* 'that': thus, they are no more than traditional relative-clause constructions, and not in any sense a radically new type of exclamative construction. As for the emergence of *comment* 'how' as an 'exclamative particle', this clearly marks nothing more dramatic that the extension of an interrogative wh-adverb to a secondary function as an exclamative wh-adverb; and like (most) other wh-words, *comment* can optionally be followed by the finite complementizer *que* 'that', so giving rise to *comment que* . . . exclamatives. But far from being a new complementizer, *comment* is simply what it always was—i.e. a wh-adverb which has come to oust the more literary adverb *comme* 'how'. And finally, it seems likely that the exclamative sequence *qu'est-ce que* 'what is it that' has now become fossilized into a single word (which we might write as *quesque*): but its behaviour clearly suggests that it functions as a nominal or adverbial wh-word, and not as a complementizer. Thus, while it is true that there has been a tendency to replace *combien* by *qu'est-ce que* and *comme* by *comment*, this does not represent the replacement of a wh-word by a complementizer, but rather the replacement of one wh-word by another wh-word. But this is surely no more than a case of 'New lamps for old!' (the lamps illuminating the history of French in this case being the relevant exclamative wh-words).

References

ALLAN, W. S. (1984). 'The Role of the Lexicon in Syntactic Change', Ph.D. thesis, University of Edinburgh.

ANDERSON, J. M. (1965). 'A Grammar of the Verb Phrase in English', dissertation, Diploma in General Linguistics, University of Edinburgh.

—— (1969). 'A Note on "Rank" and "Delicacy"', *Journal of Linguistics*, 5: 129–35.

—— (1971a). *The Grammar of Case: Towards a Localistic Theory*, Cambridge: Cambridge University Press.

—— (1971b). 'Outline of a Proposal for the Lexicalisation of Complex Structures', *Studia linguistica*, 15: 1–8.

—— (1972). 'Remarks on the Hierarchy of Quasi-predications', *Revue roumaine de linguistique*, 17: 23–44, 121–40, 193–202, 319–35.

—— (1973a). *An Essay Concerning Aspect*, The Hague: Mouton.

—— (1973b). 'Universal Quantifiers', *Lingua*, 31: 125–76.

—— (1974). 'Existential Quantifiers', *Acta linguistica Hafniensia*, 15: 1–27.

—— (1976). *On Serialisation in English Syntax*, Ludwigsburg Studies in Language and Linguistics, 1.

—— (1977). *On Case Grammar: Prolegomena to a Theory of Grammatical Relations*, London: Croom Helm.

—— (1978). 'Deep Structure Change? The History of the Modals in English', presented to the English Department, University of Lund.

—— (1979a). 'On Being without a Subject', Indiana University Linguistics Club.

—— (1979b). 'Serialisation, Dependency and the Syntax of Possessives in Moru', *Studia linguistica*, 33: 1–25.

—— (1980a). 'Towards Dependency Morphology: The Structure of the Basque Verb', in Anderson and Ewen 1980b: 227–71.

—— (1980b). 'Anti-unaccusative, or: Relational Grammar is Case Grammar', *Revue roumaine de linguistique*, 25: 193–225.

—— (1984). *Case Grammar and the Lexicon*, University of Ulster: Occasional Papers in Linguistics and Language Learning, 10.

—— (1985a). 'Structural Analogy and Dependency Phonology', *Acta linguistica Hafniensia*, 19: 5–44.

—— (1985b). 'The Case System of Old English: A Case for Non-modularity', *Studia linguistica*, 39: 1–22.

—— (1986). 'Structural Analogy and Case Grammar', *Lingua*, 70: 79–129.

—— (1987). 'The limits of Linearity', in Anderson and Durand 1987b: 199–220.

—— (forthcoming a). 'Grammaticalisation and the English Modals'.

—— (forthcoming b). 'The Tradition of Structural Analogy', in Ross Steele and Terry Threadgold (eds.), *Language Topics*, Amsterdam: Benjamins.

—— (forthcoming c). 'Old English Morphology and the Structure of Noun Phrases', *Folia linguistica historica*, 7.

—— and DURAND, J. (1986). 'Dependency Phonology', in Durand 1986: 1–54.

—— —— (1987a). Introduction to Anderson and Durand 1987b: 1–14.

—— —— (eds.) (1987b). *Explorations in Dependency Phonology*, Dordrecht: Foris.

—— and EWEN, C. J. (1980a). Introduction: 'A Sketch of Dependency Phonology', in Anderson and Ewen 1980b: 9–40.

—— —— (eds.) (1980b). *Studies in Dependency Phonology*, Ludwigsburg Studies in Language and Linguistics, 4.

—— —— (1987). *Principles of Dependency Phonology*, Cambridge: Cambridge University Press.

—— —— and STAUN, J. (1985). 'Phonological Structure: Segmental, Suprasegmental and Extrasegmental', *Phonology Yearbook*, 2: 203–24.

ANDERSON, S. R. (1971). 'On the Role of Deep Structure in Semantic Interpretation', *Foundations of Language*, 7: 387–96.

—— (1985). 'Typological Distinctions in Word Formation', in Shopen (ed.) 1985c: 3–56.

ANTINUCCI, F., DURANTI, A., and GEBERT, L. (1979). 'Relative Clause Structure, Relative Clause Perception, and the Change from SOV to SVO', *Cognition*, 7: 145–76.

ARONOFF, M. (1976). *Word Formation in Generative Grammar*, Cambridge, Mass.: MIT Press.

ASANO, A. (1979). 'On Strategies for Processing Japanese Relative Clauses', unpublished MA thesis, International Christian University, Tokyo.

ASHER, R. E. (1985). *Tamil*, London: Croom Helm.

ATKINSON, R. M., KILBY, D. A., and ROCA, I. (1982). *Foundations of General Linguistics*, London: George Allen & Unwin.

BABBY, L. H. (1986). 'The Locus of Case Assignment and the Direction of Percolation: Case Theory and Russian', in R. D. Brecht and J. S. Levine (eds.), *Case in Slavic*, Columbus: Slavic Publishers, 170–219.

BACH, E. W. (1986). 'Natural Language Metaphysics', in *Logic, Methodology and Philosophy of Science VII*, Proceedings of the 7th International Congress of Logic, Methodology and Philosophy of Science, Salzburg, 1983, Amsterdam: North Holland, 573–97.

BACHE, C. (1978). *The Order of Pre-modifying Adjectives in Present-day English*, Odense: Odense University Press.

BAKER, C. L., and MCCARTHY, J. J. (eds.) (1981). *The Logical Problem of Language Acquisition*, Cambridge, Mass.: MIT Press.

BAKER, G. P., and HACKER, P. M. S. (1984). *Language, Sense and Nonsense*, Oxford: Blackwell.

BAMBERG, M. (1986). 'A Functional Approach to the Acquisition of Anaphoric Relationships', *Linguistics*, 24: 227–84

BARWISE, J., and PERRY, J. (1983). *Situations and Attitudes*, Cambridge, Mass.: MIT Press.

BEVER, T. G. (1970). 'The Cognitive Basis for Linguistic Structures', in J. R. Hayes (ed.), *Cognition and the Development of Language*, New York: Wiley & Sons, 279–352.

BHATTACHARYA, S. (1957). *Ollari: A Dravidian Speech*, Department of Anthropology, Government of India, Memoir no. 3, 1957, Delhi: Manager of Publications.

BLANSITT, E. L., jun. (1984). 'Dechticaetiative and Dative', in Plank (ed.) 1984b: 127–50.

BLOOMFIELD, L. (1930). 'Sacred Stories of the Sweet Grass Cree', Bulletin 60, Anthropological Series 11, Ottawa: National Museum of Canada.

—— (1933). *Language*, New York: Holt, Rinehart and Winston.

BOLINGER, D. (1980). '*Couple*: An English Dual', in Sidney Greenbaum, Geoffrey Leech, and Jan Svartvik (eds.), *Studies in English Linguistics for Randolph Quirk*, London: Longman, 30–40.

BOWERMAN, M. (1983). 'How do Children Avoid Constructing an Overly General Grammar in the Absence of Feedback about what is not a Sentence?' *Papers and Reports on Child Language Development*, 22: 23–35.

BRAME, M. (1983). 'Ungrammatical Notes', *Linguistic Analysis*, 11: 277–80.

BRESNAN, J. W. (1970). 'On Complementisers: Toward a Syntactic Theory of Complement Types', *Foundations of Language*, 6: 297–321.

—— (1972). 'Theory of Complementation in English Syntax', Ph.D. dissertation, MIT, Cambridge, Mass.

—— (1976). 'On the Form and Functioning of Transformations', *Linguistic Inquiry*, 7: 3–40.

—— (ed.) (1982). *The Mental Representation of Grammatical Relations*, Cambridge, Mass.: MIT Press.

BURROW, T., and BHATTACHARYA, S. (1953). *The Parji Language: A Dravidian Language of Bastar*, Hertford: Austin.

BURTON-ROBERTS, N. (1976). 'On the Generic Indefinite Article', *Language*, 52: 427–8.

CARNAP, R. (1956). *Meaning and Necessity*, 2nd edn., Chicago: University of Chicago Press.

CHOMSKY, C. (1969). *The Acquisition of Syntax in Children from 5 to 10*, Cambridge, Mass.: MIT Press.

CHOMSKY, N. (1965). *Aspects of the Theory of Syntax*, Cambridge, Mass.: MIT Press.

—— (1968). *Language and Mind*, New York: Harcourt, Brace & World.

—— (1973). 'Conditions on Transformations', in S. R. Anderson and P. Kiparsky (eds.), *A Festschrift for Morris Halle*, New York: Holt, Rinehart and Winston, 232–86.

—— (1977). 'On Wh-movement', in P. W. Culicover, T. Wasow, and A. Akmajian (eds.), *Formal Syntax*, New York: Academic Press, 71–132.

—— (1980). 'On Binding', *Linguistic Inquiry*, 11: 1–46.

—— (1981). *Lectures on Government and Binding*, Dordrecht: Foris.

—— (1982). *Some Concepts and Consequences of the Theory of Government and Binding*, Cambridge, Mass.: MIT Press.

—— (1986). *Barriers*, Cambridge, Mass.: MIT Press.

—— (1988). *Language and the Problems of Knowledge*, Cambridge, Mass.: MIT Press.

—— and Lasnik, H. (1977). 'Filters and Control', *Linguistic Inquiry*, 8: 425–504.

Christophersen, P. (1939). *The Articles: A Study of their Theory and Use in English*, Copenhagen: Ejnar Munksgaard.

Chung, S. (1976). 'An Object-creating Rule in Bahasa Indonesian', *Linguistic Inquiry*, 7: 41–87.

Clancy, P. M., Lee, H., and Zoh, M. (1986). 'Processing Strategies in the Acquisition of Relative Clauses: Universal Principles and Language-specific Realizations', *Cognition*, 24: 225–62.

Classification nominale (1967). *La Classification nominale dans les langues négro-africaines*, Paris: Centre national de la recherche scientifique.

Clements, G. N. (1980). 'Vowel Harmony in Nonlinear Generative Phonology', Indiana University Linguistics Club.

Comrie, B. (1978). 'Ergativity', in Lehmann (ed.) 1978: 329–94.

—— (1981). *Language Universals and Linguistic Typology*, Oxford: Blackwell, and Chicago: University of Chicago Press.

—— (1982). 'Grammatical Relations in Huichol', in Hopper and Thompson (eds.) 1982: 95–115.

—— and Thompson, S. A. (1985). 'Lexical Nominalization', in Shopen (ed.) 1985c: 349–98.

Coopmans, P. (1984). 'Surface Word-order Typology and Universal Grammar', *Language*, 60: 55–69.

Corbett, G. G. (1979). 'The Agreement Hierarchy', *Journal of Linguistics*, 15: 203–24.

—— (1981). 'Syntactic Features', *Journal of Linguistics*, 17: 55–76.

—— (1983). *Hierarchies, Targets and Controllers: Agreement Patterns in Slavic*, London: Croom Helm.

—— (1991). *Gender*, Cambridge: Cambridge University Press.

—— and Hayward, R. J. (1987). 'Gender & Number in Bayso', *Lingua*, 74: 195–222.

Cosmas, N. (1981). 'Grammatical Gender in Modern Greek', *Revue roumaine de linguistique*, 26: 549–57.

—— (1982). 'Grammatical Gender in Ancient Greek', *Revue roumaine de linguistique*, 27: 47–50.

CRESSWELL, M. J. (1985). *Structured Meanings: The Semantics of Propositional Attitudes*, Cambridge, Mass.: MIT Press.

CRUSE, D. (1973). 'Some Thoughts on Agentivity', *Journal of Linguistics*, 9: 11–23.

CRYSTAL, D. (1985). *A Dictionary of Linguistics and Phonetics*, 2nd edn., Oxford: Blackwell (1st edn. 1979).

GULICOVER, P., and WILKINS, W. (1986). 'Control, PRO, and the Projection Principle', *Language*, 62: 120–57.

CUTLER, A., HAWKINS, J. A., and GILLIGAN, G. (1985). 'The Suffixing Preference: A Processing Explanation', *Linguistics*, 23/5: 723–58.

DALEWSKA-GREŃ, H., and FELESZKO, K. (1984). 'Mesto brojeva u određivanju gramatičkog roda i broja u srpskohrvatskom i polskom jeziku', *Naučni Sastanak Slavista u Vukove Dane: Referati i saopstenja* (Belgrade), 13/1: 29–40.

DAVIDSON, D., and HINTIKKA, J. (eds.) (1969). *Words and Objections: Essays on the Work of W. V. Quine*, Dordrecht: Reidel.

DENCH, A. (1983). 'The Strange Case of Objects in Martuthunira', paper delivered to Annual Conference of Australian Linguistic Society.

—— (1987). 'Martuthunira: a language of the Pilbara region of Western Australia', Ph.D. thesis, Australian National University.

DEŠERIEV, JU. D. (1953). *Bacbijskij jazyk: Fonetika, morfologija, sintaksis, leksika*, Moscow: AN SSSR.

DE WOLF, P. (1971). *The Noun Class System of Proto-Benue-Congo*, The Hague: Mouton.

DIK, S. C. (1978). *Functional Grammar*, Amsterdam: North Holland.

DIXON, R. M. W. (1972). *The Dyirbal Language of North Queensland*, Cambridge Studies in Linguistics, 19, Cambridge: Cambridge University Press.

—— (1977). 'Where Have All the Adjectives Gone?' *Studies in Language*, 1: 19–80. (Reprinted in R. M. W. Dixon, *Where Have All the Adjectives Gone? And Other Essays in Semantics and Syntax*, The Hague: Mouton, 1982.)

—— (1979). 'Ergativity', *Language*, 55: 59–138.

—— (1982). *Where have All the Adjectives Gone? And Other Essays in Semantics and Syntax*, The Hague: Mouton.

—— (1988). *A Grammar of Boumaa Fijian*, Chicago: University of Chicago Press.

—— (forthcoming). *A New English Grammar, on Semantic Principles*.

DRYER, M. S. (1980). 'The Positional Tendencies of Sentential Noun Phrases in Universal Grammar', *Canadian Journal of Linguistics*, 25/2: 123–95.

—— (1983). 'Indirect Objects in Kinyarwanda Revisited', in D. M. Perlmutter (ed.), *Studies in Relational Grammar*, Chicago: University of Chicago Press, 1: 129–40.

DUBOIS, J., GIACOMO, M., and GUESPIN, L. (1972). *Dictionnaire de linguistique*, Paris: Larousse.

DURAND, J. (ed.) (1986). *Dependency and Non-linear Phonology*, London: Croom Helm.

DURANTI, A., and BYARUSHENGO, E. R. (1977). 'On the Notion of "Direct Object"', in E. Byarushengo, A. Duranti, and L. Hyman (eds.), *Haya Grammatical Structure*, Los Angeles: Dept. of Linguistics, University of Southern California, 45–71.

DURIE, M. (1987). 'Grammatical Relations in Acehnese', *Studies in Language*, 11, 365–439,

EATHER, B. (forthcoming). 'A Grammar of Nakkara', Ph.D. thesis, Australian National University.

EMENEAU, M. B. (1955). *Kolami: A Dravidian Language*, University of California Publications in Linguistics, 12, Berkeley and Los Angeles: University of California Press.

FALTZ, L. M. (1978). 'On Indirect Objects in Universal syntax', *Papers from the 14th Regional Meeting of the Chicago Linguistic Society*, 76–87.

—— (1985). *Reflexivization: A Study in Universal Syntax*, New York: Garland Publishing, Inc.

FILLMORE, C. J. (1969). 'The Case for Case', in E. Bach and R. T. Harms (eds.), *Universals in Linguistic Theory*, New York: Holt, Rinehart and Winston.

FODOR, I. (1959). 'The Origin of Grammatical Gender', *Lingua*, 1: 1–41; 2: 186–214.

FODOR, J. D. (1983). 'Constraints on Gaps: Is the Parser a Significant Influence?' in B. Buterworth, B. Comrie, and O. Dahl (eds.), *Explanations for Language Universals*, Berlin: Mouton, 9–34.

FOLEY, W. A., and VAN VALIN, R. D. (1984). *Functional Syntax and Universal Grammar*, Cambridge Studies in Linguistics, 38, Cambridge: Cambridge University Press.

FRAZIER, L. (1978). 'On Comprehending Sentences: Syntactic Parsing Strategies', Ph.D. dissertation, University of Connecticut.

—— (1979). 'Parsing and Constraints on Word Order', in J. Lowenstamm (ed.), University of Massachusetts Occasional Papers in Linguistics, 5: 177–98.

—— (1985). 'Syntactic Complexity', in D. R. Dowty, L. Karttunen, and A. M. Zwicky (eds.), *Natural Language Parsing: Psychological, Computational and Theoretical Perspectives*, Cambridge: Cambridge University Press, 129–89.

—— and RAYNER, K. (1982). 'Making and Correcting Errors during Sentence Comprehension: Eye Movements in the Analysis of Structurally Ambiguous Sentences', *Cognitive Psychology*, 14: 178–210.

GARY, J. O., and KEENAN, E. L. (1977). 'On Collapsing Grammatical Relations in Universal Grammar', in P. Cole and J. M. Sadock (eds.),

Syntax and Semantics, viii: Grammatical Relations, New York: Academic Press, 83–120.

GAZDAR, G. (1981). 'Unbounded Dependencies and Coordinate Structure', *Linguistic Inquiry*, 12: 155–84.

—— (1982). 'Phrase Structure Grammar', in G. Pullum and P. Jacobson (eds.), *The Nature of Syntactic Representation*, Dordrecht: Reidel, 131–86.

—— and PULLUM, G. (1982). 'Generalised Phrase Structure Grammar: A Theoretical Synopsis', Indiana University Linguistics Club.

GÉRARD, J. (1980). *L'Exclamation en français*, Tübingen: Niemeyer.

GIL, D. (1984). 'On the Notion of "Direct Object" in Patient Prominent Languages', in Plank (ed.) 1984b: 87–108.

GIVÓN, T. (1972). *Studies in ChiBemba and Bantu grammar*, Studies in African Linguistics 3, Supplement 3, Los Angeles: Department of Linguistics and African Studies Centre, University of California.

—— (1979). *On Understanding Grammar*, New York: Academic Press.

—— (ed.) (1983). *Topic Continuity in Discourse: A Quantitative Cross-language Study*, Amsterdam: Benjamins.

—— (1984a). *Syntax: A Functional-typological Introduction*, Amsterdam: Benjamins.

—— (1984b). 'Direct Object and Dative Shifting: Semantic and Pragmatic Case', in Plank (ed.) 1984b: 151–82.

GLADKIJ, A. (1969). 'K. opredeleniju ponjatij padeža i roda suščesvitel'nogo', *Voprosy jazykoznanija*, 2: 110–23.

—— (1973a). 'Popytka formal'nogo opredeleniju ponjatij padeza i roda suščestvitel'nogo', in A. A. Zaliznjak (ed.), *Problemy grammatičeskogo modelirovanija*, Moscow: Nauka, 24–53.

—— (1973b). 'An Attempt at the Formal Definition of Case and Gender of the Noun', in K. Kiefer (ed.), *Mathematical Models of Language*, Stockholm: Skriptor, 159–204.

GOLDSMITH, J. (1985). 'Vowel Harmony in Khalkha Mongolian, Yaka, Finnish and Hungarian', *Phonology Yearbook*, 2: 253–75.

GRAUR, A. (1937). 'Sur le genre neutre en roumain', *Bulletin linguistique publié par A. Rosetti*, 5: 5–11.

GREENBERG, J. H. (1966). 'Some Universals of Grammar with particular Reference to the Order of Meaningful Elements', in J. H. Greenberg (ed.), *Universals of Language*, Cambridge, Mass.: MIT Press (2nd edn.; 1st edn. 1963), 73–113.

—— (1978a). 'Some Generalisations Concerning Final and Initial Consonant Clusters', in J. H. Greenberg, C. A. Ferguson, and E. A. Moravcsik (eds.), *Universals of Human Language*, ii: *Phonology*, Stanford: Stanford University Press, 243–79.

—— (1978b). 'How Does a Language Acquire Gender Markers?' in J. H. Greenberg, C. A. Ferguson, and E. A. Moravcsik (eds.), *Universals of*

Human Language, iii: *Word Structure*, Stanford: Stanford University Press, 47–82.

—— (1978c). 'Generalizations about Numeral Systems', in J. H. Greenberg, C. A. Ferguson, and E. A. Moravcsik (eds.), *Universals of Human Language*, iii: *Word Structure*, Stanford: Stanford University Press, 249–96.

GROSS, M. (1968). *Grammaire transformationelle du français: Syntaxe du verbe*, Paris: Larousse.

GROSU, A., and THOMPSON, S. (1977). 'Constraints on the Distribution of NP Clauses', *Language*, 53, 104–51.

HAEGEMAN, L. (1983). '*Die* and *Dat* in West-Flemish Relative Clauses', in H. Bennis and W. U. S. van Lessen Kloeke (eds.), *Linguistics in the Netherlands 1983*, Dordrecht: Foris, 83–91.

HAIMAN, J. (1974). *Targets and Syntactic Change*, The Hague: Mouton.

—— and MUNRO, P. (eds.) (1983). *Switch-reference and Universal Grammar*, Typological Studies in Language, 2, Amsterdam: Benjamins.

HAKUTA, K. (1982). 'Grammatical Description *Versus* Configurational Arrangement in Language Acquisition: The Case of Relative Clauses in Japanese', *Cognition*, 9: 197–236.

HALL, B. (1965). 'Subject and Object in Modern English', Ph.D. dissertation, MIT.

HALL, R. A. (1965). 'The "Neuter" in Romance: A Pseudo-problem', *Word*, 21: 421–7.

HALLIDAY, M. A. K. (1966). 'Some Notes on "Deep Grammar" ', *Journal of Linguistics*, 2: 110–17.

HANKAMER, J. (1973). 'Unacceptable Ambiguity', *Linguistic Inquiry*, 4: 17–68.

HARADA, S. I., UYENO, T., HAYASHIBE, H., and YAMADA, H. (1976). 'On the Development of Perceptual Strategies in Children: A Case Study of the Japanese Child's Comprehension of Relative Clause Constructions', in *Annual Bulletin of the Research Institute of Logopedics and Phoniatrics, University of Tokyo*, 10: 199–224.

HARTMANN, R. R. K., and STORK, F. C. (1972). *Dictionary of Language and Linguistics*, London: Applied Science Publishers Ltd.

HAWKINS, J. A. (1982). 'Language Universals and the Logic of Historical Reconstruction', *Linguistics*, 20/5–6: 367–90.

—— (1983). *Word Order Universals*, New York: Academic Press.

—— (1984). 'Modifier-head or Function-argument Relations in Phrase Structure? The Evidence of Some Word Order Universals', *Lingua*, 63: 107–38.

—— (1986). *A Comparative Typology of English and German*, Austin: University of Texas Press, and London: Croom Helm.

HEINE, B. (1968). *Die Verbreitung und Gliederung der Togorestsprachen*, Kölner Beiträge zur Afrikanistik, 1, Berlin: Reimer.

—— (1982). 'African Noun Class Systems', in H. Seiler and C. Lehmann (eds.), *Apprehension: Das sprachliche Erfassen von Gegenständen*, i: *Bereich und Ordnung der Phänomene*, Tübingen: Gunter Narr, 189–216.

HETZRON, R. (1970). 'Towards an Amharic Case Grammar', *Studies in African Linguistics*, 1: 301–54.

HJELMSLEV, L. (1953). *Prolegomena to a Theory of Language*, Madison, Wisconsin: University of Wisconsin Press. (Trans. F. J. Whitfield from *Omkring sprogteoriens grundlaeggelse*, Ejnar Muksgaard, Copenhagen, 1943.)

—— (1956). 'Animé et inanimé, personnel et non-personnel', *Travaux de l'Institut de linguistique de la Faculté des lettres de l'Université de Paris*, 1: 155–99. (Repr. (1959) in *Travaux du Cercle linguistique de Copenhague*, 12: 211–49; also repr. (1971) in *Essais linguistiques*, Paris: Les Éditions de Minuit, 220–58.)

HOCK, H. H. (1985). 'Sanskrit Double-object Constructions: Will the Real Object Please Stand up?' *Praci-Bhasha-Vijnan: Journal of Indian Linguistics*, 12: 50–70.

HOPPER, P. J., and THOMPSON, S. A. (eds.) (1982). *Syntax and Semantics*, xv: *Studies in Transitivity*, New York: Academic Press.

HORROCKS, G. (1986). *Generative Grammar*, London: Longman.

HOUSEHOLDER, F. W. (1973). 'On Arguments from Asterisks', *Foundations of Language*, 10: 365–76.

HUNTLEY, D. (1980). 'The Evolution of Genitive-accusative Animate and Personal Nouns in Slavic Dialects', in J. Fisiak (ed.), *Trends in Linguistics*, xv: *Historical Morphology*, The Hague: Mouton, 189–212.

HYMAN, L. M. (1980). 'Babanki and the Ring Group', in L. M. Hyman and J. Voorhoeve (eds.), *Les Classes nominales dans le bantou des grassfields* (vol. i of *L'Expansion bantoue: Actes du Colloque international du CNRS: Viviers (France) 4–16 avril 1977*), Paris: Société d'études linguistiques et anthropologiques de France, 225–58.

—— and DURANTI, A. (1982). 'On the Object Relation in Bantu', in Hopper and Thompson (eds.) 1982: 217–39.

ICKOVIČ, V. A. (1980). 'Suščestvitel'nye oduševlennye i neoduševlennye v sovremennom russkom jazyke (norma i tendencija)', *Voprosy jazykoznanija*, 4: 84–96.

INGRAM, D. (1978). 'Typology and Universals of Personal Pronouns', in J. H. Greenberg, C. A. Ferguson, and E. A. Moravcsik (eds.), *Universals of Human Language*, iii: *Word Structure*, Stanford: Stanford University Press, 213–48.

JACKENDOFF, R. (1977). *X-bar Syntax: A Study of Phrase Structure*, Cambridge, Mass.: MIT Press.

—— (1983). *Semantics and Cognition*, Cambridge, Mass.: MIT Press.

JAKOBSON, R. (1959). 'On the Rumanian Neuter', *Mélanges linguistiques offerts à Émil Petrovici* (= *Cercetări de Lingvistică* iii). (Repr. in *Selected Writings*, ii: *Word and Language*, The Hague: Mouton, 187–9.)

JAYASEELAN, K. A. (1983). 'Prepositions as Deletion-triggers', *Linguistic Analysis*, 11: 429–37.

JESPERSON, O. (1924). *The Philosophy of Grammar*, London: Allen & Unwin.

—— (1937). *Analytic Syntax*, Copenhagen: Munksgaard.

JESSEN, M. E. (1975). 'A Semantic Study of Spatial and Temporal Expressions in English', Ph.D. thesis, University of Edinburgh.

JOHNSON, D. E. (1977). 'On Keenan's Definition of "Subject of"', *Linguistic Inquiry*, 8: 673–92.

JONES, M. A. (1983). 'Getting "Tough" with Wh-movement', *Journal of Linguistics*, 19: 129–59.

JUUL, A. (1975). *On Concord of Number in Modern English*, Publications of the Department of English, University of Copenhagen, 1, Copenhagen: Nova.

KADAGIDZE, D., and KADAGIDZE, N. (1984). *Cova-tušinsko-gruzinsko-russkij slovar*', Tbilisi: Mecniereba.

KAYNE, R. S. (1972). 'Subject Inversion in French Interrogatives', in J. Casagrande and B. Saciuk (eds.), *Generative Studies in Romance Languages*, Rowley, Mass.: Newbury House, 70–126.

—— (1976). 'French Relative *Que*', in F. Hensey and M. Lujan (eds.), *Current Studies in Romance Linguistics*, Washington, DC: Georgetown University Press, 255–99.

—— and POLLOCK, J.-Y. (1978). 'Stylistic Inversion, Successive Cyclicity, and Move NP in French', *Linguistic Inquiry*, 9: 595–621.

KEENAN, E. L. (1976). 'Towards a Universal Definition of "Subject"', in Charles N. Li (ed.), *Subject and Topic*, New York: Academic Press, 305–33.

—— (1978). 'Language Variation and the Logical Structure of Universal Grammar', in H. Seiler (ed.), *Language Universals*, Tübingen: Gunter Narr, 89–124.

—— (1979). 'On Surface Form and Logical Form', *Studies in the Linguistic Sciences*, 8/2, Special Issue, 1–41.

KIBRIK, A. E. (1972). 'O formal'nom vydelenii soglasovatel'nyx klassov v arčinskom jazyke', *Voprosy jazykoznanija*, 1: 124–31.

—— (1979). *Materialy k tipologii èrgativnosti*, ii: *Lakskij jazyk*; iii: *Čiragskij jazyk* (Predvaritel'nye publikacii 127), Moscow: Institut russkogo jazyka AN SSSR.

KILBY, D. A. (1973). 'Notational Variance in Generative Semantics', *Edinburgh Working Papers in Linguistics*, 2: 66–75.

—— (1974). 'A Little Bit of *Give* and *Take*', *University of Essex Dept. of Language & Linguistics Occasional Papers*, 15: 5–24.

—— (1976a). 'A Semantic Approach to the Accusative Case in Russian', *UEDLLOP* 18: 46–67.

—— (1976b). 'Strategies to Order', *UEDLLOP* 18: 68–96.

—— (1977a). *Deep and Superficial Cases in Russian (Speciminae Philologiae* Slavicae 14), Frankfurt-am-Main: Kubon & Sagner.

—— (1977b). 'What Might a Universal Theory of Cases Look like?' *UEDLLOP* 20: 59–86.

—— (1981). 'On Case Markers', *Lingua*, 54: 101–33.

—— (1982a). 'A Functional Approach to Case in Russian', *Papers in Slavonic Linguistics*, Birmingham: University of Aston, 1: 73–90.

—— (1982b). 'On Lexical Approaches to the Passive', *UEDLLOP* 25: 72–99.

—— (1982c). 'Universal and Particular Properties of the Ewenki Case System', in B. Comrie (ed.), *Studies in the Languages of the USSR*, Edmonton: Linguistic Research, 45–74.

—— (1983). 'Russian Language', *Year's Work in Modern Language Studies 1982*, 44: 1159–68.

—— (1984). *Descriptive Syntax and the English Verb*, London: Croom Helm.

KIMENYI, A. (1976). 'A Relational Grammar of Kinyarwanda', Ph.D. dissertation, UCLA.

KING, L. D. (1983). 'The Semantics of Tense, Orientation and Aspect in English', *Lingua*, 59: 101–54.

KLIMOV, G. A. (1974). 'On the Character of Languages of Active Typology', *Linguistics*, 131: 11–25.

KOOPMAN, H. (1984). *The Syntax of Verbs*, Dordrecht: Foris.

KRISHNAMURTI, BH., and SARMA, P. S. (1968). *A Basic Course in Modern Telugu*, Hyderabad: Bh. Krishnamurti.

KUNO, S. (1974). 'The Position of Relative Clauses and Conjunctions', *Linguistic Inquiry*, 5: 117–36.

LAMB, S. M. (1964). 'On Alternation, Transformation, Realization and Stratification', in *Monograph Series on Language and Linguistics*, ed. C. I. J. M. Stuart, Washington DC: Georgetown University Press, 17: 105–22.

LANGACKER, R. (1982). 'Space Grammar, Analysability and the English Passive', *Language*, 58: 22–80.

LEHMANN, C. (1984). *Der Relatizsatz*, Tübingen: Gunter Narr.

LEHMANN, W. P. (ed.) (1978). *Syntactic Typology: Studies in the Phenomenology of Language*, Austin: University of Texas Press.

LEMAIRE, M. (1983). 'Un Aspect de l'échange des arguments du verbe: Les Verbes à double régime de l'objet en latin', *Bulletin de la Société de linguistique*, 78: 283–324.

LEVI, J. N. (1973). 'Where do All those Other Adjectives Come from?' *Papers from the 9th Regional Meeting of the Chicago Linguistic Society*, 332–45.

LEVIN, L. S. (1982). 'Sluicing: A Lexical Interpretation Procedure', in Bresnan (ed.) 1982, 590–654.

Lewis, D. (1972). 'General Semantics', in D. Davidson and G. Harman (eds.), *Semantics of Natural Language*, Dordrecht: Reidel, 169–218.

Li, C. N. and Thompson, S. A. (1981). *Mandarin Chinese: A Functional Reference Grammar*, Berkeley and Los Angeles: University of California Press.

Lightfoot, D. (1979). *Principles of Diachronic Syntax*, Cambridge: Cambridge University Press.

Luxt, L. I. (1970). *Sravnitel'no-sopostavitel'naja grammatika romanskix jazykov: Rumynskij jazyk*, Moscow: Nauka.

Lyons, J. (1966a). 'Towards a "Notional" Theory of the "Parts of Speech"', *Journal of Linguistics*, 2: 209–35.

—— (1966b). 'Review of Chomsky "Aspects of the Theory of Syntax"', *Philosophical Quarterly*, 16: 393–5.

—— (1968). *Introduction to Theoretical Linguistics*, Cambridge: Cambridge University Press.

—— (1977). *Semantics*, Cambridge: Cambridge University Press.

—— (1981). *Language, Meaning and Context*, London: Collins/Fontana.

—— (1987). 'Semantics'. In J. Lyons, R. Coates, M. Deuchar, and G. Gazdar (eds.), *New Horizons in Linguistics*, ii, London: Penguin, 152–78.

McCloskey, J. (1979). *Transformational Syntax and Model Theoretic Semantics*, Dordrecht: Reidel.

Magomedbekova, Z. M. (1967). 'Karatinskij jazyk', in E. A. Bokarev and K. V. Lomtatidze (eds.), *Jazyki narodov SSSR*, iv: *Iberijsko-kavkazskie jazyki*, Moscow: Nauka, 323–35.

Mallinson, G. (1984). 'Problems, Pseudo-problems and Hard Evidence: Another Look at the Rumanian Neuter', *Folia linguistica*, 18: 439–51.

Malone, J. L. (1985). 'On the Feminine Pronominalization of Irish and English Boat Nouns', *General Linguistics*, 25: 189–98.

Marcus, S. (1962). 'Le Genre grammatical et son modèle logique', *Cahiers de linguistique théorique et appliquée*, 1: 103–22.

—— (1963). 'A Synchronic Analysis of the Grammatical Gender', *Revue de linguistique* (Bucharest), 7/1: 99–111.

—— (1967). *Algebraic Linguistics: Analytical Models*, New York: Academic Press.

—— (1970). 'Les Modèles mathématiques et l'opposition romane-slave dans la typologie du genre grammatical', in A. Rosetti (ed.), *Actele celui de-al XII-lea Congres international de lingvistică si filologie romanică I*, Bucharest: Editura Acadiemi Republicii Socialiste România, 247–52.

Matthews, P. H. (1981). *Syntax*, Cambridge: Cambridge University Press.

Miller, J. (1985). *Semantics and Syntax*, Cambridge: Cambridge University Press.

Milner, J.-C. (1978). *De la syntaxe à l'interprétation: Quantités, insultes, exclamations*, Paris: Éditions du Seuil.

Miranda, R. V. (1975). 'Indo-European Gender: A Study in Semantic and Syntactic Change', *Journal of Indo-European Studies*, 3: 199–215.

Montague, R. (1974). *Formal Philosophy: Selected Papers of Richard Montague*, edited with an Introduction by R. Thomason, Newhaven, Conn.: Yale University Press.

Nesfield, J. C. (1939). *Manual of English Grammar and Composition*, rev. edn., London: Macmillan (1st edn. 1898).

Nichols, J. (1983). 'Switch Reference in the Northeast Caucasus', in Haiman and Munro (eds.) 1983: 245–65.

Noonan, M. (1985). 'Complementation', in Shopen (ed.) 1985b: 42–140.

Obenauer, H.-G. (1976). *Études de syntaxe interrogative du français*, Tübingen: Niemeyer.

Oehrle, R. T. (1977). Comments on Selkirk (1977) in P. Culicover, T. Wasow, and A. Akmajian (eds.), *Formal Syntax*, Academic Press, 317–25.

Pike, K. L. (1943). *Phonetics*, Ann Arbor: University of Michigan Press.

—— (1967). 'Grammar as Wave', *Georgetown University Monographs on Language and Linguistics*, 20: 1–14.

Plank, F. (1984a). 'The Modals Story Retold', *Studies in Language*, 8: 305–64.

—— (ed.) (1984b). *Objects: Towards a Theory of Grammatical Relations*, New York: Academic Press.

Priestly, T. M. S. (1983). 'On "Drift" in Indo-European Gender Systems', *Journal of Indo-European Studies*, 11: 339–63.

Quine, W. V. O. (1960). *Word and Object*, Cambridge, Mass.: MIT Press.

—— (1963). 'The Problem of Meaning in Linguistics', in *From a Logical Point of View*, New York: Harper Row, 47–64.

Quirk, R., Greenbaum, S., Leech, G., and Svartvik, J. (1972). *A Grammar of Contemporary English*, London: Longman.

—— and Greenbaum, S. (1973). *A University Grammar of English*, London: Longman.

—— —— Leech, G., and Svartvik, J. (1985). *A Comprehensive Grammar of the English Language*, London: Longman.

Radford, A. (1979). 'The Functional Basis of Transformations', *Transactions of the Philological Society*, 1–42.

—— (1981). *Transformational Syntax: A Student's Guide to Chomsky's Extended Standard Theory*, Cambridge: Cambridge University Press.

—— (1982). 'The Syntax of Verbal Wh-exclamatives in Italian', in N. B. Vincent and M. B. Harris (eds.), *Studies in the Romance Verb*, London: Croom Helm, 185–204.

Richards, J., Platt, J. T., and Weber, H. (1985). *Longman Dictionary of Applied Linguistics*, London: Longman.

ROSENBAUM, P. S. (1967). *The Grammar of English Predicate Complement Constructions*, Cambridge, Mass.: MIT Press.

ROSETTI, A. (1965). *Linguistica*, The Hague: Mouton.

—— (1983). *Études de linguistique générale*, Bucharest: Univers.

ROSS, J. R. (1967). 'Constraints on Variables in Syntax', Ph.D. dissertation, MIT (published (1986) as *Infinite Syntax*, Norwood, New Jersey: Ablex Publishing Corp.).

—— (1969). 'Guess Who?' *Papers from the 5th Regional Meeting of the Chicago Linguistic Society*, 252–86.

—— (1973). 'Nouniness', in O. Fujimura (ed.), *Three Dimensions of Linguistic Theory*, Tokyo: TEC, 137–257.

RUDE, N. (1982). 'Promotion and Topicality of Nez Perce Objects', *Berkeley Linguistics Society Proceedings*, 8: 463–83.

RŮŽIČKA, R. (1983). 'Remarks on Control', *Linguistic Inquiry*, 14: 309–24.

SARI, N. (1984). 'Banjarese Verbal Morphology', MA thesis, Australian National University.

SCHACHTER, P. (1985). 'Parts-of-speech Systems', in Shopen (ed.) 1985a: 3–61.

SCHENKER, A. M. (1955). 'Gender Categories in Polish', *Language*, 31: 402–8.

SCHLESINGER, I. M. (1979). 'Cognitive Structures and Semantic Deep Structures: The Case of the Instrumental', *Journal of Linguistics*, 15: 307–24.

SELKIRK, E. (1977). 'Noun Phrase Structure', in P. Culicover, T. Wasow, and A. Akmajian (eds.), *Formal Syntax*, New York: Academic Press, 285–316.

SERZISKO, F. (1982a). 'Gender, Noun Class and Numeral Classification: A Scale of Classificatory Techniques', in R. Dirven and G. Radden (eds.), *Issues in the Theory of Universal Grammar* (Tübinger Beiträge zur Linguistik 196), Tübingen: Gunter Narr, 95–125.

—— (1982b). 'Numerus/Genus/Kongruenz und das Phänomen der Polarität am Beispiel einiger ostkuschitischer Sprachen', in H. Seiler and F. J. Stachowiak (eds.), *Apprehension: Das sprachliche Erfassen von Gegenständen*, ii: *Die Techniken und ihr Zusammenhang in Einzelsprachen*, Tübingen: Gunter Narr, 179–200.

SHAUMJAN, S. K. (1965). *Strukturnaja lingvistika*, Moskva: Izdatel'stvo Nauka.

SHOPEN, T. (ed.) (1985a). *Language Typology and Syntactic Description*, i: *Clause Structure*, Cambridge: Cambridge University Press.

—— (ed.) (1985b). *Language Typology and Syntactic Descritpion*, ii: *Complex Constructions*, Cambridge: Cambridge University Press.

—— (ed.) (1985c). *Language Typology and Syntactic Description*, iii: *Grammatical Categories and the Lexicon*, Cambridge: Cambridge University Press.

SIEGEL, M. E. A. (1983). 'Problems in Preposition Stranding', *Linguistic Inquiry*, 14: 184–8.

SLOBIN, D. (1973). 'Cognitive Prerequisites for the Development of Grammar', in C. Ferguson and D. Slobin (eds.), *Studies in Child Language Development*, New York: Holt, Rinehart and Winston, 175–208.

SMITH, C. (1983). 'A Theory of Aspectual Choice', *Language*, 59: 479–501.

SPRINGHETTI, A. (1962). *Lexicon linguisticae et philologiae*, Latinitas perennis, 6, Roma: Pontifica universitas Gregoriana.

STAROSTA, S. (1982). 'Case Relations, Perspective and Patient Centrality', University of Hawaii Working Papers in Linguistics 14.1, 1–33.

STASSEN, L. (1985). *Comparison and Universal Grammar*, Oxford: Blackwell.

THORNE, J. P. (1972). 'On the Notion "definite" ', *Foundations of Language*, 8: 562–8.

—— (1982). 'A Note on the Indefinite Article', in J. M. Anderson (ed.), *Language Form and Linguistic Variation: Papers Dedicated to Angus McIntosh*, Amsterdam: Benjamins, 475–84.

THRANE, T. (1980). *Referential-semantic Analysis: Aspects of a Theory of Linguistic Reference*, Cambridge: Cambridge University Press.

VAN RIEMSDIJK, H. (1978). *Syntactic Markedness*, Lisse: Peter de Ridder Press.

—— and WILLIAMS, E. (1986). *An Introduction to the Theory of Grammar*, Cambridge, Mass.: MIT Press.

VENNEMANN, T. (1974). 'Theoretical Word Order Studies: Results and Problems', *Papiere zur Linguistik*, 7: 5–25.

VOORHOEVE, J. (1968). 'Noun Classes in Bamileke', *Lingua*, 21: 584–93.

—— (1980). 'Noun Classes in Adere', in L. M. Hyman (ed.), *Noun Classes in the Grassfields Bantu Borderland* (Southern California Occasional Papers in Linguistics, 8), Los Angeles: Department of Linguistics, University of Southern California, 57–72.

WARNER, A. R. (1983). Review article on Lightfoot 1979, *Journal of Linguistics*, 19: 187–209.

WASOW, T. (1981). 'Major and Minor Rules in Lexical Grammar', in T. Hoekstra, H. van der Hulst, and M. Moortgat (eds.), *Lexical Grammar*, Dordrecht: Foris, 285–312.

WATTERS, J. R. (1980). 'The Ejagam Noun Class System: Ekoid Bantu Revisited', in L. M. Hyman (ed.), *Noun Classes in the Grassfields Bantu Borderland* (Southern California Occasional Papers in Linguistics, 8), Los Angeles: Department of Linguistics, University of Southern California, 99–137.

WEXLER, K., and CULICOVER, P. W. (1980). *Formal Principles of Language Acquisition*, Cambridge, Mass.: MIT Press.

WIENOLD, G. (1967). *Genus und Semantik*, Meisenheim am Glan: Anton Hain.

WIERZBICKA, A. (1980). *The Case for Surface Case*, Ann Arbor: Karoma.

WILLIAMS, E. (1981). 'On the Notions "Lexically Related" and "Head of a Word"', *Linguistic Inquiry*, 12: 245–74.

—— (1983). 'Semantic vs. Syntactic Categories', *Linguistics and Philosophy*, 6: 423–46.

WINDISCH, R. (1973). *Genusprobleme im Romanischen: Das Neutrum im Rumänischen* (Tübinger Beiträge zur Linguistik 31), Tübingen: Gunter Narr.

XAJDAKOV, S. M. [=KHAIDAKOV, S. M.] (1963). 'Principy raspredelenija imen suščestvitel'nyx po grammatičeskim klassam v lakskom jazyke', *Studia Caucasica*, 1: 48–55.

—— (1980). *Principy imennoj klassifikacci v dagestanskix jazykaz*, Moscow: Nauka.

ZALIZNJAK, A. A. (1964). 'K voprosu o grammatičeskix kategorijax roda i oduševlennosti v sovremennom russkom jazyke', *Voprosy jazykoznanija*, 4: 25–40.

ZIRKOV, L. I. (1955). *Lakskij jazyk: Fonetika i morfologija*, Moscow: AN SSSR.

ZSILKA, J. (1967). *The System of Hungarian Sentence Patterns*, Bloomington: Indiana University.

—— (1973). *Sentence Patterns and Reality*, The Hague: Mouton.

ZWICKY, A. M. (1985). 'Heads', *Journal of Linguistics*, 21: 1–29.

Authors' Index

Language Index